CLANSHIP TO CROFTERS' WAR
The social transformation of the Scottish Highlands

T. M. Devine

MANCHESTER UNIVERSITY PRESS
Manchester and New York

distributed exclusively in the USA and Canada by St. Martin's Press

Copyright © T. M. Devine 1994

Published by Manchester University Press
Oxford Road, Manchester M13 9NR, UK
and Room 400, 175 Fifth Avenue, New York, NY 10010, USA

Distributed exclusively in the USA and Canada
by St. Martin's Press, Inc., 175 Fifth Avenue, New York,
NY 10010, USA

British Library Cataloguing-in-Publication Data
A catalogue record for this book is available from the British Library

Library of Congress Cataloging-in-Publication Data
Devine, T. M. (Thomas Martin)
    Clanship to crofter's war : the social transformation of the Scottish Highlands /
T.M. Devine.
    p.   cm.
    ISBN 0–7190–3481–7 (cloth). — ISBN 0–7190–3482–5 (pbk.)
    1. Highlands (Scotland)—History.   2. Highlands (Scotland)—Social conditions.
    I. Title.
    DA880.H6D37   1993   93–30886
    941.1'507—dc20   CIP

ISBN 0 7190 3482 5 *paperback*

Reprinted 1996, 1998

Photoset in Linotron Clearface
by Northern Phototypesetting Co. Ltd, Bolton

Printed in Great Britain
by Bell & Bain Limited, Glasgow

CLANSHIP TO CROFTERS' WAR

This important book charts the story of the people of the Scottish Highlands
from before the '45 to the great crofters' rebellion in the 1880s – a powerful
story of defeat, social dissolution, emigration, rebellion and cultural revival.

   T. M. Devine argues that the Highlands in the eighteenth and nineteenth
centuries saw the wholesale transformation of a society, at a pace without
parallel anywhere else in Western Europe. Beginning with the decline of
clanship before and after Bonnie Prince Charlie's Jacobite rebellion, he
explores themes in the process of fundamental social change: the development
of the crofting economy, the clearances, transatlantic emigration, the great
Highland famine and the emergence of the 'new' Highland landed class. He
juxtaposes the 'making of Highlandism', with its tartan paraphernalia, with
the harsh realities of the crofting way of life and explores the vibrant and
persistent Gaelic culture. Finally he offers a full-scale examination of the
uprising which played a vital role in reasserting the Gaelic identity, the
Crofters' War.

CONTENTS

LIST OF COLOUR PLATES

LIST OF FIGURES

MAPS

The maps were drawn by Peter Clapham

FOR MY BROTHER AND SISTER
JAMES AND ANNE

PREFACE

The eighteenth and nineteenth centuries saw immense social changes throughout Europe. It was a period of enormous industrial expansion, accelerating growth in the towns and cities and rising population. To a greater or lesser extent, most European countries were affected by these developments, but few regions were transformed as rapidly or as completely in these years as the Scottish Highlands. There, within the space of a few generations, an ancient clan-based society collapsed and was replaced by one where modern economic and social priorities became dominant. Elsewhere in Britain, traditional rural structures were also subject to profound changes as agriculture became ever more responsive to the needs of burgeoning urban and industrial markets for more foods and raw materials. In the Highlands, however, this radical change of direction had a cataclysmic impact on the people of the region, and the social costs of the economic revolution were very high. Like the Irish, the Scottish Gaels suffered the trauma of famine, emigration and eviction and the breakup of traditional social connections and relationships in the nineteenth century.

This book studies the origins, nature and effects of that experience. It seeks to synthesise and interpret the important academic research which has been carried out on eighteenth and nineteenth century Highland history over the last few decades and which has produced new perspectives and insights on old themes. Part of the fascination of the subject, however, is the controversy which still rages among scholars on most of the major issues. Highland history is alive with debate and dispute, and I have not therefore attempted to write a 'balanced' if bloodless account but rather my own evaluation of the results of recent historical research in a manner which it is hoped can make it accessible to a wider readership. The transformation of Scottish Gaeldom is a story too extraordinary to be confined to a small circle of scholars. Chapters 5, 9, 12 and 13 are based on my own work and have appeared in somewhat different form elsewhere.

Much of the history of the Highlands has for long been shrouded in romance and myth through the ingenious efforts of Victorian writers who virtually invented a Gaelic past which fitted in with the assumptions and expectations of their readers. The revolution in Highland historiography of the last three decades has started to put together a much more compelling and fascinating story based on careful examination of contemporary documentary evidence and oral tradition. It is hoped that some of the excitement and interest of this new work comes across in the pages that follow.

Tom Devine
University of Strathclyde
March 1993

ACKNOWLEDGEMENTS

My primary debt is to the scholars whose researches have helped to transform Highland history in recent years. Their works form an important basis for this book and I hope that they will be interested in my interpretations of their conclusions even if they do not necessarily always agree with them.

I am grateful also to Dr Ewen Cameron of the University of Edinburgh for allowing me to read and quote from his invaluable Ph.D. thesis on 'Public policy in the Highlands in the later nineteenth century'. Dr Allan Macinnes of the University of Glasgow kindly let me see a copy of his article on the Crown and the Highlands in the early seventeenth century before its publication in *Northern Scotland*. Reading these two important pieces of research has shaped my thinking in chapters 1 and 15.

Mrs Jean Fraser of the University Strathclyde not only typed the book with her usual skill and efficiency and produced the index but encouraged the project to a successful conclusion by gently reminding the author to accelerate the speed of his composition.

Thanks is due to institutions and individuals who assisted in locating illustrations and granted permission for their use.

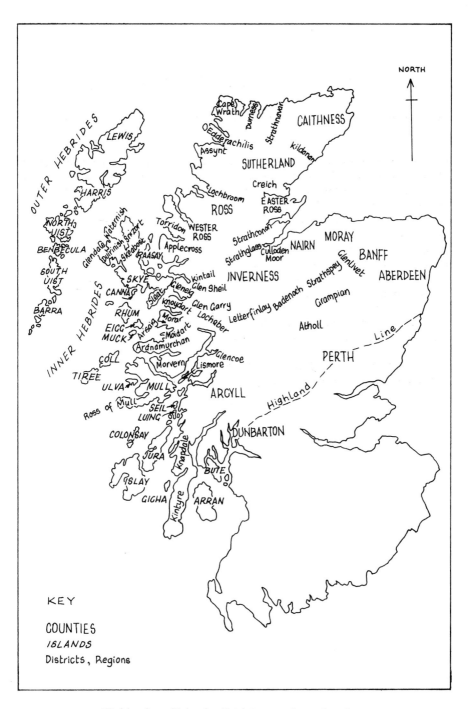

Highlands and Islands: districts counties and regions

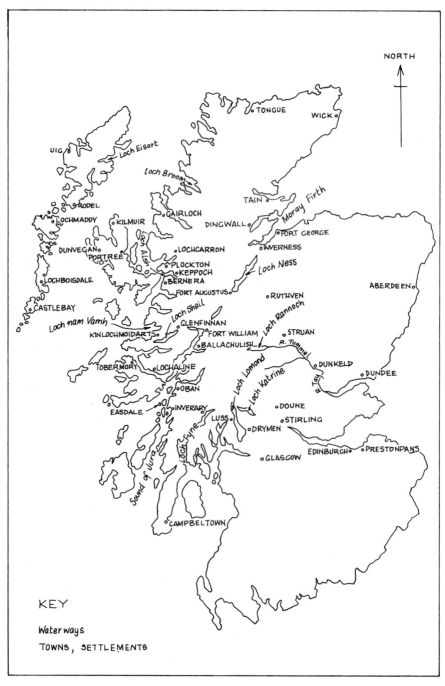

NORTH

TONGUE   WICK

UIG

Loch Eisort

Loch Broom

TAIN   Moray Firth

RODEL   GAIRLOCH

LOCHMADDY   KILMUIR   DINGWALL   FORT GEORGE

DUNVEGAN   LOCHCARRON   INVERNESS

PORTREE

Loch Alsh

PLOCKTON   Loch Ness

LOCHBOISDALE   KEPPOCH

BERNERA

FORT AUGUSTUS   ABERDEEN

CASTLEBAY   RUTHVEN

Loch nam Vamh   Loch Sheil   Loch Rannoch

GLENFINNAN

KINLOCHMOIDART   FORT WILLIAM   STRUAN

BALLACHULISH   R. Tummel

TOBERMORY   LOCHALINE   DUNKELD

R. Tay   DUNDEE

OBAN   Loch Lomond   Loch Katrine

EASDALE   INVERARY   DOUNE

LUSS   STIRLING

DRYMEN

Loch Fyne   EDINBURGH   PRESTONPANS

GLASGOW

Sound of Jura

CAMPBELTOWN

KEY

Waterways

TOWNS, SETTLEMENTS

Highlands and Islands: towns, settlements and waterways

1

CLANSHIP

The conventional and familiar division of Scotland into 'Highlands' and 'Lowlands' is a comparatively recent development. Before the later fourteenth century there was apparently little consciousness of the 'Highlanders' as a people with a distinctive language, customs, dress and social structure. The inhabitants of the north of Scotland and the Western Isles did not yet possess a special identity, and Gaelic was still spoken widely in districts as far south as Fife in the east and Galloway in the west. The state did not govern in terms of Highlanders and Lowlanders and the charters of William the Lyon (1156–1214) described his subjects simply as 'French, English, Scots, Welsh and Gallovidian'. In the twelfth and thirteenth centuries royal authority was making its presence felt throughout the land and even, from the 1230s, penetrating the remotest areas of the north-western seaboard and outer isles. The most effective instrument for this systematic extension of state power was the creation of a loyal class of feudal landed families who acknowledged royal supremacy. A by-product of the development of feudalism was the acquisition of landed property, especially in the north-east, by Anglo-Norman families. The entire process suggested the development of a unitary kingdom with little in the way of racial or cultural distinctions. Yet, before long, the first perceptions of Scotland as a country split between the Highlands and the Lowlands were beginning to emerge.

The first and most famous enunciation of Scotland as a land of two cultures came from the pen of the Aberdeen chronicler, John of Fordun, in 1380. Fordun drew several distinctions, one of which was linguistic. He noted that two languages were spoken by the Scots, 'the Scottish and the Teutonic', the latter being associated with 'the seaboard and the plains' while the former was the speech of 'the highlands and outlying islands'. The two peoples also differed profoundly in behaviour. The 'people of the coast' were 'of domestic and civilised habits, trusty, patient and urbane . . . affable and peaceful, devout in Divine worship' and were also 'decent in their attire'. The Highlanders on the other hand were beyond the pale of civilisation and Fordun denounced them bitterly. They were 'a savage and untamed nation, rude and independent, given to raping . . . exceedingly cruel'. In addition, they were unsightly in dress'.[1]

After Fordun most medieval Scottish chroniclers, such as Andrew Wyntoun, Walter Bower and John Major, continued to draw these distinctions between the 'wild Scots' and the 'domestic Scots'. But in Fordun there was already encapsulated all the elements which for centuries thereafter distinguished the Highlander in the Lowland mind. The differences in both speech and dress were clear but even more significant, however, was the perceived savagery and lawlessness of the Highlander. He was a figure of menace who did not share the 'domestic' and 'civilised' virtues of the Lowland people. 'Wyld wykkd Helandmen', as Wyntoun described them, were viewed as racially and culturally inferior to other Scots and were seen as a threat to the more peace-loving inhabitants of the rest of the country. Above all, Fordun seemed to imply, Highlanders were a different race, who as he put it, were hostile to 'the English people and language'.[2]

The accuracy of Fordun's remarks is not really the important issue. Their significance, and those of later commentators, is rather that they reveal a quite remarkable transformation in the Lowland cultural perception of the society of northern Scotland. The Highlanders were for the first time revealed as a separate people with a distinct identity who were also regarded as less 'civilised' than the inhabitants of other areas of the country. It was a belief which endured for several centuries and was to have an enormous impact on Highland history.

The new perception originated in a variety of cultural, social and political changes. In the fourteenth century the inexorable advance of English speech in the south and east meant that Gaelic was no longer the language of most Scots. Instead it became especially associated with the Highlands and Islands and the east coast area north of Inverness. A correlation seemed to develop between the geographical division of the high and low country and the linguistic divide between Gaelic and English. Moreover, the retreat of Gaelic came to an end at the Highland line. Over the subsequent four centuries there was little further erosion of the language in the upland and insular heartlands of northern Scotland. The later Middle Ages also experienced a resurgence in Gaelic culture, particularly associated with the 'Lordship of the Isles', in the fourteenth and fifteenth centuries. The continued strength of the language within its new geographical focus led to an even sharper awareness of the cultural division developing in Scottish society and, at the same time, the association of Gaelic with the Highland people served to enhance the belief that they were culturally inferior to other Scots. English was not simply expanding territorially in much of Scotland, it was also increasingly the language of the aristocracy, court and government by the early fifteenth century: 'For much of the Middle Ages, vernacular English and Gaelic had probably had equally low status after official Latin and aristocratic French, but once English was the establishment language, Gaelic alone may have seemed second rate.'[3]

It is difficult to believe, however, that language differences alone can account for the crystallisation of new attitudes towards Highland society in the later fourteenth century. It is significant, for instance, that both Fordun and later commentators placed considerable stress on the savagery of the Highlanders. They were identified as violent, cruel and 'untamed', quite different from the more peace-loving and 'civilised' inhabitants of the plains. Highland society was seen as a threat, menacing the more stable areas of the country. In part this may have been because two of the main contemporary institutions associated with law and order, the Christian Church and the burghs, were less well developed in the Highlands than elsewhere in Scotland. But the fears of Highland barbarism first became apparent at a particular period in the later fourteenth century and must have been influenced by contemporary developments. In addition, even Fordun admitted that the people of the Highlands and Islands were not innately barbarous and indeed, he stressed that, 'if properly governed', they were 'faithful and obedient to their king and country and easily made to submit to law'.[4] The implication was that the Highlands had become anarchic as a result of a failure in control by the state which can be traced to the collapse in the fourteenth century of the attempt by central government effectively to absorb the north of Scotland as an integrated and loyal part of the kingdom.

In the thirteenth century royal power was extended even into the remotest parts of the western Highlands by a combination of military force and the creation of a dependent elite of feudal landowners of both Gaelic and Anglo-French origin. In return for formal grants of land through charters, these families promised to uphold the power of the crown in their territories. The feudal contract was commonplace elsewhere in Scotland and was a potentially effective instrument for national unity and organisational cohesion. Unfortunately, however, in the century after the death of Robert the Bruce in 1329, 'feudalism collapsed as a vehicle for unity and became instead a vehicle of faction'.[5] A succession of misfortunes befell the institution of monarchy which alone could provide the political and administrative backbone of the feudal system. David II (1329–71) and James I (1406–37) were imprisoned in England for almost thirty years, while Robert II (1371–90) and Robert III (1390–1406) were notorious incompetents. Warfare with England, which fluctuated in intensity from the 1330s, compounded the difficulties of governance. In the western Highlands the structure of local authority was further weakened as several major families died out in the male line, so disrupting a key element in the system of administrative control which had developed in the thirteenth century.

Out of the resulting upheavals there emerged two new power groupings, each of which was manifestly independent from the Scottish state and pursued territorial ambitions outside its immediate sphere of influence by force of arms. The first was the MacDonald Lordship of the Isles which at the height of its power included all the Hebrides, except Bute and Arran, together with Kintyre, Lochaber and Morvern in the mainland. In addition, it sought to expand eastwards towards the regions of Ross and Moray. The Lordship brought stability to the Western Isles and over the 150 years of its existence created the context for a veritable golden age of Gaelic culture. But its very success made it appear menacing to the rest of Scotland, especially since the MacDonald Lords had considerable expansionist ambitions. The Lordship was almost a state within a state, an independent kingdom which, though deeply imbued with feudal influences from the Lowlands, seemed an overtly Gaelic institution with a distinctive culture. It probably helped to shape lowland perceptions of the western Highlands and Islands as an alien world. In addition, when the Lordship collapsed in the later fifteenth century, due to internal discord and forfeiture by James IV in 1493, a period of turmoil ensued which endured until the early seventeenth century. It was this cycle of violence more than any other which imprinted the Highland reputation for lawlessness in the Lowland mind.

The rise of MacDonald power in the west in the fourteenth century had produced a degree of regional stability. In the north east, however, the collapse of royal authority led to disorder and faction. The power of the state in eastern Inverness, Moray and Nairn had depended upon the co-operation and support of three leading families and their kindred, the Randolphs (created earls of Moray), the Murrays and the earls of Ross. The Randolphs were pivotal and held the entire province of Moray as lords of regality giving them, *inter alia*, complete criminal jurisdiction in the region. In the later fourteenth century, all these families died out in the senior male line and a struggle for power began. Alexander Stewart, third son of Robert II, and self-styled 'Wolf of Badenoch', was triumphant and became the dominant force in the area, but rather than main-taining law and order he used violence to extend his influence on a systematic basis. His chosen instruments were the tribal hosts of the upland districts or, as the chronicler described them, 'wyld wykked helend-men', and his most notor-ious act of plunder, the destruction of the town of Elgin in 1390, with its churches, manses, books, charters and other valuables. Stewart had in a sense become a bandit chief using armed gangs to pursue his ambitions relentlessly. It is significant that his reign of terror coincides in both time and place with some of the early recorded perceptions of Highland barbarism and lawlessness. John of Fordun, for instance, was writing from Aberdeen, in the north east, in 1380, precisely at the time when the Wolf of Badenoch, and other lords who also used bands of Highland warriors to carry out plundering expeditions, were at their most active. It was therefore not surprising that it was in this frontier zone between the upland areas and the more stable districts to the south that the Highlanders first achieved their reputation as men of violence.

II

Strangely, however, fourteenth century chroniclers who noted differences in culture, dress, speech and social behaviour between the Highlands and the Lowlands failed to comment on clanship as a distinguishing characteristic. During the Wars of Independence against England, soldiers from the Highlands fought on the Scottish side but were not given clan affiliations. In contemporary accounts of the Battle of Bannockburn (1314) the lists of the Scottish forces make no reference to any clan, but this is hardly surprising as the essence of the clan was a real or assumed kin relationship between chief, ruling families, cadet branches and followers. In the medieval and for much of the early modern period, however, such kin-based groupings were not unique to the Highlands. They were to be found throughout Scotland and were especially strong in areas such as the Borders and the north east where state authority was often at its weakest. It was common for noblemen and greater lairds to surround them-selves with networks of lesser gentlemen who bore their name and promised loyalty and service in return for protection. Social structures throughout Scotland were designed for defence and security and the martial ethos was not confined to the Highlands. One illustration of this is that clan ruling families in Gaeldom and Lowland magnates both used the system of 'bonds of manrent' to extend their influence and create further networks of loyalty and military solidarity. These contracts created 'effective' rather than real kin with each party agreeing to act together as though they indeed had family ties.[6]

The penetration of feudal structures into the Highlands also blurred the distinction between clanship and social systems elsewhere in Scotland and many of the greatest clan chiefs were feudal lords as well as tribal leaders. This can be best illustrated from the history of the Lordship of the Isles. Successive heads of the MacDonald dynasty practised primogeniture, issued feudal charters to major landowners in the lordship and employed feudal rules in marital contracts. Feudal structures also reinforced the authority which clan elites derived from kinship and traditional connections. In feudal theory the monarch was regarded as the owner of all land in the kingdom which he divided among his most significant followers through formal charters in return for specific obligations. These charter holders could then parcel out their estates among dependants through the process of 'subinfeudation'. Feudal forms of tenure, such as the *wadset* (pledge of lands in security for a debt) and the *feu farm* (a type of tenure by which the possessor held the land for a perpetual fixed payment and other obligations), were both heritable and gave their holders the opportunity to establish landed families in perpetuity. They also confirmed in law the ownership of land as the possession of the ruling family. In the feudal tradition, the notion of clan lands was therefore a legal nonsense. Highland elites like their counterparts in other parts of Scotland from the later Middle Ages possessed land by crown charters which gave them virtually absolute control over their territories. Property was vested in the ruling family and not surprisingly, when estate rentals became available from the sixteenth century, most Highlanders are listed as tenants or undertenants of these proprietors, holding land at will or by agreement from feudal superiors.

But social relationships in the Highlands did not become wholly contractual or legalistic until the eighteenth century. In most areas, and especially along the western seaboard and throughout the islands, blood, kin, personal loyalty and traditional allegiance still counted for more than feudal charters. The Scottish state had neither the military resources or the political will until the seventeenth century to try to establish effective government in a region of scattered settlement, poor communications and difficult terrain. In addition, two important institutions which made for more stable administration in much of the Lowlands, the church and the burghs, had less impact in the Highlands than elsewhere. Social control within the region continued to be exercised by dominant clans and their allies, and after the disintegration of the MacDonald empire in the later fifteenth century more than a century of intermittent warfare ensued over much of the western districts of Gaeldom which powerfully strengthened clan bonds and loyalties. While life in the Lowlands was gradually becoming more stable, the militaristic nature of Highland society seemed to become more pronounced.

The inner core of the clan consisted of the chiefs and their leading gentry, the *fine*, or clan elite, who tended for the most part by the sixteenth century to hold their lands under crown charters. The lesser clan gentry, *doine-uaisle*, was composed of leaseholders or tacksmen, *fir-tacsa*, who managed and supervised the townships worked by clansmen. Along the western seaboard and throughout much of the Hebrides, the lesser gentry were split between the *fir-tasca* and the *buannachan*, or household men. The latter were the warrior class of the clan

whose basic function was the defence and protection of clan territories, and also
the main source of supply of Highland mercenaries to Ireland. Native Irish
chiefs, especially in the north of the country, faced with continuous English
attempts throughout the sixteenth century to impose supremacy, obtained
considerable mercenary assistance from their kindred among the Scottish clans.
This was a profitable business for the clan elites of the west because the Irish paid
for the military service of the *buannachan* in both food and money and, there
was an obvious incentive therefore to maximise the fighting strength of their
clans. One English estimate of the 1590s suggested that there was a military
class of well over 6,000 men in the Western Isles, quite distinct from those
clansmen who were usually employed in 'labouring of the ground'. Mercenary
service was also a means of employing younger sons of the clan gentry who were
unlikely to succeed to land or leases in their own right. The existence of the class
of *buannachan* helped to limit downward social mobility from the elite while at
the same time perpetuating and intensifying the martial ethos of the clans.

    The dominant families liked to trace their origin from a heroic figure of
antiquity in order to give prestige, status and legitimacy to their position while
at the same time providing the ordinary clansmen with a common sense of
identity with the elite. Most of these pedigrees were created and recreated with
scant regard for historical accuracy. It was a pragmatic business designed to
enhance family pride, accommodate changing alliances and absorb other clans.
Among the common ancestors claimed by the MacGregors was Pope Gregory the
Great while the Campbells included King Arthur among their 'name-fathers'.

    The reality was more prosaic. The Grants, for instance, who were probably
of Anglo-Norman stock, did not become prominent until after the marriage in
the fifteenth century of Iain Ruadh (Red John) to Matilda, the heiress of
Glencairnie which allowed the acquisition of lands in Moray and Inverness.
Thereafter Grant expansion relied heavily on the family's close association with
the Gordons, earls of Huntly, which allowed consolidation and extension of their
landed interest and clan power in the central Highlands. The McKenzies became
important when they gave assistance to the crown in its attempt to subdue the
Lords of the Isles. After its forfeiture, the head of the family received a crown
charter in 1476 for the lands of Strathconnan and Strathgarve in central
Ross-shire and thereafter the MacKenzies increased their powers until they
became second only to the mighty Campbells in influence by the later seventeenth century. The McNeills had a pedigree which went back to Niall, a
Knapdale warlord of the eleventh century, but they seem only to have emerged
as a significant entity in the turmoil which followed the Norwegian ceding of the
Western Isles to the Scottish crown in 1246 and the beginning of the Wars of
Independence with England. At that time they became established in Barra, but

through their association with Alexander MacDonald, Lord of the Isles, obtained Boisdale in South Uist by charter and by the middle decades of the fifteenth century they were also esconsed in Gigha and in part of Knapdale on the Argyll mainland.

As the larger clans extended their territory through conquest, marriage and the acquisition of crown charters, effective control of the new lands became difficult, especially since large areas could be obtained very quickly in time of war. The strategic response to this problem, set within the context of a kin-based society, was to lease or make life-grants to members of the ruling family and establish new lines of descent and cadet branches of the main clan. Once consolidated, these kin groups would then infiltrate the existing landed hierarchy of the newly acquired territories and steadily replace the native elites with their own kindred. This was widespread practice among such imperialistic clans as the MacDonalds in the heyday of the Lordship of the Isles and the Campbells and McKenzies in the seventeenth century. As Clan Donald expansion accelerated in the Western Isles, members of the *fine* were settled in different districts; eventually no less than seventeen different branches, or *sliochden*, became established. Each was linked with a particular part of the Clan Donald empire, such as Glencoe, Ardnamurchan, Sleat and Knoydart. Even these sub-hierarchies split into further branches controlling smaller areas: from the MacDonalds of Clanranald, for example, there developed the cadets of Knoydart, Glengarry, Morar and Kinlochmoidart. There was a similar dynamic in other clans. Five branches of the Frasers were documented in 1650, but by 1745 there were thirty. The Clan Donachy or Robertson is noted as being in possession of lands in Strowan, Perthshire, in 1451, and each of the twenty-four branches of the clan became divided and controlled a sub-area within the broader district.

This description of clan evolution makes nonsense of any claim that the clans were united through ties of blood. The territorial possessions of many clans were often in a state of constant flux as small kinship groups were overwhelmed and absorbed by the expansion of greater rivals, and it was inevitable that in such cases there were changes of allegiance and that individuals adopted the identity of locally dominant clans for sound reasons of security and survival. In addition, it was common for weaker units to develop close alliances with the stronger. For instance, the MacRaes and MacLennans followed the MacKenzies and the MacColls, the Stewarts of Appin. The blood ties between the ruling families and the ordinary clansmen were largely mythical but the assumption of consanguinity, suggested in the very word *clann*, i.e. children, gave an emotional bond which helped to cement social cohesion within clanship. A clan therefore did not consist of those of the same kindred or surname, because surnames did not become at all common until the seventeenth century when clanship was already in decline. Rather it was made up of those who followed the same chief whatever their own lineage.

Clan structures were inherently unstable and constantly under threat from changing circumstances. In the early seventeenth century the crown determined on the forcible removal of the *fine* of Clan Donald South from Islay, Kintyre and Jura. As a result the heads of the MacBraynes, MacKays and MacEacherns, formerly loyal to the MacDonalds, bound themselves to become 'dewtiful kinsmen and obedient tennentis' to the Campbells of Cawdor.[7] The kin-based society was itself very volatile. As one scholar has put it, '. . . consequent upon the weakening of the ruling family a province becomes wide open either to a takeover by the kindred within its bounds or to inroads by powerful neighbours'.[8] Weakness or incapacity among the *fine* could precipitate aggression and conquest of clan territory by expansionist forces in the locality. One of the main reasons for the successful expropriation of several clans, such as the Clan Leod and Clan Donald South, by the government of James VI in the early seventeenth century was open dissent among their *fine*. The penetration of feudalism into Gaeldom created other causes of dispute without ensuring enforcement of central justice or sound government and, as seen above, chiefs increasingly sought to give a legal basis to their territorial acquisitions by securing charters of possession. However, these often exacerbated social conflict at the local level. Rebellion could mean forfeiture by the crown of a chief's lands and encourage clans more loyal to the king to annex them. In addition, chiefs who held their territory directly from a great lord rather than the crown were sometimes faced with divided loyalties especially if lands were held from more than one superior. It was also common for clansmen to give their loyalties to the chiefs who were not their landlords. Out of this conflict of interest and allegiance between clanship and feudalism there developed some notorious and enduring feuds such as that between Clan Mackintosh and the earls of Huntly in Badenoch.

It was against this background of endemic insecurity and constant rivalry punctuated by episodes of outright violence and aggression that many aspects of clan society can be understood. Self-evidently military preparedness was axiomatic and Martin Martin writing in the later seventeenth century recalled how courage and prowess in war were the vital qualities of a chief. In the Western Isles, he described how it was common for the young heirs to the chiefdoms to demonstrate a 'publick specimen of their valour' before they could be accepted by their people. This was carried out by the chieftain and other members of the *fine* of the clan undertaking 'a desperate Incursion upon some Neighbour or other that they were in Feud with' and to 'bring by open force the Cattle they found in the Lands they attack'd or to die in the Attempt'.[9] The militarism of the western clans was also illustrated by the widespread practice of *soring*, the forcing by fighting men of food and hospitality from tenants within the clan territory or, indeed, on the lands of other clans with whom a feud existed. *Soring* suggested the existence of a parasitic class which was not engaged in regularly labouring the land but in preparing for or making war, and even when clanship was in decline, an official estimate in 1724 suggested that twenty-six chiefs of Highland clans could still call out a total of 18,890 warriors.

In turn, the effective deployment of military resources depended on the depth and integrity of the social relationships between clan elites and followers. The clan virtues were loyalty, courage, obedience and a sense of common identity between the ruling family and those below with whom they had few blood ties. Social cohesion came from a variety of sources. The bards, genea-logists and orators provided the historical identity of the clan and enhanced the prestige of the present chief by recounting the epic deeds of his ancestors. In addition, the rentals in kind of cattle, sheep, meal, cheese, hens and geese which were paid to the chief by clansmen in their role as tenants were sometimes converted back into the provision of subsistence support in seasons of shortage and here the elites were acting as a source of social insurance in a society where harvests could be erratic because of an inhospitable environment. Feasting also had a vital social purpose. As well as demonstrating the chief's capacities for generosity and hospitality it also generated a sense of communal harmony which involved all clansmen no matter what their rank. The feasts of the medieval period were often lavish affairs with the consumptions of enormous amounts of meat and drink. Even in the early seventeenth century, some of the old traditions survived. When the daughter of MacLeod married the heir of Clanranald the feasting was maintained for six days and some of those who had taken part dimly recollected that 'we were twenty times drunk every day, to which we had no more objection than he had'.[10]

Ultimately of even more significance than support in times of subsistence crisis and the provision of hospitality was the issue of land. As feudal lords the clan elites had the same absolute rights of ownership over their property as proprietors anywhere else in Scotland, but within the kin-based society the territory of the clan was governed by a quite different set of assumptions which were in conflict with the legal realities of private landownership. The areas settled by each clan were regarded as their collective heritage, or *duthchas*, and the gentry were seen not as the individual masters of these territories but as their guardians, protectors and trustees. Real or nominal kinsmen within these lands felt they possessed a prior claim to clan holdings as a result of their loyalty to and connection with the ruling family. For example, a Clanranald rental of 1718 for the Isle of Eigg shows the Captain of Clanranald asserting his 'power of keeping in his own Kinsmen and tenents on this Isle'.[11]

There seems to have been a general understanding that the chief should provide land for his clansmen rather than that they had rights to specific individual holdings in perpetuity. Captain Edward Burt, an officer of engineers, sent to the Highlands as a road contractor under General Wade in 1730, noted how chiefs commonly divided township lands for this purpose and that this was a reflection of the economic needs of the people on the one hand and the military imperative to establish a large following on the other. Nevertheless, some chiefs apparently moved clansmen about as circumstances required. When Sir James MacDonald was attempting to make peace with the crown in the early seventeenth century he at first offered to remove elements of Clan Donald South from Kintyre to Islay. Subsequently, he went further and undertook to move them anywhere that the state wished. Commonly, as a result of inter-clan feud and fear of annexation, entire townships were abandoned and lay unoccupied for many years. There seems also to have been in some areas a considerable turnover of tenants, even in townships under continuous settlement. R. A. Dodgshon has examined a series of rentals for Kintyre between 1502 and 1605 and concluded that no family held the tack (or lease) of a township over the whole period. Elsewhere, however, in Harris, Seil and Luing after 1660 Frances Shaw discovered more tenant stability. But this conflicting evidence notwithstanding, the cultural force of *duthchas* was pervasive in Gaeldom and was central to the social cohesion of the clan because it articulated the expectations of the masses that the ruling families had the responsibility to act as their protectors and guarantee secure possession of land in return for allegiance, military service, tribute and rental. It was a powerful and enduring belief which lived on long after the military rationale of clanship itself had disappeared and tribal chiefs had shed their ancient responsibilities and become commercial landlords.

III

It used to be thought that Highland clanship died on Culloden Moor in 1746 and was effectively buried by the punitive legislation imposed on Gaeldom after the final defeat of the last Jacobite rebellion. Recent research, however, has painted a less simple and more intriguing picture. It is now clear that clan society was undergoing a process of gradual and protracted decline long before the '45 and that the climax to this was reached in the decades after the failure of the rebellion. The roots of decay stretched well back into the seventeenth century and were first associated with the effective extension of state power in the Highlands in that period. As the government steadily built up more authority in

Gaeldom, so the practical basis of the kin-based society, the uniting chiefs and followers for the purposes of mutual defence, was gradually undermined. The process, however, was very slow, piecemeal and varied in its extent between different parts of the Highlands. As the '45 demonstrated, the military capabilities of many clans were maintained into the middle decades of the eighteenth century.

From the later sixteenth century, the government of James VI was seeking to impose more political and administrative control on the Highlands by employing the techniques which had successfully been tried on that other recalcitrant region, the Borders. From 1587 certain Highland landowners were required to find sureties ranging from £2,000 to £20,000 for the good behaviour of their tenants, but this sanction had only limited effect because many clansmen looked to chiefs who were not their landowners for protection. In other words, the policy did not address the complexity of Highland clanship. The more decisive initiatives came after the Union of the Crowns in 1603 because the clans were then confronted by the awesome naval and military power of a unified and expansionist British state which could co-ordinate strategy much more effectively against the two Gaelic societies of the Highlands and Ireland. The ruthlessly efficient annexation of native lands in the six counties of Ulster and the establishment of the colonial plantation there forcibly brought home to the chiefs in the western Highlands, who had strong kinship links with Irish landed

Men of Mackay's regiment at Stettin in 1630

families, the considerable danger of resisting the authority of the state. More directly, the end of rebellion in Ulster markedly reduced the opportunities for mercenary service by the Highland *buannachan*, or household men, the warrior class who had long survived on the opportunities of booty and military employment across the Irish Sea.

The government of James VI and I did not undertake the draconian policy of wholesale annexation in the Highlands that it had initiated in Ireland. Instead, a variety of strategies were executed and partial expropriation of those clans which were considered to be especially delinquent was undertaken. The main victims were Clan Donald South, the Clan Leod of Lewis, the MacIains of Ardnamurchan, and Clan Gregor. A policy of colonisation was designed to drive a further wedge of stability between Gaelic Ireland and Scotland and plans were made to establish colonies of 'answerable inlands subjects' in Lewis, Lochaber and Kintyre, although only the last settlement was even partially successful. Much more effective was the launching of military and naval expeditions along the western seaboard in 1596, 1599, 1605, 1607 and 1608. This direct intervention was paralleled by the award of judicial commissions to lieutenants, drawn mainly from 'trustworthy' magnate families on the Highland–Lowland frontier, such as the Gordon earl of Huntly and the Campbell earl of Argyll, to demand bands of surety from lawless clans.

These, however, were all traditional techniques which had long been employed in the Borders. The state also embarked on a novel attempt to produce a final solution to the Highland problem by tackling what were seen as the social roots of disorder, the strategy of 'planting civilitie' which James himself had outlined in his *Basilikon Doran* and which was laid out in 1609 in the Statutes of Iona to which all the major chiefs in the Hebrides gave their consent. The nine statutes ranged from the suppression of beggars and vagabonds to the control of wine and whisky, from the limitation of the chief's retinue to the strengthening of the reformed church, from sending the heirs of men of substance to the Lowlands for education to the prohibition of ordinary clansmen from carrying arms. Not only were the chiefs bound to observe these statutes but they were also directed to appear personally before the Privy Council at stated intervals. The statutes were a comprehensive attempt to impose lowland values on Gaeldom, destroy the basis of lawlessness and control the perceived excesses of clanship.

There has been considerable historical debate about the actual impact of these initiatives, and whatever their effects as a whole, it is plain that they did have a powerful influence on the clan elites. It has been remarked that 'central government's main priority was to educate the *fine* about their responsibilities as members of the Scottish landed classes, not to denigrate their status'.[12] Only the gentry were permitted to wear arms and armour and they also were given the monopoly licence to bring wines and spirits to the Western Isles. Thus, if anything, the statutes gave further legal confirmation of their elite position, but in return the chiefs were expected to become partners with the state in the maintenance of order and were also held to account for the conduct of their clansmen. This was achieved through the exaction of substantial sureties and the demand from 1616 that chiefs appear annually before the Privy Council. Attendance at Edinburgh was rigorously enforced from then until the outbreak of the Scottish Revolution in 1638.

These strategies of political control resulted in substantial changes within clanship. Heavy economic burdens were placed on the *fine*; for example, the sureties recommended in the Statutes of Iona varied in the 1610s from £3,000 to £18,000 sterling. The expenses of appearing before the Privy Council in Edinburgh on an annual basis were also considerable and those who attended could be detained for up to six months. Sir Rory MacLeod of Dunvegan complained to James VI in 1622 that his annual appearances meant that he was away from his estates for more than half the year and this made it difficult for him to manage them effectively. Sojourns in Edinburgh also led to expenditure on lawyers and agents and an increased appetite for the more sophisticated lifestyle of the capital. The accounts of seventeenth century Highland families, such as the MacDonalds of Clanranald and the MacLeods of Dunvegan, indicate significant and growing outlays on expensive clothing, furniture and exotic foods. Increasingly, they were being assimilated into Scottish landed society.

The outbreak of civil war in 1638 ended the compulsory annual attendances in Edinburgh, but inflicted new and greater costs through the impact of land devastation and economic dislocation. The bloodiest fighting occurred during the Wars of the Covenanters in the central and south-western Highlands, especially after the arrival of Alasdair MacColla with his Irish-Catholic troops from Ulster in 1644. Whole districts were despoiled by pillage and numerous townships laid waste through the marching and counter-marching of royalist and covenanting forces. During the Cromwellian Union further systematic destruction was inflicted on the area from Lochaber to Wester Ross by General Monck during his suppression of the rebellion led by the earl of Glencairn in 1653–4. The long-term economic impact of the wars on some localities is demonstrated from the MacLean estates in Mull, Morvern and Tiree. Sir Hector McLean of Duart fell with around 700 of his clansmen at Inverkeithing in 1651. One thousand men had originally been raised and the losses were so great that the functioning of the estate economy was disrupted for years with a rental of 1674 revealing 32 out of 140 McLean townships still lying waste. Nor did the Restoration bring much respite. The new taxation regime which was established affected landowners in the Highlands as it did the rest of Scotland. The land tax

(1665), the cess (1667) and the excise (1661) were additional and exacting fiscal burdens. Moreover, from 1661, chiefs were once again compelled to attend Edinburgh to account to the authorities for the conduct of their clansmen.

The fifty years after the Statutes of Iona saw a massive increase in the indebtedness of the Highland elites as a result of the combined forces of state action, absenteeism and conspicuous consumption. The debts of the MacLeods of Dunvegan rose to £66,700 Scots in 1649 and climbed again to £129,000 by 1663, and in 1700, an account of Clanranald's debts to his kinsman, MacDonald of Sleat, stood at £64,000. Two decades previously fourteen leading gentry of the clan had put their names to a document described as 'the Oath of the Friends' to protect the finances of their chief from inevitable ruin. The problem of debt was a structural one which plagued most of the ruling families of Gaeldom. It produced various responses, including a huge increase in wadsetting (giving a pledge of lands in security for a debt), growing dependence on Edinburgh and Glasgow merchants for bonded loans and a more commercial approach to the management of lands. It was the last reaction which was of profound significance for clanship because the determination of chiefs and leading gentry to extract more income from their lands was at some point likely to conflict directly with their patriarchal responsibilities.

It is significant, for instance, that the old traditions of feasting, heroic drinking and collective hospitality seem to have been in decline throughout the seventeenth century. In the 1690s, Martin Martin regarded these practices as belonging to the past. At the same time, on several estates, rentals in kind or 'victual' rents, were gradually being converted to a cash value, and clearly this implied that food rents, many of which were formerly consumed internally, were now being marketed. On the MacLeod estates in Harris and Skye rents were mainly paid in kind until the 1640s. By the 1680s, however, money rents made up half the value of the total and by the 1740s over three-quarters. The most important export commodity was black cattle which reflected the pastoral emphasis of the agrarian economy and the fact that the beasts could easily make their way to market on the hoof. The needs of the Royal Navy for salt beef, urban demand in Lowland Scotland and England, the impact of the new common market after 1707 and late seventeenth century controls on Irish beef imports were also significant factors in the rapid expansion of droving. By 1723 as many as 30,000 cattle were driven south for sale at the great fair at Crieff. Income could also increasingly be augmented from the sale of timber, fish, slate and other produce as part of the drive to control debt and support absenteeism and consumerism.

By the early eighteenth century, therefore, the Highlands were already a society in transition. The resolution of clan feuds by force of arms had begun to die out. It is reckoned that the last major clan battle took place near Spean Bridge in 1688 and the fact that the times were more peaceful is one explanation for the horrified contemporary reaction to the Massacre of Glencoe in 1692. Acts of collective violence which were commonplace in the sixteenth century had become exceptional a hundred years later. For the same reason, clans such as the MacGregors were denounced as barbaric in the early eighteenth century for their banditry and cattle rieving, and stood out as dangerous and threatening in a world that had moved on. For the most part cattle raiding and protection rackets were confined to particular areas, such as Highland/Lowland periphery and the more inaccessible parts of the Lochaber region. The growing cost of warfare in the age of gunpowder also made chiefs less willing or less able to arm their clansmen properly with muskets, pistols and shots. It is a remarkable fact that most Highlanders who fought in the Jacobite rebellions between 1688 and the '45 had never been in action before in the uprisings and before the battle of Killiecrankie in 1689 the Jacobite commander, Viscount Dundee, was concerned how his raw troops would react under fire. Daniel Defoe, in his *Tour Through the Whole Island of Great Britain*, in the early eighteenth century was impressed by the changes. While noting that the people of the central Highlands were 'a fierce, fighting and furious kind of men' he went on to add that they were also 'by the good conduct of their chiefs and heads of clans, much more civilised than they were in former times'.[13]

The social cohesion of the clans was also under stress as the new emphasis on economy imposed increasing strains, and the bards lamented the growing habit of chiefs who spent longer periods in Edinburgh and even London. Rent rises were becoming more common on some properties. Archibald Campbell of Knockbuy raised his rental fourfold between 1728 and 1788 on the profits from the cattle trade. First in Kintyre about 1710 and then elsewhere on his properties in 1737, the second Duke of Argyll offered leases to the highest bidder, thus substituting competition for clanship on the largest Highland estate. In the 1730s came the first significant emigrations from Argyll, Sutherland and the central Highlands to Georgia and the Carolinas. Around the same time Norman MacLeod of Dunvegan of Dunvegan and Sir Alexander MacDonald of Sleat, the two most powerful chiefs in Skye, devised a scheme to deport some of their tenants, together with wives and children, to America there to be sold as cheap indentured labour for the plantations. In the resulting scandal both of them were threatened with prosecution and it seemed that the ethic of clanship was already being abandoned in favour of profit.

But the point can be pressed too far. Commercial values were not yet paramount and tenancies on most estates were still allocated on the basis of kin and traditional affiliation. Agrarian improvements were largely confined to the estates of the Campbells and a few other families. The new ethos powerfully influenced the clan gentry and that explains their energetic exploitation of even greater commercial opportunities in the later eighteenth century. The process of conversion to commercial landlordism was far advanced before 1750, but the ordinary clansmen were still by and large insulated from the economic transition because it was the elites who undertook most of the business of selling cattle and other produce to Lowland markets. It seems clear, therefore, that while the gentry were undergoing a profound metamorphosis, the clansmen still maintained traditionalist expectations. These were not yet disappointed, however, because the limited scale of commercialisation before the 1760s meant that the elites were able to extract more income from the land without wholly compromising their hereditary functions as protectors and guardians of their people. That uneasy equilibrium was soon to change radically.

NOTES

1 Quoted in P. Hume Brown, ed., *Scotland before 1100 from Contemporary Documents*, Edinburgh, 1893, pp. 11–12.
2 *Ibid.*
3 A. Grant, *Independence and Nationhood: Scotland 1306–1469*, London, 1984, p. 202.
4 Hume Brown, *Scotland before 1100*, p. 12.
5 T. C. Smout, *A History of the Scottish People*, 1560–1830, London, 1969, p. 37.
6 J. Wormald, *Lords and Men in Scotland*, Edinburgh, 1985, p. 78.
7 A. I. Macinnes, 'Crown, clans and *fine*: the "civilising" of Scottish Gaeldom', *Northern Scotland*, 13, 1993.
8 J. W. M. Bannerman, 'The Lordship of the Isles' in J. M. Brown, ed., *Scottish Society in the Fifteenth Century*, London, 1977, p. 213.
9 M. Martin, *A Description of the Western Isles of Scotland*, 2nd edn, 1716, p. 101.
10 Quoted in R. A. Dodgshon, 'West Highland chiefdoms, 1500–1745' in R. Mitchison and P. Roebuck, eds, *Economy and Society in Scotland and Ireland 1500–1919*, Edinburgh, 1988, p. 31.
11 Quoted in R. A. Dodgshon, "Pretense of blude" and "place of thair duelling": the nature of Scottish clans, 1500–1745' in R. A. Houston and I. D. Whyte, eds, *Scottish Society 1500–1800*, Cambridge, 1989, p. 181.
12 Macinnes, 'Crown, clans and *fine*'.
13 D. Defoe, *A Tour Through the Whole Island of Great Britain*, London, 1971 edn, p. 663.

FURTHER READING

Anon., *The Seventeenth Century in the Highlands*, Inverness, 1986.
J. W. Bannerman, 'The Lordship of the Isles' in J. M. Brown, ed., *Scottish Society in the Fifteenth Century*, London, 1977.
E. Cregeen, 'The changing role of the House of Argyll in the Scottish Highlands' in N. T. Phillipson and R. Mitchison, eds, *Scotland in the Age of Improvement*, Edinburgh, 1970.
R. A. Dodgshon, 'West Highland chiefdoms, 1500–1745' in R. Mitchison and P. Roebuck, eds, *Economy and Society in Scotland and Ireland*, 1500–1939, Edinburgh, 1988.
R. A. Dodgshon, ' "Pretense of blude" and "place of thair duelling": the nature of Scottish clans, 1500–1745' in R. A. Houston and I. D. Whyte, eds, *Scottish Society, 1500–1800*,

Cambridge, 1989.

A. Grant, *Independence and Nationhood: Scotland 1306–1469*, London, 1984.

I. F. Grant, *The Macleods*: The History of a Clan, 1200–1956, London, 1959.

P. Hopkins, *Glencoe and the End of the Highland War*, Edinburgh, 1986.

L. Leneman, *Living in Atholl: A Social History of the Estates, 1685–1785*, Edinburgh, 1986.

A. I. Macinnes, 'The impact of the civil wars and interregnum: political disruption and social change within Scottish Gaeldom' in R. Mitchison and P. Roebuck, eds, *Economy and Society in Scotland and Ireland, 1500–1939*, Edinburgh, 1988.

A. I. Macinnes, 'Crowns, clans and *fine*: the "civilising" of Scottish Gaeldom, 1587–1638', *Northern Scotland*, 13, 1993.

L. Maclean, ed., *The Middle Ages in the Highlands*, Inverness, 1981.

A. G. Macpherson, 'An old Highland genealogy and the evolution of a Scottish clan', *Scottish Studies*, 10, 1966.

R. G. Nicholson, *Scotland: the Later Middle Ages*, Edinburgh, 1974.

F. J. Shaw, *The Northern and Western Islands of Scotland: Their Economy and Society in the Seventeenth Century*, Edinburgh, 1980.

D. Stevenson, *Alasdair MacColla and the Highland Problem in the Seventeenth Century*, Edinburgh, 1980.

A likeness notwithstanding the Disguise that any Person who Secures the Son of the Pretender is Intitled to a Reward of 30.000 £.

Reward poster for Prince Charles Edward Stewart

David Morier's famous painting depicting the battle of Culloden

2

JACOBITISM AND THE '45

I

The term Jacobitism comes from the Latin 'Jacobus' meaning James. The Jacobites were committed to the restoration of the Stewart dynasty which had lost the thrones of England, Ireland and Scotland in 1688–9 when James VII and II was overthrown by the Dutch prince, William of Orange, in the so-called 'Glorious Revolution'. James had invited opposition because he seemed bent on imposing a more authoritarian government in his realms, threatened to bring back Catholicism and convinced the ruling classes of England that the gains they had achieved against the monarchy in the civil wars were now in jeopardy. The widespread alienation against his policies on the part of the aristocracy and the urban elites led to his downfall and the successful invasion of William of Orange in November 1688. The continuity of the revolution and the exclusion of the Stewarts were confirmed in 1714 when the German Elector of Hanover was crowned King George I after the death of Queen Anne. Those who remained loyal to the royal house of Stewart were the Jacobites.

At the heart of Jacobitism was a belief in the hereditary and indefeasible rights of kingship which remained sacrosanct and inviolate whatever the actions of a particular monarch might be. The dynasty's right to rule was based on the law of God and that took precedence over the laws of men. But over time Jacobitism was also stimulated by economic, social, religious and political developments which attracted adherents, especially in Ireland, northern England and Scotland for pragmatic as well as ideological reasons. Jacobitism became the refuge of the disaffected who held a grudge against the post-1688–9 regime and the force of this argument can be seen from the history of Jacobitism in Scotland. By 1688 James VII had managed even to alienate the majority of his conservative supporters and his huge unpopularity can be judged by the fact that the first attempt at an armed restoration of the Stewarts by Viscount Dundee in

1689 attracted only a couple of thousand men and no leading member of the nobility. By 1715, however, the Jacobite star was in the ascendant. The rebellion of that year attracted considerable magnate support together with enthusiastic commitment from all parts of Scotland north of the Tay, including the towns of that region.

What had happened in the interim years was that Jacobitism had evolved into a broad-based movement of political and religious dissent which had many roots one of which was religious in origin. The decision in 1690 to impose a presbyterian settlement on the Scottish kirk drove non-juring episcopalians into the Jacobite camp alongside catholics and the heartland of Scottish episcopalianism in the north-east lowlands of Aberdeenshire and Banffshire long remained a bastion of Jacobitism. The failure of the Union of 1707 to satisfy expectations also fuelled support and it became patriotic to be Jacobite because only a counter-revolution could break the Union. Scotland not only failed to gain immediately in economic terms but rising fiscal demands through the malt, salt and linen taxes caused widespread discontent. The Scottish aristocracy was discomfited by the refusal of the Westminster House of Lords to accept Scots peers on the basis of their British titles as well as by the more general economic problems after 1707. Jacobitism also gained enhanced credibility in these years because it had become clear that it had the sympathy and potentially the armed support of most of catholic Europe, especially France, Spain, Austria and the Italian principalities. The assistance of France was especially critical. It was the European superpower of the day and had given a clear commitment to the exiled Stewarts when it provided safe refuge for the royal family and in 1701 proclaimed 'James VIII and III' lawful king of Scotland, England and Ireland on his father's death. For much of the eighteenth century France and Britain were engaged in a titanic struggle for world commercial and political supremacy, and the existence of Jacobitism gave the French an opportunity to intervene directly in British domestic politics and destabilise the Hanoverian régime. It was a threat which never materialised into full-scale invasion but the French factor, despite its volatility, made Jacobitism a much more formidable force than it would otherwise have been.

It is against this background that Highland Jacobitism can be considered. In a sense, support in the Highlands was an vital as the diplomatic connection with France because the clans provided the military muscle of Jacobitism. In the three major rebellions of 1689, 1715 and the '45 it was the Highlanders who were the backbone of the Jacobite armies. It was reckoned that in the early eighteenth century a host of 30,000 clansmen might be raised for the Stewarts, though nothing like that number ever took the field and Charles Edward Stewart reached Derby in 1745 with less than 5,000. Only in the Highlands in the eighteenth century could a force of armed irregulars be quickly mobilised for action and, given the absence of a standing army in Britain and the recurrent need to despatch regular troops for European combat, even a small and determined force could make a dramatic impact. This was demonstrated in the '45 when, after a battle lasting only around fifteen minutes at Prestonpans, the Jacobites with a few thousand men crushed Sir John Cope's Hanoverian army and effectively became the military masters of Scotland. As the Earl of Islay wrote early in the rebellion, the Highlanders,

> are the only source of any real danger than can attend the disaffection of the Enemies to the Protestant Succession. Several thousand men armed and used to arms, ready upon a few weeks call is what might disturb any government. The Captain of Clanranald . . . has not £500 a year and yet has 600 men with him.[1]

English officers were less complimentary, contemptuously dismissing the Highlanders as mere rabble bent on plunder. In 1746, the *Gentleman's Magazine* published a letter from an inhabitant of Derby who had had clansmen quartered in his house and this faithfully captures the southern contempt for the 'northern yahoos':

> About 6 o'clock on Wednesday evening, were quarter'd on me, six officers (one a major as they stiled him) and forty private men, with eight pick'd up shabby horses, some without saddles or bridles, others with halters, and pieces of bridles, and ropes about their heads and necks, and poor saddles, or a sort of padds stuffed with straw upon 'em. Most of the men, after their entrance into my house, look d like so many fiends turn'd out of hell, to ravage the kingdom, and cut throats; and under their plaids nothing but a various sort of butchering weapons were to be seen: the sight at first must be thought very shocking and terrible. But these wretches being fatigued with their long march from Leek that day, soon after they came into my house, stuffed themselves well with bread, cheese, and ale, and then about 20 of them, before a great fire in my hall order'd by them, called for a large quantity of straw, and nestled into it for repose; and the remainder of them did the like in a large landry-room belonging to my house, before two great fires likewise order'd to be made there. The officers took possession of my parlour, and chambers they liked best, commanded what supper and liquor they would have, and expected me, my wife and whole family, to wait on them, as if they had been so many petty princes; yet one of the officers was tolerably civil and communicative, and redressed some complaints made about the ill behaviour of his men. My hall (after these vagabond creatures began to be warm, by such numbers under the straw, and a great fire near them) stunk so of their itch, and other nastinesses about them, as if they had been so many persons in a condem'd hole, and 'twill be very happy if they ve left no contagion behind them . . .
>
> Their dialect (from the idea I had of it) seemed to me, as if an herd of hottentots, wild monkes in a desart, or vagrant gypsies, had been jabbering, screaming, and

howling together; and really this jargon of speech was very properly suited to such
a sett of banditti.

I cannot omit taking notice of the generous present they made me at parting on
Friday morning, for the trouble and expence I was at, and the dangers undergone,
(tho' by the by, I wished for no other compensation than the escape of my family
with their lives, and of my house being plunder'd) which was a regiment of lice,
several loads of their filthy excrements, and other ejections of different colours,
scatter'd before my door, in the garden, and elsewhere about my house.[2]

But comments such as these, however, wholly underestimated the military
capabilities of the lightly-armed Highland soldiers who were able to endure
greater hardship and were more mobile than regular forces. The clan hosts were
also organised into 'regiments' and officered by gentlemen, some of whom were
veterans of service in the armies of France, the Holy Roman Empire and Russia
and were well acquainted with contemporary military technique. Lord George
Murray, a younger brother of the Duke of Atholl and a commander of the
Jacobite forces in the '45, was acknowledged as one of the outstanding military
tacticians of his day. His army won virtually every skirmish and full-scale battle
against regular troops in 1745–6 except Culloden. Indeed one reason for the
decision to stand and fight there was Charles's belief in the invincibility of his
clansmen against regular troops. The ensuing disaster was as much due to the
incompetence of his leadership, the unsuitable nature of the ground for irregulars and the hungry and exhausted condition of the Jacobite army as to any other
factor. The Hanoverian commander, the Duke of Cumberland, fully understood
the lethal potential of the Highland charge, as the following extract from his
Orderly Book shows:

> Edinburgh, 11th January, 1745–6
> Sunday parole, Derby. – Field-officer for the day; to-morrow, Major Wilson. The
> manner of the Highlanders' way of fighting, which there is nothing so easy to resist,
> if officers and men are not prepossessed with the lyes and accounts which are told of
> them. They commonly form their front rank of what they call their best men, or
> true Highlanders, the number of which being always but few. When they form in
> battalions, they commonly form four deep, and these Highlanders form the front of
> the four, the rest being Lowlanders and arrant scum. When these battalions come
> within a large musket shott or threescore yards, this front rank gives their fire, and
> immediately throw down their firelocks and come down in a cluster with their
> swords and targets, making a noise and endeavouring to pierce the body or
> battalion before them, – becoming twelve or fourteen deep by the time they come
> up to the people they attack . . . if the fire is given at a distance, you probably will be
> broke, for you never get time to load a second cartridge, and, if you give way, you
> may give your foot for dead, for they being without a firelock, or any load, no man
> with his arms, accoutrements, etc., can escape them, and they give no quarter.[3]

The Highland support for Jacobitism gave it a degree of military credibility in the same way that the French connection boasted its political and diplomatic standing, but the commitment of the clans seems paradoxical. As the previous chapter showed, three of the four Stewart kings of the seventeenth century were bent on policies of repression and control against the clans, and it seems indeed strange that their successors should have generated such loyalty among the Highlanders. Certainly not all the clans were Jacobite, especially in areas where presbyterianism had made an impact in the eighteenth century such as Argyll, Sutherland and Caithness, and clans Campbell, MacKay, Munro, Ross and Gunn were usually likely to favour the House of Hanover. Again, even if there was latent sympathy for the cause, active support for the rebellions in the Highlands varied very significantly over time, space and within clan groupings. Some families were split on points of political and religious principle and few clans were committed to either side in their entirety, if only because it was prudent to keep a foot in both camps to try to ensure that family lands would be secured whatever happened. Thus the first Duke of Atholl was a staunch supporter of the revolution of 1688–9 but three of his sons fought for the Jacobites under the Earl of Mar in 1715. Over time militant Jacobitism in the Highlands came to focus on the Grampian region and parts of western Inverness-shire. The clans of the inner and outer Hebrides played little part in the '45. The refusal of the chiefs of the MacDonalds and MacLeods in Skye to take part was a particularly bitter blow to Charles Edward Stewart, but the insular clans were more cautious because they were more exposed to attack by the Royal Navy. The political unreality of the '45 made even committed Jacobites opt for prudent neutrality. The 'Young Pretender' landed in the Outer Hebrides in the summer of that year with seven companions, some arms and 4,000 French gold coins, despite the estimates of the Jacobite leadership in Scotland that he needed to bring with him a war chest of 30,000 French gold pieces, arms for 10,000 men and a force of 6,000 soldiers to have even a reasonable chance of military success. Not surprisingly many found it difficult to reconcile Jacobite loyalties with the facts of life and the resulting uncertainties help to explain why several families had members on both sides. One extraordinary illustration of this was the experience of the Chisholms. The youngest son of Roderick Chisholm of Chisholm led the clan for Prince Charles and perished at Culloden, but his father stayed at home and had two other sons who fought in the Royal Scots Fusiliers on the Hanoverian side in the same battle. Entire clans were also divided. William Mackintosh of that Ilk tried to raise his men for the government, but all except nine deserted to join the 600 clansmen recruited by his wife, Lady Anne Mackintosh, for the Jacobites! Ewen MacPherson of Cluny, one of the most brilliant regimental commanders of the '45, was unable to bring out his entire clan in 1745 as its most powerful cadet branch, the MacPhersons of Invereshie, remained neutral throughout the rebellion. In all the rebellions, but particularly in the '45, chiefs used strong-arm tactics to force their clansmen out. Sending the 'fiery cross', the traditional call to battle, around their lands was not always enough.

However, the complex nature of shifting loyalties and divided responses does not answer the central question of why so many of the clans maintained a commitment to the restoration of the Stewart dynasty for so long. The religious factor was doubtless fundamental. After 1690 the association of the revolution of 1688 with presbyterianism swung episcopalians and roman catholics in favour of the Stewarts in the Highlands as it did in the north-east Lowlands. Only through the removal of the revolutionary regime of 1688 and, after 1714, the house of Hanover, could the full rights of non-jurors be restored and toleration for catholics ensured. Such episcopalian clans as the Camerons and Stewarts of Appin were therefore almost intuitively Jacobite, as were the catholic populations of Barra, South Uist, Morvern, Moidart, Arisaig, Morar and Knoydart. The tiny catholic enclave on the mainland was not only loyal, but its remoteness also left it virtually immune from Hanoverian incursion until after the failure of the '45. It was no coincidence that it was here at Loch nan Uamh, between Arisaig and Moidart, that the Young Pretender (i.e. claimant to the throne) made his first landing on the Scottish mainland at the start of his ill-fated expedition in the summer of 1745. But the religious factor was not always decisive. The Protestant MacKenzies came out on the Jacobite side during the 1715 rebellion as did the Whig Campbell of Glenorchy and Earl of Breadalbane and in that rising there were plenty of Protestant Campbells in the Jacobite camp. Religious faith did not always ensure clan unity as the example of the Chisholms, a normally Catholic clan discussed above, demonstrates.

Religion gave a stiffening and a sense of moral purpose to Highland Jacobitism, but its roots also lay in the political and economic realities of seventeenth century Scotland. It is possible to trace the identification of some clans with the house of Stewart back to the 1640s when they had fought under Alasdair MacColla and Montrose on the king's side against the Covenanters during the civil wars. This was a connection which was also in large part based on the hostility of many western clans to the continued expansion of Clan Campbell which during these wars was overtly anti-Stewart. These were alliances and hostilities which were to become an integral part of the later struggle between Jacobite and Hanoverian forces and were already being fashioned in this earlier period. As one scholar has put it, 'If Highland Jacobitism was born in the 1680s it had been conceived in the 1640s'.[4]

At one level, the appeal of Jacobitism for the clans may have been based on the fact that they could readily identify with the values of kinship and hereditary right which were shared by both monarchy and clanship. But James VII, while still Duke of York, did much to enhance this relationship and build a kind of bridge between the older Stewart policy of repression and a newer strategy of co-operation with the clan chiefs, and this was the approach he adopted when he came to Scotland in 1682. What almost certainly endeared him even more to clans such as the Camerons, MacLeans and some branches of Clan Donald, was that during his short period of government in Scotland, Archibald Campbell, the ninth Earl of Argyll and chief of Clan Campbell, was executed in 1685 for treason after his abortive rebellion against James. The monarchy in general terms and James and the Stewarts in particular were seen as effective checks on the rampant imperialism of Clan Campbell. Those clans along the western seaboard and in the islands who were steadily losing both lands and feudal superiorities to the earls of Argyll had little choice but to support the crown because only it had the legitimacy and resources to counter Campbell power. As the Marquis of Hamilton remarked to Charles I in 1638, the western Highlanders would ally with the royalist forces during the civil war, 'not say for anie greatt affection they cayrie to your Majestie bot because of ther splen to Lorne (i.e. Campbell) and will dou if they durst just contrarie to whatt his men doueth'.[5] In 1688–9 the removal of the Stewarts was paralleled by the full restoration of the Campbells. Their forfeiture was rescinded, the tenth Earl of Argyll personally administered the coronation oath to William and Mary at Westminster and the family was later rewarded with a dukedom. It was inevitable, therefore, that in the western Highlands, therefore, the revolution of 1688–9 became associated with the triumph of Campbell hegemony. Support for the exiled Stewarts was the only practical response and the connection between Jacobitism and anti-Campbell sentiment was thereafter a powerful and enduring one. However, even here there was complexity. The huge Campbell empire itself contained political diversity and the Breadalbane and Glenlyon branches, for instance, were sympathetic to the Stewarts in the 1715 rebellion. Marital relationships between Cameron and Campbell and MacDonald and Campbell existed alongside family and political divisions. But, overall, the vigorous support of the earls of Argyll for the Protestant Succession 1688, and later, for the house of Hanover, helped to swing their traditional rivals and mortal enemies in favour of the Stewarts.

The economic origins of Highland Jacobitism are more difficult to determine. Some writers have argued that the rebellions can be seen as a basic struggle between tribalism and capitalism when the archaic clan society of the Highlands was confronted by the dynamic, mercantile world of the Lowlands in a long drawn out struggle which ended when Gaelic society was finally crushed in the aftermath of the '45. This thesis is not very convincing. For a start,

Jacobite sympathies transcended the Highland/Lowland frontier and the Stewarts attracted support from most areas, both Lowland and Highland, north of the Tay, including the towns of that region. In addition, throughout Gaeldom, though Jacobite clans were in a majority, others were loyal to the Hanoverians. More fundamentally, the image of a backward region, mainly insulated from commercial forces, is in conflict with the evidence presented in chapter 1 of growing tensions within clanship as a result of the economic developments taking place in the seventeenth century Highlands. The expansion of droving was one of the most important Scottish commercial developments of the early modern period and could not have taken place on such a scale if there had not been more stability in the north. Some Jacobite chiefs were also notable for their entrepreneurial activities; they were not simply the tribal patriarchs or warrior leaders of legend. The chiefs of Clan Cameron, one of the most committed Jacobite clans, had interests in American land, timber exportation, the Caribbean plantations and the Edinburgh money market. MacDonnell of Glengarry was heavily involved in the provision of timber for charcoal for the production of iron. On his lowland estates, the Earl of Mar, the incompetent leader of the 1715 rebellion, had a range of industrial investments, including coal and glass. Robertson of Struan ran an extensive commercial forestry operation and deals produced from local timber and his estate around Loch Rannoch were floated down to the rivers Tummel and Tay and from there to lowland markets. The Duke of Perth, who was prominent in the '45, was a noted improver who was actively engaged in agricultural innovation on his estate in highland Perthshire in the early 1740s.

At the same time, however, there was evidence of a close correlation between political disaffection and financial difficulty. During the '45 it was estimated that twenty-two clans were 'out' for the Pretender and only ten for the government but, overall, the Hanoverians had the more prosperous clans on their side. Three Jacobite clans, MacDonnells of Keppoch, the MacGregors and MacDonalds of Glencoe, were either landless or possessed only marginal property. They tended mainly to make ends meet by cattle rieving and running protection rackets. A high proportion of other chiefs who committed themselves to Prince Charles in 1745 were in acute financial difficulty, much of it as a result of the attempt to live in the style of eighteenth century gentlemen on the limited revenue from a Highland estate. One contemporary, writing in the *Caledonian Mercury*, claimed that the yearly income of the clans numbered in the Jacobite army did not exceed £1,500, which if divided equally among the estimated 4,000 rebels was only 7s 6d a year each and less than a farthing a day!

Government was itself partly at fault for allowing financial hardship to fuel disaffection and a more generous programme of patronage to chiefs of Jacobite inclination might have brought rich dividends. In the reign of Queen Anne in the early eighteenth century, Westminster did pay annual pensions of £360 to such chiefs as Stewart of Appin, Cameron of Lochiel and Glengarry in return for good behaviour and, in addition, in the few years before the '45, the Mackintoshes and MacPhersons were given captaincies of the newly-created government Independent Companies. However, for the most part, pensions, posts and sinecures were not deployed in the Highlands as a means of shoring up Hanoverian support and most of the spoils that were available went to the Whig clans. In addition, in the years between the '15 and the '45 the state effectively created a power vacuum in Gaeldom. For the most part, the rebels of 1715 were treated leniently, mainly on the grounds that Jacobitism in Scotland was far too common for draconian action to be taken against it. The Disarming Act of 1725, passed after the abortive rising of 1719 and rumours of further plots, had more impact on the Whig clans than on the Jacobites. Around the same time, General Wade came north to begin an ambitious programme of road and fort construction. Between 1725 and his departure from Scotland in 1740 he claimed to have built 250 miles of road to facilitate government troop movements throughout the disaffected region. These routes were also designed to link the forts of Fort William, Fort Augustus, Bernera and Ruthven which were to act as the government's eyes and ears in the Jacobite districts. The whole basis of Wade's plan, however, was undermined from the later 1730s when the government stripped the forts of adequate garrisons in order to enhance the supply of troops for the European war, later known as the War of Jenkin's Ear. Wade's roads remained and helped to expedite the march of the Young Pretender's Jacobite army in 1745.

II

The early phase of the '45 rebellion culminating in the victory at Prestonpans and the march into England, was a remarkable triumph for the small Jacobite army of a few thousand men. To a significant extent, however, Charles's success not only reflected the martial *élan* of the clans but the weaknesses of the Scottish state and its virtual paralysis in the summer of 1745. The abolition of the Scottish Privy Council in 1708 had long since removed the executive structure as well as the main agency for intelligence gathering. When the Stewart standard was raised at Glenfinnan at the north end of Loch Sheil in August 1745 the government commander in Scotland, Sir John Cope, had a mere 3,000 troops at his disposal throughout the entire country. Even the Campbells, the government's crucial strategic buffer in the western Highlands, had been weakened as a fighting force by the second Duke of Argyll's estate reforms after 1737. These eroded the position of the tacksmen and made competition rather than clanship the main factor in the allocation of leases.

Yet the very potency of the threat posed by the advancing Jacobites ensured that the government soon responded with determination and vigour and battle-hardened regiments were speedily withdrawn from the European theatre. The retreat of the Highlanders from Derby was a reaction of Charles's Council of War to the knowledge that the Brigade of Guards now stood between them and London and that three separate armies were massing to advance. There was also a recognition that they had failed to attract any significant support for the Jacobite cause in the north of England and retreat seemed the most sensible option. The return to Scotland, outnumbered by the enemy and marching through hostile territory, was itself an outstanding exploit. However, after a further victory at Falkirk, the Jacobite forces retreated again into the Highlands, thus ensuring that they were unable to obtain funds through levies and taxation on the richer Lowland counties and towns. Indeed, the central, and especially the western Lowlands, the economic heart of Scotland, were always con-spicuously hostile and the presbyterian church openly and stridently opposed. Sources of Jacobite revenue inevitably contracted and this fundamental problem was compounded by the failure of the French treasure ships, especially *Le Prince Charles*, to get through to Scotland with vital financial support. It would appear that the Young Pretender decided to turn and fight at Culloden on ground which favoured regular infantry and artillery and put the clan regiments at a positive disadvantage, because his cause was, in the literal sense, bankrupt. It was not only fatigue, after an attempted night attack on the government army at Nairn, which weakened the Highlanders on that fateful day in April 1746. Hunger also played an important part. A significant proportion of the army was away foraging for food and took no part in the battle, and Charles's decision to stand and fight despite all this reflected his own desperation and the complete financial collapse of his cause.

The rout of the Jacobites at Culloden was the prelude to a massive military, judicial and political assault on the clan society which had spawned subversion. There were two key differences from the aftermath of the '15 rebellion. First, a huge regular army, supported by naval units, had been drawn into the very heart of the Highlands and could be used in effective combination for punitive action against the clans. Second, the '45 rebellion had come too close to success and the very social system which had produced the attempted counter-revolution had to be destroyed. The Duke of Cumberland, the Hanoverian commander, contended that there had been a missed opportunity after the '15 to destroy clanship and this mistake was not to be repeated again. Underpinning the eventual ferocity of the government's response was the belief that the Gaels were a deadly poison threatening the body politic which had to be rooted out by radical surgery. Six years before the rebellion, the following appeared in a London magazine:

> In this great Extent of Country, [the Highlands] Ignorance and Superstition greatly prevail; In some Places the Remains even of Paganism are still to be found, and in many others the Reformation from Popery has never yet obtained. The Parishes where Ministers are settled, are commonly of very great Extent, some 30, 40, 50 Miles long, and generally divided by unpassable Mountains and Lakes; so that most of the Inhabitants being destitute of all Means of Knowledge, and without any Schools to educate their Children, are entirely ignorant of the Principles of Religion and Virtue, live in Idleness and Poverty, have no Notion of Industry, or Sense of Liberty, are subject to the Will and Command of their Popish disaffected Chieftains, who have always opposed the propagating Christian Knowledge, and the English Tongue, that they might with less Difficulty keep their miserable Vassals in a slavish Dependance. The poorer sort have only the Irish Tongue, and little Correspondence with the civilized arts of the Nation, and only come among them to pillage the more industrious Inhabitants; they are brought up in Principles of Tyranny and Arbitrary Government, depend upon foreign Papists as their main Support, and the native Irish as their best Correspondents and Allies. This has been the Source of all the Rebellions and Insurrections, in that Country, since the Revolution.[6]

The onslaught began with the systematic pillage of western mainland Inverness-shire and the adjacent islands by the army and Royal Navy in which even Highland communities loyal to the crown suffered extensive depredations. In due course, the military road system was considerably extended until by 1767 over a thousand miles had been built. Between 1748 and 1769 one of the greatest bastion artillery fortresses in Europe was constructed at Ardersier, east of Inverness, and named Fort George. It was a permanent physical demonstration of the state's commitment that the clans would never again rise to menace the protestant succession. Through the passage of a series of Acts of Parliament, an attack was launched on the culture of the Gael and the system of clanship: Highland dress and the playing of the pipes were proscribed as the symbols of militarism; heritable jurisdictions, the private courts held by the landowners, were abolished; and the carrying of weapons was forbidden and estates of rebels declared forfeit to the crown. Forty-one properties were forfeited in all, but significantly, in the light of earlier discussion about the financial pressures which fuelled disaffection, the vast majority were sold by the Barons of Exchequer by auction to pay creditors. Thirteen, however, were inalienably annexed and managed between 1752 and 1784 by a Commission in order to promote 'the Protestant Religion, good Government, Industry and Manufactures, and the Principles of Duty and Loyalty to His Majesty'. The thinking was that protestantism would induce ideological conformity while prosperity would remove the alienation which had caused rebellion.

It is tempting to regard this ambitious legislative programme as a major watershed in Highland history, especially since the second half of the eighteenth century did see the rapid disintegration and collapse of clanship. But the temptation to see a clear cause and effect relationship should be resisted. As one historian has put it, 'The fact that there never was another Jacobite after 1745 owed more to a disinclination to rebel than to the government's repressive measures'.[7] The savagery of the Hanoverian forces seems to have produced little more than stubborn defiance in a people inured to hard times. Indeed, in the short run, there were more disturbances than usual in the Jacobite areas. The Earl of Albemarle, Cumberland's successor, became so frustrated that he concluded the only way to ensure permanent stability was to devastate whole areas and deport large numbers of their inhabitants. Equally significantly, his reports show there was still an expectation in some areas that a French landing would eventually provide support and succour and this suggests that suppression in the later 1740s kept the spirit of Jacobitism alive rather than destroyed it. The proscription of wardship and heritable jurisdictions made little impact as clan loyalties were matters of the mind and heart rather than the law, and the abolition of the private jurisdictions mainly affected the Lowland nobility and not the clan chiefs. Military land tenures such as wardship had been rendered obsolete already due to the commercial developments of the seventeenth and early eighteenth centuries. The Commission for Annexed Forfeited Estates strove to improve agriculture, establish industry and develop communications. Not all the effort was in vain and there was significant progress in the building of roads and bridges, but no social and economic revolution was achieved because of the profound constraints of poor land endowment, remoteness and social suspicion. One Commissioner, Lord Kames, admitted that in the final analysis much of the resources poured into the Highlands had been 'no better than water spilt on the ground'.[8]

But the society did seem to change in the decades after Culloden. Dr Samuel Johnson during his tour of the Western Isles in 1773 pronounced the death of clanship: 'the clans retain little now of their original character. Their ferocity of temper is softened, their military ardour is extinguished, their dignity of independence is depressed, their contempt for government subdued, and their reverence for their chiefs abated'.[9] But whether all of this was due, as Johnson contended, to 'the late conquest and subsequent laws' is debatable. As chapter 1 demonstrated the Highlands were in the throes of a long transition from clanship to commercialism well before the '45. More and more the gentry of the clans were showing the characteristics of landlords rather than of chieftains and the final pacification of the Highlands accelerated this process, but it was effective precisely because clanship was already in decline. In the last analysis, however, neither legislation nor military occupation was critical. What finally and irrevocably transformed social relations in the Highlands were the irresistible market pressures emanating from Lowland industrialisation and urbanisation in the second half of the eighteenth century. That is why social change in Gaeldom did not gather speed until the 1760s and 1770s because it was precisely in these decades that the economic revolution in the south really began.

NOTES

1 Quoted in R. Mitchison, 'The government and the Highlands, 1707–1745' in N. T. Phillipson and R. Mitchison, eds, *Scotland in the Age of Improvement*, Edinburgh, 1970, p. 31.
2 Extract of a letter from a 'Gentleman at Derby', 13 December 1745, *Gentleman's Magazine*, XVI, January 1746.
3 Quoted in P. Anderson, *Culloden Moor*, Stirling, 1920, p. 57.
4 D. Stevenson, *Alasdair MacColla and the Highland Problem in the Seventeenth Century*, Edinburgh, 1980.
5 Quoted in A. I. Macinnes, 'Scottish Gaeldom, 1638–1651: the vernacular response to the covenanting dynamic' in J. Dwyer, R. A. Mason and A. Murdoch, eds, *New Perspectives on the Politics and Culture of Early Modern Scotland*, Edinburgh, n.d., p. 84.
6 *Gentleman's Magazine*, IX, June 1739.
7 W. A. Speck, *The Butcher*, London, 1981, p. 183.
8 Quoted in B. Lenman, *The Jacobite Risings in Britain 1689–1746*, London, 1980, p. 281.
9 S. Johnson, *A Journey to the Western Islands of Scotland*, Oxford, 1924 edn, p. 51.

FURTHER READING

P. Hopkins, *Glencoe and the End of the Highland War*, Edinburgh, 1986.
B. Lenman, *The Jacobite Risings in Britain 1689–1746*, London, 1980.
B. Lenman, *The Jacobite Clans of the Great Glen, 1650–1784*, London, 1984.
F. McLynn, *The Jacobite Army in England, 1745: The Final Campaign*, Edinburgh, 1983.
F. McLynn, *The Jacobites*, London, 1985.
F. McLynn, *Charles Edward Stuart: A Tragedy in Many Acts*, Oxford, 1991.
R. Mitchison, 'The government and the Highlands, 1707–1745', in N. T. Phillipson and R. Mitchison, eds, *Scotland in the Age of Improvement*, Edinburgh, 1970.
A. M. Smith, *Jacobite Estates of the Forty-Five*, Edinburgh, 1982.
W. A. Speck, *The Butcher: the Duke of Cumberland and the Suppression of the '45*, London, 1981.
A. J. Youngson, *The Prince and the Pretender*, London, 1985.

3

THE TRANSFORMATION OF GAELDOM

I

Gaelic society and clanship were in decay long before the later eighteenth century. However, in the 1760s and 1770s there was a marked acceleration in the rate of social change and, in subsequent decades, material, cultural and demographic forces combined to produce a dramatic revolution in the Highland way of life. In simple terms traditional society was destroyed in this period and a new order based on quite different values, principles and relationships emerged to take its place. Before this time, elite attitudes were changing, commercial influences were on the increase and government pressures on clanship in the aftermath of the '45 were intensifying. However, the basic structure of Gaelic society in most areas remained broadly unaltered. What happened in the last quarter of the eighteenth century was a decisive change of pace which was brought about by an enormous expansion in the rest of Britain for such Highland produce as cattle, kelp, whisky, wool, mutton, timber, slate and a host of other commodities. The irresistible forces which were unleashed transformed the Highlands forever.

Commerce, and in particular the export of cattle and the import of meal, had long been vital to Gaelic society. But in this period southern markets began to exert such a dominant influence that the Highland region effectively became an economic satellite with its population increasingly dependent for survival on demand for products from the industries and cities of the Lowlands and England. A full-scale process of commercialisation was under way. and one important indicator was the movement of rentals. Starting in the 1760s, but speeding up drastically during the Napoleonic Wars, rentals through the region soared to unprecedented levels to catch the surplus from rising prices. It was the speed and scale of rent inflation that was new and different from the earlier eighteenth century and, in addition, most of it reflected surging external demand rather than a return on landlord improvement investment. Skye rents trebled in the third quarter of the eighteenth century while those of Torridon in Wester Ross rose tenfold between 1777 and 1805. On the Lochiel estate in Inverness, the rental jumped from £560 in the 1760s to £863 in 1774, an increase of 45 per cent with even more dramatic rises later. Glengarry rentals stood at £732 in 1768, but by 1802 had spiralled by 472 per cent to £4,184.

The raising of rents to this extent demonstrated that the Highland elites were now subordinating their lands to market production and new commercial imperatives, and a revolution in the attitude to and function of land took place. The growing commercial economy of the decades before about 1760 could be uneasily accommodated with the old social structure, but the traditional order was no longer compatible with wholehearted agricultural production for the market at competitive prices. Important consequences ensued. First the transition of clan chiefs and gentry to landed gentlemen, which had been under way for several generations, was finally accomplished and the heritable trusteeship of clan elites, obliging them to secure and maintain the landed possessions of their kindred and associates within their territories, was abandoned in favour of other priorities. Land came to be allocated through competition to the bidder able and willing to offer the highest return. It was the resolute imposition of these new standards when tenancies were available for reletting which was one factor in stoking up the social tensions stimulating wave after wave of emigration from the western Highlands in the later eighteenth century.

Secondly, there was a sustained and widespread assault on the traditional township or *baile*. These group settlements of multiple tenant farmers, cottars, and servants had formed the basic communities of Gaeldom from time immemorial, but over the space of two to three generations, starting in Argyll and Highland Perthshire in the 1760s and quickly spreading north and west in subsequent decades, the *baile* was broken up and virtually eliminated. By the 1830s and 1840s only a few remnants of a once universal pattern of settlement and cultivation remained. But the new structure which emerged to take its place was far from simple and reflected not only the strategies of individual landowners but varying natural endowment, climatic advantage and market potential. Thus in much of Argyll, Highland Perthshire and the eastern parishes of Inverness, lands were often consolidated into single tenant farms, some pastoral but many arable, with their dependent servants and labourers. In this region too there were the crofts or smallholdings which were more typical of the north and west. The heartland of the new 'crofting' society, however, was the western seaboard to the north of Fort William and extending to all the Inner and Outer Hebrides. In this region the communal townships were steadily replaced by individual smallholdings or crofts with the arable land possessed by single small tenants and the grazing land still held in common. The core of the new structure, however, was division of the scattered strips or rigs of arable, which were the basis of the old system of joint farming, into separate holdings of only a few acres. In addition, throughout the whole Highland area, but especially before 1815 in the central and western mainland, commercial pastoral farms were advancing rapidly. The coming of the *Na Caoraidh Mora* or 'big sheep', as the Gaels called the Blackface and Cheviots which stocked these holdings in the eighteenth century Highlands, posed a particular threat to the old society. Before the 1750s there were few commercial, specialist sheep ranches anywhere in the Highlands. Yet, as early as 1802, an official report of the Highland Society described how the hill country of Perth, Dumbarton and Argyll and the entire west coast from Oban to Lochbroom were already under sheep. Most of Mull had been invaded and the sheep frontier was also starting to advance in Skye. The report concluded ominously that 'In Ross and northwards all parts capable of sheep are or soon will be occupied'.

Third, there were important effects on social structure. This was partly to do with the impact of the crofting revolution. The delicate and graduated social hierarchies of the *baile* were shattered and replaced by the virtually uniform small tenancies of the new crofting townships and it was in large part for this reason that the transformation from *baile* to croft caused such widespread anxiety and hostility throughout the Highlands. Equally significantly, the traditional tacksman class was gradually reduced in number and social significance as the deliberate destruction of subtenure became a central theme of landlord policy from the 1770s. The action of the Duke of Argyll against the tacksmen of his estate had been unusual in the 1730s, but fifty years later it was commonplace as the landed classes sought to absorb the middlemen rentals. The demise of the tacksmen varied in speed and extent from estate to estate. Some who were wadsetters, that is gentlemen who had received lands from their chief as security in return for providing loans, were bought out. Others were placed in difficulty by having their rights to subletting reduced. Sharp increases in rental also put acute pressure on many, as in the 1750s much of the rent on many Highland estates would be paid by the tacksmen. A century later, they were but a minor part of the social structure and the displacement of this class was one of the clearest demonstrations of the death of the old Gaelic society. The new middle class in many areas were invariably southern sheep farmers and cattle ranchers with little hereditary or ethnic connection with the people.

Fourthly, the new landlord priorities and incessant market pressures produced a massive and relentless displacement of population. Eviction and forced removal became an integral part of the destruction of the traditional settlements throughout the Highlands and this was the most direct violation of *duthchas*, the obligation on clan elites to provide protection and security of possession for their people within their lands. 'Clearance', as the process of dispossession became known to later generations, was far from simple. Too often it is equated only with the removals resulting from the creation of large sheep farms. But displacement took place by other means and for other reasons. The carving out of the monotonous lines of crofts from the scattered rigs of the *baile* led to the eviction of entire communities. It also became almost routine for estates in the north west and islands to move people from inland glens to the sea and to areas of moorland where new crofts were planted in the waste and the settlers encouraged to reclaim it by potato cultivation. Removal of the *bailtean* to create larger arable holdings was a marked feature of the southern Highlands, and today at Auchindrain in Argyllshire there still survive many of the buildings of an old farming township in a marvellous open-air museum. But in the 1760s between Auchindrain and the half dozen miles to Inveraray, there were no fewer than a further six such settlements. By the nineteenth century they had all disappeared.

This was a vivid illustration of the subordination of the human factor to the new needs of productive efficiency. Possession of individual areas of land had never been permanent in the old society when clan territory had been lost by conquest, annexation and insolvency. It was common for subtenants and cottars, and even principal tenants, to be moved from one farm to another. The later eighteenth century, however, brought dispossession on a truly unprecedented scale all over Gaeldom with people on the move everywhere. Sometimes the pressures did not come by direct removal. The jacking up of rentals in a peasant economy where the balance between sufficiency and failure was a fine and precarious one caused immense strain. The detailed research by Marianne McLean on western Inverness-shire shows that often rent increases were pushed above the rise in cattle prices and when the markets collapsed, as they did in 1772–3 and again in 1783–4, rent arrears spiralled and small tenants came under great pressure to surrender their holdings. Similarly, when farms were offered for letting at higher rents, which reflected the new commercial realities of the time, the poorer men had profound difficulty in competing. Loss of land was an inevitable result.

Undoubtedly, however, it was large-scale pastoral husbandry which led to the greatest social dislocation. Extensive cattle ranching was increasingly practised in parts of Argyll, Dumbarton and Perthshire and dislodged many peasant communities. One contemporary, John Walker, estimated that as a result of conversion of small farms into large cattle holdings, population had fallen in seventeen parishes in these counties since 1750. Much more significant, however, was sheep-farming. The new Blackface and Cheviot breeds were greedy for land and required different levels and types of land for the different ages and sexes of the flocks. The Cheviots in particular had special needs. Initially they enabled sheep-farmers to pay twice the rent that was usually possible on land grazed by Blackfaces, but they could not easily survive the Highland climate without access to low ground for wintering and this posed a potent threat to the arable lands of the traditional townships. At the same time, the sheep competed for grazing with the small tenants' black cattle. The sheiling grounds where stock were taken into the hill country during the summer months while crops were growing on the arable land which was so vital to the functioning of the traditional cattle economy were especially at risk. Sheep-farming therefore weakened the basis of the old economy by other means than direct clearance. Thus in two sheep-grazing parishes in Sutherland (Creich and Assynt) between 1790 and 1808, the numbers of cattle fell from 5,140 to 2,906 while sheep increased from 7,840 to 21,000.

Much more cataclysmic, however, was the extensive and direct removal of peasant communities to make way for the big sheep farms. The new order and the old pastoral economy were fundamentally incompatible as not only was there intense competition for scarce land, but the rental return from sheep was significantly higher than that from cattle. This was not only because of price differences in the market resulting from the new industrial demand for wool, but it was also because sheep used land more intensively *and* extensively than cattle. They were able to graze in areas formerly under-utilised in the old pastoral economy. In addition, landlords stood to gain from more secure returns. Sheep farms were normally run by big graziers who could guarantee the proprietor a regular and rising income in most years, whereas small tenants were much less dependable: their rent payments fluctuated with the weather and the state of the cattle markets. Nor could the indigenous tenantry hope to participate in the sheep economy in large numbers, as pastoralism was most efficient when practised on a large scale and this created an insurmountable financial barrier for most Highland tenants. There is evidence, for example, on the estates of MacDonnell of Glengarry and Cameron of Lochiel in Inverness-shire of some townships building up small flocks of Blackface in the 1770s, but the landlords were too impatient for the massive profits to be obtained from grazing on a large scale, especially since there were now plenty of ambitious and enterprising farmers from the pastoral districts of Ayrshire, the Borders and Northumberland eager for Highland leases. The unexploited lands of the north had become too valuable to be let to the inexperienced native tenantry.

As the sheep frontier advanced, so also did clearance. The most notorious removals took place on the Sutherland estate and between 1807 and 1821 the factors of the Countess of Sutherland and her husband Lord Stafford removed between 6,000 and 10,000 people from the inner parishes to new crofting settlements on the coast in the most extraordinary example of social engineering in early nineteenth century Britain. Old men looking back from the 1880s could still give the names of forty-eight cleared townships in the parish of Assynt alone. In its scale and level of organisation no other clearance matched that of Sutherland. Indeed, the vast majority of removals probably only involved a few people at a time until the more draconian episodes of the 1840s and 1850s during the potato famine. Gradual and relentless displacement rather than mass eviction was the norm, but taken together the numbers involved were very great and suggest a systematic process of enforced movement on an unprecedented scale.

What is clear, nevertheless, is that most clearances before 1815 were not designed to expel the people. The conventional eighteenth century assumption that a rising population was an economic benefit was only slowly being questioned with, more practically, most landowners and improving theorists taking the view that the evicted represented an important resource who should not simply be discarded. A dual economy was envisaged, each part of which would in time be a source of increasing revenue. Thus the people from the inner straths and glens should be moved to the coast where they might find employment in kelp or fishing and the interior districts would then become extensive sheep farms. This became the pattern along the whole west coast north of Fort William as the entire traditional settlement structure was fundamentally changed in the later eighteenth and early nineteenth centuries. On the Reay estate in northwest Sutherland the inland population was settled on the coast in the 1810s and further south in Wester Ross and western Inverness similar forced movements from the inland areas occurred in Glensheil, Glenelg, Morvern and other districts. The people no longer had traditional guarantees of land and the old social order was destroyed forever.

II

The social experience of the Scottish Highlands in the decades after c. 1760 had its distinctive characteristics, but it was far from being unique in Europe as all over the continent and the British Isles ancient social systems were increasingly under pressure. The eighteenth and nineteenth centuries were an epoch of persistent rise in population, urban growth and industrial expansion and in virtually every European country the rural economy had to produce more food and raw materials at acceptable prices to feed and support the growing urban masses. To a greater or lesser extent the new market orientation of agriculture imposed enormous strains on the older social patterns and in some regions caused considerable dislocation. The most potent threat came from the recognition that land was now principally to be seen as an asset and a productive resource to be managed according to its capacity for earning profit rather than a basic source of support for the rural population. Enclosure and consolidation was the principal means by which this radical change was accomplished, and these brought to an end the old order in which several members of a community had rights of use to a new condition in which single occupants possessed complete control. There were echoes of this dramatic transition in the wave of clearances and land improvements which swept across the Scottish Highlands from the last quarter of the eighteenth century.

But there was also profound regional variation in western Europe to these changes in markets and ideologies. The peasant social order, where the majority of the people retained some rights of access to land, survived in most European countries, partly due to the varying impact and intensity of market demand but more fundamentally to the widespread nature of peasant proprietorship on the continent. To disturb land interests sanctified by both law and custom would have threatened to unleash massive social disorder, and thus it was only in a few countries and areas that the full impact of the new agronomy and its revolutionary effect on traditional patterns of life and settlement was experienced. These included England, Scotland, Denmark, the Low Countries, Catalonia in Spain, some German states, such as Pomerania and Brandenburg, and parts of Sweden, and even in these regions there was great diversity in the pace, nature and structure of agrarian change. This demonstrates that though the pressures making for reform of the rural economy were common across Europe, the responses to them depended ultimately on the particular political, legal, social, cultural and economic characteristics of each country. The case of Denmark, for instance, highlights the peculiar features of the revolution in land in northern Scotland. The Danes also mounted a sustained attack on communal agriculture and 'inefficient' patterns of landholding, but the whole revolution was supported by the state and managed in a way which markedly reduced the social costs which otherwise might be incurred as a result of the huge upheaval in peasant agriculture. State regulation was involved from the start when a Danish Royal Commission in 1757 produced a series of recommendations, later incorporated as state decrees, which provided for consolidation, rated the costs among individual villages and established a fund to help cover the costs of reform. But the striking feature of the Danish case was the degree of social benevolence employed to ensure social stability as the new structure was steadily built up and those who suffered loss from the reforms were to be compensated by a leasehold of four to six acres. Other legislation banned division of lands into areas too small to support a family.

The case of the Scottish Highlands could not have been more different. There state action and control were minimal and landlords virtually allowed complete freedom of action. Indeed, from the seventeenth century in Scotland the balance of law had swung even more decisively towards the interests of private property. Acts of the Scottish Parliament in 1661, 1669, 1685 and 1695 created the legal framework for land division and the consolidation of runrig and an Act of the Court of Session of 1756 clarified the legal procedures for removal of tenants, which could relatively easily be accomplished through application to a local sheriff court at least forty days before Whitsun. The system of land tenure in Scotland was well suited to the exercise of landlord authority as small peasant proprietors of the type who dominated the social structure of many European countries did not extend to any great extent. The overwhelming majority of the Highland population in the eighteenth century had no absolute legal right to land. They were either tenants whose rights were finite and limited by lease or agreement or they belonged to the growing underclass of semi-landless cottars and servants who possessed no legal security of tenure whatsoever. It was the legal and customary defencelessness of the people which made the clearances possible in the Highlands, and which simply would not have been feasible in many regions of the continent where peasant ownership and legal rights and privileges built up over centuries were formidable obstacles to radical and rapid agrarian modernisation.

There were, however, similarities with patterns of social change in the Scottish Lowlands, as there too there was considerable population displacement. Just as the Highland *bailtean* were broken up, so also were the *ferm touns* of the traditional Lowland society. Over time multiple tenancies and communal farming were steadily eliminated and by the early nineteenth century in most districts farms leased by individual husbandmen had become dominant. In several ways there were intriguing and close analogies with the Highland experience. From the middle decades of the seventeenth century Border cattle and sheep ranching had expanded rapidly on the basis of the new demands from the urbanising and industrialising areas of the north of England which led to extensive farm consolidation, annexation of peasant arable and grazing lands to feed and winter stock, and inevitably the removal of many small communities in a manner similar to what happened later in the Highlands.

Clearance and dispossession were, therefore, not uniquely Highland. The whole of Scotland in the last quarter of the eighteenth century was in turmoil as the new order took shape and for too long the 'Lowland Clearances' have been neglected by historians at the expense of concentration on events in the north and west. Old tenurial rights, ancient patterns of settlement and traditional habits of working the land were being transformed everywhere in Scotland in these decades to a greater or lesser extent. But, nevertheless, there were distinctive aspects of the changes in the Highlands which mark the Gaelic experience out from the broader movement to agrarian improvement elsewhere in Scotland.

The movement from multiple to single tenancy occurred over many decades in the south while in Gaeldom the breakup of the *bailtean* was concentrated in the later eighteenth century. The Highland experience, outside the southern and eastern fringes, was therefore more traumatic. The terrain of most of the north and west was best suited to large-scale pastoral husbandry which required much land but little labour, whereas over much of the Lowland areas farming was based on a mix of arable cultivation and stock rearing which required more hands. Again, in the western Highlands and Islands, no successful alternative to agriculture developed. In the eighteenth century, kelp, fishing, distilling and quarrying all prospered but after 1815 they went into rapid decline. In the Lowlands, on the other hand, the booming textile industries, many of them located in rural districts, and the creation of the elaborate new urban and agrarian infrastructures, offered employment to those threatened with dispossession as a result of agrarian improvement.

One suspects also that the Gaels were more vulnerable to mass removal. The rural social system in the Lowlands, even before the Age of Improvement, depended on the tenant farmers who paid the rents to the landlord and employed the cottars and servants. This class had legal rights to their holdings over a given period, usually between eight to fifteen years, which was defined clearly in written leases which were enforceable at law and this made instant, comprehensive and widespread removal of entire tenant communities virtually impossible. Proprietors had to proceed with patience and weed out surplus tenants slowly as leases lapsed. In many highland districts, however, the majority were much more vulnerable as possession was invariably by custom or short annual leases which posed little obstacle to the enthusiastic improver. Not surprisingly, therefore, in a society where legal security was minimal, clearances spread alarm and anxiety throughout areas still undisturbed and helped to push people into making preparation for emigration long before they faced the direct threat of removal.

The cultural distinction was also vital in understanding the impact of clearance on the psyche of the Gael. There was a quite different social relationship between elites and people in the two regions of Scotland by the middle decades of the eighteenth century. Due in large part to the much earlier pacification and hence more thorough-going commercialisation of the Lowlands, landowners were no longer regarded as heads of kindred groups or personal, feudal followings and were simply proprietors. The rights and privileges of the tenants of their estates were defined in the written lease and although labour duties were still required the main factor in the relationship between lessor and lessee was the rental, either paid in cash or kind, and increasingly in the former. Tenants had no right to land beyond the terms of the lease and could be removed from it as a result of a breach of the agreement or for persistent rent arrears. At the end of term, it was common for holdings to change hands and the connection between landlord and tenants was, therefore, a commercial and economic one. Land was property and there was a social acceptance of this fundamental fact by both parties.

As noted earlier in this book, this was not at all the pattern in Gaelic society. Even if the clan elites had new commercial assumptions and priorities, the people still clung to the principles of *duthchas* in which the landlord had a basic duty as protector and the guarantee of land possession was central to this role. Not only, therefore, was the scale of removal greater and faster in the Highlands, but the cultural trauma of dispossession by 'landlord-protectors' was much more devastating for the people. It is hardly surprising that the relentless violation of the values of clanship caused enormous collective disorientation throughout the Gaelic world and hence a basic difficulty in resisting landlord action in any effective fashion. As one recent author has put it:

> That the occupiers of the soil adhered tenaciously to the traditionalist concept of *duthchas* long after clanship had been abrogated by the conduct of chiefs and leading gentry is testimony more to the cultural disorientation rather than outright cultural alienation occasioned by the first phase of Clearance. Unlike contemporaneous Irish Gaels who were able to direct polemical attacks against the alien English forces of government, the landowning classes and the established church, Scottish Gaels seem prisoners of their own culture, thoroughly perplexed, demoralised and disorientated by the process of anglicisation effected by the assimilation of the clan elite into the British establishment. The criticisms of the poets – still the main outlets for public opinion within Scottish Gaeldom – were usually expressed deferentially through misplaced strictures against factors, legal agents, tacksmen, incoming tenant farmers and even sheep. On the rare occasions when landlords were indicted as instigators of Clearance, citations were depersonalised, the amorphous 'they' being held responsible.[1]

III

While the processes and outcomes of agrarian modernisation may have differed between Highlands and Lowlands the origins of social change were not dissimilar. Britain was the first industrial nation and the demands on the rural economy for more food and raw materials were considerable, but in Scotland rapid economic change came later than in England and agrarian modernisation took place within a shorter time scale. In the early eighteenth century around one Scot in eight lived in a town of more than 5,000 in population, by the 1820s this was more like one in three. This rapid pattern of urban expansion suggests an economy experiencing massive structural change with inevitable results for agricultural producers. In simple terms the depth and extent of the markets for all that the Highlands could export was transformed and the commercial forces were so powerful that social change in Gaeldom became irresistible.

Demand for traditional staples boomed. Cattle prices quadrupled in the course of the eighteenth century and total exports of cattle from the region probably quintupled. In Argyll, albeit to a lesser extent further north, commercial fishing of herring became even more significant with, for example, some 600 to 800 boats engaged annually in Loch Fyne alone. Due to changes in government revenue legislation and enhanced Lowland markets, demand increased persistently for illicit whisky, and the exploitation of Highland slate quarries at Easdale and Ballachuilish and elsewhere, and of woodland on many estates continued apace. Textile production began to expand in Highland Perthshire, Argyll and eastern Inverness and in parts of Ross and Cromarty and Sutherland, and the production of linen cloth stamped for sale in the Highland counties rose steadily from 21,972 yards in 1727/8 to 202,006 yards by 1778.

Southern industrialisation had an insatiable and voracious appetite for Highland raw materials in the later eighteenth century and thereafter, with wool being in special demand. The Lowland cotton industry quickly achieved abundant supplies of raw fibre from the Caribbean and then from the southern USA, but it was more difficult for the woollen manufacturers. Overseas supply from Europe was limited and erratic during the Napoleonic Wars and it was only when Australia started to export in volume from the 1820s that overseas sources became really significant. In the interim, the gap was increasingly filled by Highland sheep-farmers and by 1828 Scottish wool accounted for just under 10 per cent of UK output and 25 per cent by the early 1840s. Behind these statistics lay the convulsion in Highland society unleashed by the inexorable advance of the sheep farms. Equally significant for a time, though in different ways, was the manufacture of kelp, an alkali seaweed extract used in the manufacture of soap and glass. Industrial demand for it was on the increase, not least because cheaper and richer sources of foreign barilla were curtailed during the French Wars, and kelp production seemed well suited to the western Highlands and Islands where the raw material was abundant. Cheap and plentiful supply of labour was vital since the process of production though essentially a simple one was very arduous with a ratio of one ton of kelp refined to twenty tons of collected seaweed. Kelp manufacture began in the west in the 1730s but not until after 1750 did it begin to take hold: 2,000 tons per annum output were reached in the 1770s and 5,000 in 1790 and thereafter the industry boomed, achieving a peak production in 1810 of about 7,000 tons. By that date its main centres had become clearly established as the Uists, Barra, Harris, Lewis, Skye, Tiree and Mull, and on the mainland there was also considerable activity in Ardnamurchan and Morvern. But to a considerable extent kelp production was concentrated in the Hebrides, especially in the Long Island, and there, as will be seen in more detail below, it had profound social consequences.

British demand was not simply confined to the foodstuffs and raw materials of the Highlands. The market for human beings was also expanding, as young adult Gaels, especially from Argyll, had taken up seasonal harvest work in lowland farms earlier in the eighteenth century. After the 1770s opportunities increased, as output rose in southern agriculture and the old cottar class, which had been the main source of harvest labour in the past, was readily reduced in size. Highland migrants also took up seasonal employment in the herring fishery of the Clyde and in the bleachfields around the textile towns and villages. An even more spectacular growth industry was the recruitment of Gaels into the British Army and Navy in the later eighteenth century. Beginning on a small scale during the Seven Years War (1756–63) and increasing during the American War, recruitment multiplied to extraordinary levels during the Napoleonic Wars when, on one estimate, the Highlands supplied around 74,000 men for regiments of the line, the Militia, Fencibles and Volunteers out of a total regional population of about 300,000. This was a quite remarkable figure, even if probably inflated and represents a *per capita* rate of military recruitment unequalled in any other region of Europe. It was eloquent testimony to the impact of population pressures at the time and of the ability of the landlords to maximise recruitment to their family regiments by coercion and the promise of land in return for service.

On a much broader scale the role of the landed classes was fundamental in accelerating social change. As earlier discussion has shown they were in a position of virtual omnipotence over their people with full legal authority to transform their estates when they willed it. In theory, however, the hereditary duties attached to their position in the clan structure was a powerful impediment. The roles of chief and capitalist landlord were completely incompatible and there is evidence in the historical record of landed families agonising over the conflicts between these two functions. However, the forces making for the triumph of landlordism over tribalism were eventually triumphant.

First, as shown in chapter 1, many Highland proprietors were increasingly acting in their own commercial interest rather than that of their clansmen before the 1750s. Second, if chiefs were becoming an integral part of the British landed elite, they could not remain immune from the material, intellectual and cultural goals of that class. Among the aristocracy and gentry the eighteenth century was an era of conspicuous consumption, of ornate and expensive building, foreign travel and a more opulent style of life. The atmosphere in elite circles was one of competitive display where a family's place was defined by the grandeur of its physical surroundings and this was the world now inhabited by the Highland landowners, one which was a constant drain on the purse and in which they could not easily survive on the paltry returns of traditional agriculture. Third, clearance and dispossession could be and were given intellectual justification. The Highland elites through education in southern schools and universities and travel elsewhere had absorbed non-Gaelic values and objectives long before the '45. Alien forces were partly responsible for the destruction of the traditional society through the post-Culloden pacification and the activities in certain districts of the Commissioners for the Annexed Forfeited Estates. Fundamentally, however, the revolution was achieved by the indigenous leaders of Gaeldom who had absorbed and accepted the ideas current among their class elsewhere in Britain. These included a view of the existing social order as 'primitive' and urgently in need of reform, an uncritical belief in the values of individualism and a contempt for the traditional patterns of life and work as demonstrating the indolence, fecklessness and inefficiency of the people. These assumptions made it much easier to reorganise their estates along more rational and profitable lines. The landlords were not simply making more money but they could also justify the abrogation of their traditional responsibilities by claiming that it was a necessary evil in order to 'civilise' and 'improve' their estates.

Fourth, the sheer force of market pressure was fundamental. Demand for Highland commodities was advancing on all fronts at such a pace that few could resist the rewards. Indeed, it was the combination of the growing financial demands on the landlord class with the emergence in the later eighteenth century of huge new opportunities to satisfy them which was the basic catalyst for accelerated change and Eric Richards has concluded that Highland rents may even have been rising at a faster rate than those elsewhere in Britain. Indeed, most proprietors achieved what were essentially windfall gains because many significant sources of profit, kelp, cattle, wool, mutton and regimental recruitment, did not require significant investment but accrued to the landlord simply because of his rights of ownership. Little wonder that the period c. 1760 to 1815 seemed a bonanza for many Highland landowners and it is scarcely surprising that the majority were tempted to remove the traditional society quickly and completely rather than embarking on the more complex and difficult task of patiently developing a fusion between the old and the new.

In the long run an even more potent threat to the traditional ways was the steady rise in regional population which was becoming apparent in the eighteenth and accelerated in the nineteenth century. This was part of a European-wide demographic revolution in which traditional levels of population rise were not only sustained but the rate of increase became greater over time. Demographers are still divided about the origins of this historic change of direction but it seems to have been based mainly on increasing food supply, rising employment opportunities as a consequence of industrialisation and some limited medical advances such as inoculation and vaccination against smallpox.

More important, however, than the causes were the social consequences for the Highlands and closer scrutiny reveals that an explosive demographic problem was emerging. The southern and eastern rim of the Highlands experienced very modest growth because of high levels of migration to the Lowlands, whereas along the western seaboard from north Argyll and in most of the Hebrides increase was more pronounced. Between 1801 and 1841 population in this region increased by 53 per cent. In 1755 the population of the island of Tiree was 1,509, but it had risen to 1,676 by 1768 and to 2,443 by 1792. The average population of each township on the island stood at 56 in 1768 but had reached 90 by 1800. Increases of this order could not have come about except through repeated divisions of tenancies and rampant subdivision much of it abetted by landlords eager to swell the ranks of kelpers and fishermen and only made possible by the rapid spread of potato cultivation. A major demographic result in the short term was to limit emigration by anchoring population on the land on splintered and insecure holdings. There can be little doubt either that population growth outstripped traditional levels of agricultural productivity and the methods evolved over centuries for ensuring a basic living from a poor land and a hostile climate. All detailed studies show that the old agrarian economy was delicately and precariously balanced between a meagre sufficiency and occasional shortage. It could not easily have survived the population upsurge of the eighteenth century without substantial change.

IV

By the end of the Napoleonic Wars two divergent types of tenure and settlement were visibly seen to be replacing the traditional Highland townships. The destruction of the *bailtean* and runrig was far advanced in the southern and eastern rim of the Highlands, including much of mainland Argyll, highland Perthshire, central and eastern Inverness and the eastern parishes of Ross-shire. A distinctive social order was emerging which despite some differences within the region had a number of common characteristics. The shape of the holdings and the layout of the land was not unlike many adjacent parts of the Lowlands where landlords had consolidated rather than divided tenancies. There were therefore fewer full tenants than in the older order but significant numbers of servants, cottars, labourers and servants who were employed by the new farming elite. Large sheep and cattle holdings existed throughout the region but in other districts, especially in parts of Argyll and highland Perthshire, family farms of forty to sixty acres were engaged in mixed husbandry. There was a modest standard of comfort and little sign of the recurrent subsistence crises which occurred in the north west. The potato was an important item in diet but so also was grain and, in coastal parishes, fish. A feature of the region was the development of non-agricultural activities, such as the herring fishery of the Argyll sea lochs and the linen manufacture of Perthshire.

There can be little doubt that agrarian change in this region maintained and even improved standards of life, and partly this was because of more favourable natural endowment. Arable and mixed agriculture was possible in the great straths which run from west to east. The Highland massif is a great tableland which slopes towards the south and east and this affords good drainage for the land surfaces of the area, provides some protection against the heavy and continuous rainfall which often devastates arable farming further west and facilitates communication with the economic heart of Scotland. But material amelioration was at the expense of an enormous haemorrhage of people from the region, partly as a result of widespread population displacement during the era of transformation as well as the job opportunities emerging in the Lowlands as a result of industrialisation and urbanisation. From 1755 to the 1790s, no less than 60 per cent of the region's parishes failed to increase population at all because of the huge scale of out-migration. Agrarian reform in the south and east channelled the people out of the area in large numbers and to this day the physical evidence of that great exodus can still be seen in the ruined steadings and crumbling sheilings scattered throughout the hill country.

Nevertheless, there were real benefits for those who remained. By the 1830s a relatively balanced, more secure and much more productive economic regime had begun to form in this region. The ratio of the population to available cultivable land was higher than elsewhere in the Highlands. In the early 1840s, for instance, arable acreage per head of population was reckoned at 2.18 in mainland Argyll but a mere 0.5 in Wester Ross and Skye. Land consolidation had broken up the old townships and produced a new farming class who employed a larger number of landless and semi-landless wage labourers who derived their subsistence partly from earnings at work and partly from their crofts. In both the south-west and north-east corners dynamic fishing communities had developed. The economic backbone of the region was the small core of tenant farmers, for the most part natives of the area, and renting medium-sized holdings of from £20 to £100. This class gave the southern and eastern Highlands resilience notably lacking in the poorer parishes to the north and west and its stability was most obviously demonstrated during the potato famines of the 1840s. While the west was threatened with actual starvation the districts adjacent to the Lowlands weathered the storm and experienced only temporary difficulty. As one famine relief organisation concluded at the time:

> The population of these parishes was in an entirely different position from that of the western districts. The different classes of society were in their proper place. There was a labouring class supporting themselves and their families by remuner-ative employment – a fishing population, carrying on that branch of industry as a permanent resource – and there were all the appliances of an advanced state of society, in which purchased food forms a principal feature of the subsistence of the people. The distress among them had been occasioned by a temporary dis-proportion between the ages of labour and the price of food, and the loss of the potato, which formed but a subordinate element in their means of subsistence.[2]

However, along the western seaboard from Morvern to Cape Wrath and including most of the inner and outer Hebrides a quite different social order was developing from the traditional society. Over great tracts of the region, especially on the mainland before 1815 but extending over the islands in subsequent decades, large grazing farms devoted to the raising of blackface and cheviot sheep had become dominant. But although the advance of pastoral husbandry had caused immense social disruption and the removal of traditional communities, it did not often result in this period in planned and overt expul-sion of the inhabitants. Instead relocation, and especially relocation in crofting townships, was the favoured policy so that profit could be extracted both from the labour-intensive activities of the crofters and the more extensive operations of the big flockmasters.

Over less than two to three generations, as the *bailtean* were destroyed, the crofting system was imposed throughout the region. By the 1840s at least 86 per cent and in most parishes 95 per cent of holdings were rented at £20 or less. These small tenancies, only a few acres in size, were laid out in 'townships' or crofting settlements, and had certain common features because they were the product of an 'improving' philosophy which was absorbed and implemented by virtually all landowners in these districts. At the core was the arable land divided into a number of separate smallholdings and these were surrounded by grazing or hill pasture which was held in common by the tenants of the township. The most striking feature, however, was that the croft was not designed to provide a full living for the family. Sir John Sinclair, one of the most influential improving propagandists of the day, reckoned that the typical crofter had to be able to obtain at least 200 days of additional work outside his holding in order to avoid chronic destitution and crofts were in fact reduced in size in order to force the crofter and his family into other employments. The holding itself should only provide partial subsistence and to make ends meet and afford the rental the crofter and his family had to have recourse to supplementary jobs.

These non-agricultural tasks were usually seasonal in nature. The crofting system provided a convenient source of subsistence for a reserve army of labour which was only required at certain times of the year. Crofting, therefore, became the *sine qua non* for the rapid expansion of kelp manufacture (in which between 25,000 to 40,000 people were seasonally employed during the peak summer months in the Hebrides), for fishing and for illicit whisky-making. Crofts were also used to attract recruits to the family regiments of the landowners with tiny areas of land being promised in return for service. Throughout the process of transforming the joint tenancies into crofts there was one fundamental guiding principle: too much land would act as a distraction from other more profitable tasks. The crofters were to be labourers first and agriculturists only second but, in retrospect, this proved a disastrous policy for the people of the western Highlands and Islands.

Essentially the whole social system of the region became bound up with the success of the by-employments which flourished down to the end of the Napoleonic Wars. But these activities in the main were ephemeral because, like kelp manufacture and military service, they often existed only on the basis of the transitory conditions of wartime. Moreover, in their heyday, they had little positive effect on the crofting economy. Kelp, for instance, was noted for its volatile prices but because of the huge market expansion of the 1790s became the principal economic activity in the Western Isles by 1815. But the working population gained little from this short-term bonanza as landlords in the kelp islands achieved monopoly control over the manufacture and marketing of the commodity and the 'earnings' of the labour force were mainly absorbed by increased rentals and annual payments to proprietors for meal.

Indeed the economic expansion of the Napoleonic Wars, which had brought some material improvement to the southern and eastern Highlands, laid the foundations for social catastrophe elsewhere in the region. Because of the labour needs of so many activities, most landlords were happy to see the unregulated division of lands among cottars and squatters, but this fragmentation of holdings tied the people to the land and inhibited permanent migration. The impact of these policies can be clearly seen in demographic statistics. Between 1801 and 1841 along the western seaboard and the islands population increased by 53 per cent while in the south and east the average was around 7 per cent and the kelp districts in the west had also substantially higher levels of increase than the regional norm. The reckless process of subdivision also depended on an equally rapid increase in potato cultivation. Potatoes had been grown in the early eighteenth century but by 1750 were still relatively uncommon. It was only where the croft became dominant that potatoes became a central part in the diet and during the crofting revolution of the later eighteenth and early nineteenth centuries cultivation expanded on an unprecedented scale. The transformation of land structures and the adoption of the potato went hand in hand, but this was no coincidence. The potato, because of its very high yield, became the key source of support for the dense com-munities of crofters, cottars and squatters which were building up to service kelping and fishing. Sir John Sinclair reckoned that four times as many people could be supported by an acre of potatoes as by an acre of oats. The potato crop was also less vulnerable to climate as even marginal and inhospitable land could be made to yield good returns through the process of lazybed cultivation by which sandwiches of soil and seaweed were created and planted with potatoes, and this allowed a much larger population to make a living, at however basic a level, in the crofting region than ever before. But the potato also carried the enormous risk of over-dependency on a single crop and facilitated excessive subdivision of precious land resources in areas where the possibilities of a secure existence had always been delicately balanced.

V

The experience of the western Highlands is a salutary reminder that economic change is not necessarily for the better. Victorian observers were troubled by this, especially when the problems of the region degenerated into acute destitution and famine and it then became common to blame the economic failures of the area on the conservatism and indolence of the people. They were seen as having a blind attachment to the old ways and lacking the enterprise which had brought prosperity and progress elsewhere. The Highlands became a 'problem' region where economic transformation had produced difficulties rather than benefits.

This outcome seemed all the more puzzling given some of its advantages for development. The Highlands possessed an expanding and cheap labour force, it was surrounded by seas which were rich in fish and before 1815 the potential of the region as a major source of raw materials had been amply demonstrated. The possibilities for capital accumulation were also very great because so much of the area's principal asset, land, was concentrated among a small group of proprietors. The Highlands were one of the few parts of Britain where, because of their strategic importance as a source of soldiers and sailors, the state invested on a considerable scale through the Commission for Annexed Forfeited Estates, the British Fisheries Society and an ambitious programme of road and bridge building in the early nineteenth century. But all to no avail; there was little long-term impact.

However, the argument that the basic cause of failure was the social conservatism of the Gael hardly convinces. Gaelic culture and values did not prevent the successful economic adaptation of the southern, central and eastern Highlands and there is also abundant evidence of Gaelic entrepreneurship, from the commercial activities of clan gentry in the cattle, fish, grain and slate trades before the 1760s to the successful organisation of large-scale transatlantic emigration after that date. A peasant population which responded to the cultural and economic shock of clearance by rapidly adopting a new subsistence crop (the potato) and adjusting to the new realities of crofting can hardly be described as conservative or rigid. The records of the Commissioners for Annexed Forfeited Estates also show clear evidence of a willingness to adopt 'Lowland' crop rotations if they were deemed practical. So much of the approved system, however, such as enclosures and turnip husbandry, was not relevant to the Highland landscape.

However, such pools of indigenous enterprise as did exist were inhibited in a variety of ways. The destruction of the old order, resettlement and rental inflation combined to produce a context of profound insecurity which was not conducive to small tenant investment. Crofters were allocated their holdings on an annual basis and were vulnerable to removal at the end of this term. Again, before 1760, while the expansion of the cattle trade brought capital into the Highlands, it failed to filter down to any great extent and produce more commercial values across the society, whereas in the Lowlands by the 1750s the ordinary tenants sold their grain and stock directly to the market. In the western Highlands, marketing was mainly monopolised by proprietors and clan gentry, and partly for this reason and partly because of the paucity of towns in the region commercialisation before the 1760s only affected the elites in a significant way. The area lacked the large Lowland middle class of capitalist tenants, merchants, traders and manufacturers who were the shock troops of economic transformation. The emigration of tacksmen and middle rank farmers can be seen in part as a flight of capital from Gaeldom and still further diminished the entrepreneurial pool. The creation of crofting townships probably decimated the small group of tenants who had a significant surplus above sufficiency by shaving holdings down to a uniform and basic subsistence minimum.

Whether more effective management of the resources of the region by the landlord class would have resulted in a different outcome is an interesting question. Highland landlords were confronted with more formidable obstacles

Ruthven Barracks in Badenoch

The author in Auliston settlement, Morvern, Argyll, which was cleared in the 1850s

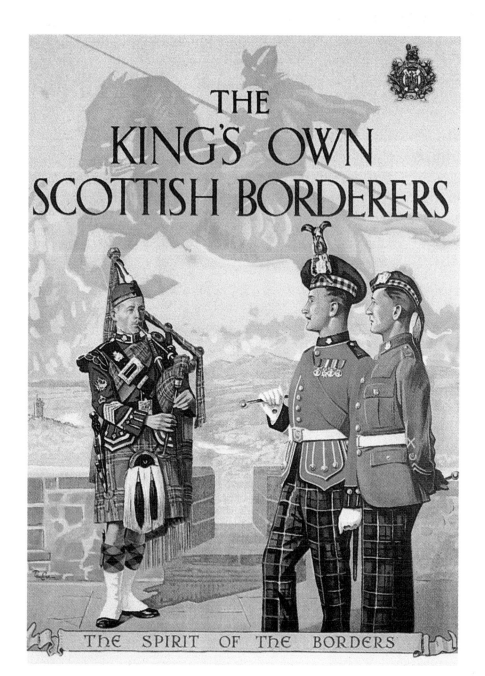

Recruiting poster for the King's Own Scottish Borderers

than their counterparts elsewhere in Britain: the climate was more oppressive and the land much poorer, they did not possess the mineral and urban rentals of many more fortunate proprietors elsewhere and intensive arable farming which might have absorbed the population more easily was not possible in the north and west. By laying down more and more land to sheep, they were playing to the region's comparative advantage in pastoral husbandry and so their actions had an inherent economic rationality but with devastating social consequences.

But impersonal forces were not the whole story; several landlords directly contributed to the malaise of the region themselves. Some seem to have been more interested in extracting profit than in sound investment and most of the windfall gains from kelp were recklessly squandered outside the Highlands. To change drastically the entire social structure of their estates around activities which were unlikely to last for much longer than the conflict with France was myopic to say the least and these policies inflicted considerable social damage on the Hebrides in particular for decades thereafter. Yet some proprietors did try to fund fishing and industrial development on an ambitious scale, the most notable examples being the 5th Duke of Argyll in the later eighteenth century and the Sutherland family in the early nineteenth century. In both cases, however, the development strategy, after some initial success, came to little and this suggests that imaginative schemes, based on considerable sources of finance, faced major problems.

In fact, the north west had little scope for adjustment by the early nineteenth century. It was locked into an economic vice which was contracting inexorably, and there were at least four major problems. First, by 1815 commercial forces had transformed the region into an economic enclave of British industry. It had become a satellite and its functions were utterly subordinate to the production of foodstuffs, raw materials and labour for the southern cities. No longer were the people of the western Highlands only dependent on the climate, the price of cattle and the returns from the land but their fate was now also inextricably bound up with the fluctuation of distant markets for a range of commodities. Commercialisation had ended their isolation and partial independence. Second, commercialisation had fashioned an insecure and vulnerable economic structure centred around crofting, the potato and by-employments and at the same time much grazing land, vital in the old society, had been absorbed by the new sheep farms which also tended to channel most of their economic gains out of the region. Commercialisation, therefore, even in the short run had profoundly negative *economic* effects on the western Highlands as well as destroying the old cohesion of society. Third, the Highlands were now an integral part of the British market economy and one consequence was that the region was fully exposed to the direct impact of competition from advanced centres of industry such as the west of Scotland and the north of England. The Highlands lacked coal reserves of any significance, had few large towns and like other British peripheral regions such as the west of Ireland and the south east of England its small-scale textile industries were soon remorselessly destroyed by competition from the manufacturing heartlands. It was forced to specialise in sectors where it had a comparative advantage within the new economic system and these were confined increasingly to sheep-farming and the provision of casual labour.

Fourth, the collapse in prices after the end of the Napoleonic Wars made it impossible for even the most skilled form of landlord management to stabilise the crisis. Most areas of the British economy were in difficulty after 1815 but in the north and west the outcome was disastrous. This was partly because in a recession peripheral areas tended to suffer worst, but it was also because so much of the Highland boom was due to ephemeral wartime conditions and much of the region's export economy fell apart with the coming of peace. Cattle prices halved between 1810 and 1830. Fishing stagnated due to the erratic migrations of the herring in the western sea lochs, the withdrawal of bounties on herring in the 1820s and the rapid decline of the Irish and Caribbean markets for cured herring. Kelp, the great staple of the Hebrides, suffered even more acutely when peace brought revived imports of foreign barilla, a cheaper and richer substitute. The reduction of the duty on foreign alkali combined with the discovery that cheaper alkali could be extracted from common salt also had a devastating effect. The price of kelp had already halved by 1820 and fell further in later years. The coming of peace also led to the demobilisation of the vast number of Highlanders who had joined the colours, and before long illicit whisky-making was also under severe pressure as a result of radical changes in the 1820s in revenue legislation. That decade was indeed a grim one for the people of the western Highlands as virtually the whole economic fabric which had been built up between 1760 and 1815 disintegrated. Even more ominously, though sheep prices stagnated they did not experience the collapse of other commodities and it looked as if only commercial pastoralism, with all its implications for clearance and dispossession, had a real future.

NOTES

1 A. I. Macinnes, 'Scottish Gaeldom: the first phase of clearance' in T. M. Devine and R. Mitchison, eds, *People and Society in Scotland, I, 1760–1830, Edinburgh, 1988, p. 72.*
2 Quoted in T. M. Devine, *The Great Highland Famine*, Edinburgh, 1988, pp. 42–3.

FURTHER READING

E. R. Cregeen, 'The changing role of the House of Argyll in the Scottish Highlands' in N. T.

Phillipson and R. Mitchison, eds, *Scotland in the Age of Improvement*, Edinburgh, 1970.

T. M. Devine, 'Social responses to agrarian "improvement": the Highland and Lowland clearances in Scotland in R. A. Houston and I. D. White, eds, *Scottish Society, 1500–1800*, Cambridge, 1989.

P. Gaskell, *Morvern Transformed*, Cambridge, 1980.

M. Gray, *The Highland Economy, 1750–1850*, Edinburgh, 1951.

J. Hunter, *The Making of the Crofting Community*, Edinburgh, 1976.

A. I. Macinnes, 'Scottish Gaeldom: the first phase of clearance' in T. M. Devine and R. Mitchison, eds, *People and Society in Scotland, I, 1760–1830*, Edinburgh, 1988.

M. McLean, *The People of Glengarry: Highlanders in Transition, 1745–1820*, Toronto, 1991.

E. Richards, *The Leviathan of Wealth*, London, 1973.

E. Richards, *A History of the Highland Clearances*, London, 1982 and 1985, 2 vols.

A. J. Youngson, *After the Forty-Five*, Edinburgh, 1973.

4

THE FINAL PHASE OF CLEARANCE

As the post-war recession deepened the crofting region saw the ebbing away of income and employment. The kelping districts in particular were badly hit and numerous townships along the west coast degenerated into congested rural slums. As profits from kelp collapsed, several landed families, such as the McKenzie earls of Seaforth and the MacDonalds of Clanranald, went to the wall, and demoralisation spread rapidly among the people of the region as accumulating rent arrears, decline in employment and the fear of arbitrary eviction induced a deep social malaise. The majority eked out a poor and precarious living on potato cultivation, intermittent fishing and the earnings from temporary migration in the Lowlands. Out-migration undoubtedly accelerated. The population of the west Highlands was rising at a rate of 1.46 per cent per annum between 1811 and 1820. From 1821 to 1830 this fell back to 0.51 per cent per annum but only declined in absolute terms by a fractional 0.03 in the following decade.

In fact the scale of the exodus did not keep pace with the contraction in income and employment and emigration was slowest from the islands where the social problems were most severe, and it was those with means who emigrated and the very poor, the cottars and the squatters were left behind. The experience of Glenelg in the western mainland was typical. The census report of the parish concluded in 1841 that:

> Within the last fifty years all the more affluent inhabitants have emigrated . . . and few remained behind, except such as have not the means of removing, but these are now crowded together on limited portions of the soil, whose produce is entirely inadequate to their support.[1]

Around the same time it was reckoned that 35 per cent of the population had no land, 51 per cent possessed an acre or less and a mere 4 per cent had more than five acres. Almost three-quarters of the families living in the parish were cottars whose names did not appear on any rent roll and were subject to instant removal by the landlord.

It was against this background of economic decay and social destitution that the final phase of clearance began in the 1820s when the death of the labour-intensive economy based on kelp, fishing and military recruitment compelled a radical change of policy. The land which was divided among crofters and cottars had now to be consolidated and made available for grazing for sheep-farming, the only sector which remained profitable. In 1827, the managers of the estates of the kelp lord, MacDonald of Clanranald in South Uist and Benbecula, resolved to reduce kelp manufacture and cattle rearing and concentrate on sheep and similar plans were being hatched on other Hebridean estates. These strategies demanded large-scale eviction of the now 'redundant' population. Sometimes this took place, as in Harris, Lewis and parts of Skye, by moving the inhabitants of entire townships to areas of marginal land through displacement and relocation rather than outright expulsion. The most notorious example occurred in Harris where thirteen townships on the fertile *machair* lands of the Atlantic coast were cleared and the entire district from Rodel to Loch Eisort, a distance of forty miles, depopulated in the course of the 1820s. Several hundred emigrated but many were also forced to settle on the island's bare and rocky east coast on the almost lunar landscape of the 'Bays' where they scraped a living by constructing the *feannagan* or lazybeds to grow potatoes. It was of these that the ecologist, Frank Fraser Darling, remarked in memorable terms:

> Nothing can be more moving to the sensitive observer of Hebridean life than these lazybeds of the Bays district of Harris. Some are no bigger than a dining-table and possibly the same height from the rock, carefully built up with turfs carried there in creels by the women and girls.[2]

But displacement in itself was not deemed sufficient because it merely exacerbated 'over-population'. The central feature of the final phase of clearance was the linkage of mass eviction with schemes of assisted emigration. The poor and destitute would be exported to the colonies, even more land released for commercial pastoralism and the growing claims of the people for landlord charity in crisis years effectively eliminated. These policies had already become part of the conventional wisdom by the 1820s as is evidenced by the numerous landlord petitions for emigration assistance dispatched from Hebridean estates to the Colonial Office in that decade. The Clanranald plan of 1827 referred to above envisaged the shipping of at least 3,000 people to British North America from South Uist and Benbecula alone.

In some areas these strategies were actually put into effect. McLean of Coll successfully transported 300 people from Rhum to Canada, and between 1838 and 1843 Lord MacDonald assisted around 1,300 people to emigrate from North Uist. In each case the emigrations were related to widespread evictions and the subsequent conversion of considerable tracts of land to sheep farms. But these cases were exceptional. The semi-bankrupt landed class of the crofting region simply could not afford to finance large-scale emigration and the government in most years was equally reluctant to provide a subvention. Until the potato famine of the 1840s clearance and expulsion were attractive to most estate factors in theory but were rarely possible in practice.

The catastrophic failure of the potatoes in 1846 and the continuation of the blight for several years thereafter was an important watershed in the history of the Highland clearances. For one thing, the great destitution seemed to demonstrate unequivocally the utter bankruptcy of crofting as an economic and social system and, in addition, much of the burden of relief during the crisis years was borne by government and external charities co-ordinated by the Central Board of Management for Highland Destitution. But the state effectively withdrew its support in 1847 and the Central Board wound up its operations in 1850. The responsibility for relieving continued destitution returned to the landed classes. There were also rumours at the time that the government was determined to

Settlement in Barra

ensure that proprietors assumed their social responsibilities by establishing an 'able-bodied poor law' in the Highlands, financed through the rates, and offering relief by right to the vast numbers of destitute in the region. All this provided a powerful incentive for landowners once and for all to rid their estates of the poor by coercive means and it was openly admitted that 'the terror of the poor rates' was the decisive factor in the wave of evictions which swept over the Hebrides between 1849 and 1854.[3]

But the changing price structure for cattle and sheep was also relevant. During the early years of the famine, from 1846 to 1852, cattle prices fell on average by more than half, but the market for wool and mutton was in dramatic contrast. The 1820s and 1830s had both been decades of fluctuating fortunes for sheep. While prices held up better than in all other Highland exports the market did not expand at anything like the rate of the later eighteenth and early nineteenth century. However, from the early 1840s there was a steep rise in the prices of both the Blackface and Cheviot breeds precisely in the years when there was a prolonged stagnation in demand for Highland cattle. Political factors also entered the equation. In the aftermath of the Repeal of the Corn Laws it was argued that grain farmers in more favoured districts would switch from arable to mixed and pastoral farming because of the anticipated increase in foreign wheat imports. In the event this fear turned out to be false but at the time it had a considerable influence because it suggested that the malaise in the Highland

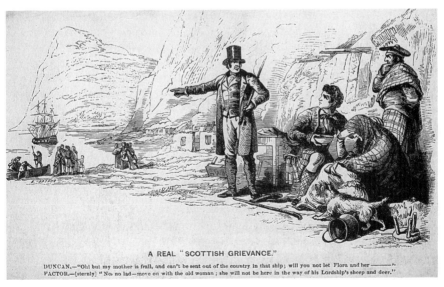

A REAL "SCOTTISH GRIEVANCE."

DUNCAN.—"Oh! but my mother is frail, and can't be sent out of the country in that ship; will you not let Flora and her ———"
FACTOR.—[sternly] " No, no lad—move on with the old woman ; she will not be here in the way of his Lordship's sheep and deer."

A contemporary cartoon depicting the classic elements in the perception of clearance

cattle economy, the main source of income for the crofters, was structural and long term rather than cyclical and short term. The economics of the famine years seemed to make mass clearance irresistible. While the rental payments of the small tenantry collapsed on most estates during the crisis, income from the big sheep-farmers remained buoyant.

That clearance would be more radical and draconian than ever before was also likely because of the changing management of Highland estates. The old landed families were by now so financially embarrassed that several were no longer masters in their own houses. By the early 1850s the three major estates in Skye, including those of Lord MacDonald and MacLeod of MacLeod, were under trust; so too was the MacDonald estate in North Uist. Sir James Riddell's lands in Ardnamurchan were also managed by trustees until they were finally put on the market in 1853. Campbell of Islay, who owned virtually the whole of that island, had gone bankrupt in 1849, and five of the smaller properties on Mull were also under trust.

These estates were administered by the agents of trustees for the creditors of the landowner and their obligation was to treat the property as an asset, run it efficiently, increase rental income and, if possible, bring it to a more solvent condition in readiness for an early sale. Under such a regime any social considerations and the welfare of the people had no relevance in law, and it was not therefore surprising that some of the most controversial clearances of the famine period were carried out on estates managed by trustees. As *The Scotsman* put it in 1849:

> When the lands are heavily mortgaged, the obvious though harsh resource is dispossessing the small tenants, to make room for a better class able to pay rent. This task generally devolves on south country managers or trustees, who look only to money returns, and who cannot sympathise with the peculiar situations and feelings of the Highland population.[4]

Financial imperatives governed the administration of these properties to the virtual exclusion of other considerations. Many estates were so burdened with debt that much income was absorbed in interest payments and the movement upwards of interest rates in the distant money markets of Glasgow, Edinburgh and London could therefore have a crucial effect on estate policy. In the first half of 1847 the rate increase sent shock waves through the western Highlands. MacLeod of MacLeod wrote despairingly to his mother at the time that: 'Interests for the next half year having risen half a per cent I am utterly unable any longer to struggle against the load of debt . . . in the course of a few weeks you will see the whole of the unentailed lands exposed for sale.'[5] Financial fluctuations in the wider economy helped to shape the policies of clearance in the later 1840s.

So also did the great transfer of west Highland and Hebridean lands to a new class of proprietor in the two decades immediately before the famine, a revolution in estate ownership which is described in detail in the next chapter. Between about 1800 and 1850, around two-thirds of Highland properties were sold to wealthy Lowland and English interests. The 'new' landed class consisted mainly of industrial tycoons, merchant princes and rich lawyers and bankers, and whole districts fell under their control. Most areas in Mull, except the Ross and a few hereditary estates elsewhere, were owned by new proprietors. All of the Long Island, apart from North Uist, had been bought up by Lord Dunmore, a Lowland laird (Harris), Sir James Matheson who made a fortune in East India trade (Lewis) and John Gordon of Cluny, an Aberdeenshire financier and land-owner (Barra and South Uist). The replacement of the old indebted families by these new interests had a crucial effect on clearance and it now became possible to put into practice on a much greater scale than ever before the policy of compulsory emigration mooted in the 1820s and 1830s by which removals were linked to the provision of assisted passages across the Atlantic for those who lost their lands. These new men could afford to finance such schemes on a massive scale: for instance, John Gordon eventually supported the emigration of almost 3,000 people from his estates to Canada and James Matheson around 2,230 from Lewis. In each case eviction and other forms of coercion were applied systematically to speed the exodus.

It is hardly surprising, given the combination of powerful forces outlined

Eviction in the later nineteenth century

above, that the clearances of the 1840s and 1850s were quite devastating in their scale and intensity, and whole areas were rapidly depopulated. Between 1847 and 1851, F. W. Clark, a Stirlingshire lawyer, and proprietor of the island of Ulva off Mull, reduced the total population of his estate from around 500 to 150 through a relentless process of eviction. In 1850 alone, 660 people were evicted in Barra and it was rumoured that 600 families in Mull were to be removed in 1848 and 1849, while on the island of Skye by the early 1850s eviction was increasing to such an extent that many heads of household feared to leave their families to trek south for work for the season. Between 1847 and 1851, Matheson of Lewis alone secured over 1,300 summonses of removal against the small tenants of his estate. Yet eviction was not the only form of coercion, though it was certainly the most feared. The Matheson administration records and those of the Dukes of Argyll in Inveraray Castle show that other methods were widely employed to loosen the grip of the people on the land. Kelp manufacture was delayed on the Argyll estate on Tiree to force migration and confiscation of cattle stocks to recoup rent arrears; delay or refusal of famine relief and controls over the cutting of peat were other favoured sanctions. The depth of the crisis in the Highlands seemed to legitimise such draconian action because, so its advocates contended, the alternative was lingering destitution and even mass starvation.

Nevertheless, such was the extent of coercion that even experienced and hardened observers of famine conditions elsewhere became alarmed. Sir Edward Pine Coffin was the lugubriously named senior government relief official in the Highlands during the crisis. He had served in the west of Ireland during the potato famine there, in Mexico and in other overseas areas, and was a career civil servant not given to alarmist claims. Yet even he was concerned about the intensity of clearance and in unusually colourful prose he condemned the landowners for seeking to bring about what he called 'the extermination of the population'. Eviction was so rampant in 1848 and 1849 that in his view it would inevitably lead to 'the unsettling of the foundations of the social system' and 'depopulate the Highlands by force'.[6]

In a sense, Pine Coffin was right. While removal and relocation had been familiar processes in the Highlands since the second half of the eighteenth century, the clearances of the famine period had several distinctive and unusual characteristics. They were very concentrated in time. Few substantial evictions occurred in 1846 and 1847, the first years of famine, when the policy seems to have been principally one of containment and relief. Mass removals started to increase in 1848 and were very common from 1849 to 1855 before receding in the later 1850s as the economy started to recover, and by 1860 large-scale clearance had become rare though the eviction of families and individuals continued. The removals were also concentrated in space. One estimate suggests that over three-quarters of the population affected lived in the Inner or Outer Hebrides. This was very much a Hebridean clearance with large-scale eviction on the mainland being confined for the most part to districts such as Knoydart and Ardnamurchan. This largely reflected the fact that sheep-farming in most other areas of the western mainland was already dominant, but it was also the consequence of a determined strategy to break up the crofting townships which had provided the labour force for the now redundant kelp manufacture. Indeed, within particular estates, considerable discrimination was employed in order to ensure the removal of the former kelp communities. On Lewis, for instance, the fishing townships were safeguarded while those attached to the old kelp shores with poor rent payers were evicted. Clearance was used not as a blunt instrument but was deployed with clinical care. The islands were also vulnerable because sheep-farming, though advancing through the Hebrides, was not yet dominant and Lewis, Mull, Tiree, Skye, Barra, Islay and South Uist were still only partially cleared in the 1840s. They represented a final and enticing frontier for sheep husbandry.

The famine removals were also different because their social costs were greater. In the past, even in the 1820s and 1830s, clearance had meant dispossession but not necessarily depopulation, but evictions during the famine were most often governed by an undisguised determination to expel the people. In addition, these clearances were unleashed on a population already ravaged by hunger and destitution and few attempts were made to provide shelter for the dispossessed. In the vast majority of cases the options were either assisted emigration or migration off the estate, sinking from the status of tenant to that of semi-landless cottar or seeking lodgings in overcrowded accommodation in slum villages like Lochcarron, Plockton, Tobermory and Lochaline, which continued to expand in size as the evictions intensified.

The famine clearances, therefore, have a special significance in the history of the Highland clearances as a whole. They were the last in the cycle of great evictions which transformed Gaelic society from the last quarter of the eighteenth century. They intensified suffering within the region and attracted bitter criticism outside it, and the more notorious episodes of clearance, such as those in South Uist, Knoydart, Sollas in North Uist and Boreraig and Suishnish in Skye were chronicled in detail in the national press, giving rise to a large and impassioned pamphlet literature. It was these large-scale removals which helped to put the crofting question firmly on the national political map and created the context for the attack on Highland landlordism later in the nineteenth century.

NOTES

1 General Register Office, Edinburgh, Census Enumerator's Schedules, Glenelg, 1841.
2 F. Fraser Darling, *West Highland Survey*, Oxford, 1955, p. 44.
3 Quoted in T. M. Devine, *The Great Highland Famine*, Edinburgh, 1988, p. 189.
4 *The Scotsman*, 25 August 1849.
5 Dunvegan Castle, Skye, Macleod Muniments, 659/23/6, Macleod to Mother, 31 December 1846.
6 Quoted in Devine, *Great Highland Famine*, p. 180.

FURTHER READING

T. M. Devine, *The Great Highland Famine*, Edinburgh, 1988.
T. M. Devine, 'Highland landlords and the Highland potato famine' in L. Leneman, ed., *Perspectives on Scottish Social History*, Aberdeen, 1988.
J. Hunter, *The Making of the Crofting Community*, Edinburgh, 1976, chs 3–5.
E. Richards, *A History of the Highland Clearances*, London, 1982 and 1985, 2 vols.

5

REVOLUTION IN LANDOWNERSHIP

I

At the end of his long career as engineer with the Scottish Fishery Board, in the course of which he travelled widely in the Highlands, Joseph Mitchell noted the transformation which had occurred in the pattern of landownership in the region since the 1820s: 'I have seen nearly two-thirds of the estates in the Highlands in my time change proprietors'.[1] Mitchell did not exaggerate. Between 1820 and 1860 Highland landed families who had held extensive territorial possessions for centuries disappeared from the scene. The empire of the MacDonalds of Clanranald, which included Arisaig and Moidart on the western mainland, the smaller islands of Eigg, Canna and Muck and South Uist in the Outer Hebrides, vanished after a series of sales between 1813 and 1838 which eventually realised more than £214,000. Walter Campbell of Islay, at one time the owner of the entire island, was forced into bankruptcy in 1848 and his estate sold off in 1853. The extensive lands of the McKenzie earls of Seaforth, in Lewis, and Kintail and Glensheil on the mainland, had almost all passed out of their possession by 1844. Knoydart, the last possession of the MacDonnels of Glengarry, was sold in the 1850s. The McNeills of Barra, MacLeod of Harris, MacDonald of Bornish and MacDonald of Boisdale, all lost their hereditary estates in the three decades after the end of the Napoleonic Wars.

But this was not all. Even those landed families who managed to survive were forced into massive sales of parts of their patrimony to maintain solvency. The estates of Lord Reay, in the western Sutherland parishes of Tongue, Durness and Edderachillis, were bought up by the Duke of Sutherland in 1829. Lord MacDonald lost North Uist but managed to preserve some of his family's possessions in Skye while the MacLeods of MacLeod were forced to sell Glenelg on the mainland and the unentailed portions of their property in Skye in order to escape a greater calamity. Even such grandees as the dukes of Argyll and the dukes of Gordon did not remain immune. The Duke of Gordon surrendered territory in Badenoch and Lochaber in the 1830s and the Argyll family put up for sale much of their possessions in Mull and all of their lands in Morvern which had been annexed from the McLeans of Duart in the later seventeenth century. The Morvern estate was exposed to sale in 1819, and from then until 1838 every single property in the parish changed hands.

By the 1850s the pattern of landownership in the western Highlands and Islands had been revolutionised. All of the Outer Hebrides had been sold out of the hands of the hereditary proprietors, and large parts of Skye, most of Mull and all of Raasay, Ulva, Islay, Lismore, Rum and Eigg in the Inner Hebrides had new owners. Only Coll, Tiree, parts of Skye and Jura remained under the control of their traditional possessors. On the western mainland, Knoydart, Moidart, Glengarry, Glensheil, Arisaig, Kintail and Morvern were all dominated by the new elite, and only in parts of Wester Ross, especially in Gairloch, Applecross and Lochbroom parishes, in the county of Sutherland and in Ardnamurchan, was there substantial continuity of ownership from earlier days. It was a social revolution quite staggering in its scale. From John Bateman's survey of British landownership, published in 1882, it is possible to calculate that at that date new purchasers had acquired 1,139,717 acres or about 60 per cent of the territory occupied by larger estates in the west Highland and Hebridean region outside the county of Sutherland and even this figure does not do full justice to the real significance of the new landed families. Bateman excluded estates of less than 3,000 acres from his survey and it is known that many new purchasers tended to acquire properties below this size in islands such as Mull and mainland parishes such as Morvern. A calculation based on his survey, therefore, is likely to exaggerate the continuity of ownership of large estates among hereditary proprietors. The entire acreage owned by new purchasers was in reality probably closer to at least 70 per cent of the mainland and insular parishes of western Argyll, Inverness and Ross by the last quarter of the nineteenth century.

Precise final figures may be in some doubt but there can be little uncertainty about the significance of what had happened. The scale of land transfer in this region was exceptional both when compared to patterns in the eighteenth century Highlands and to the general structure of the land market elsewhere in Britain in the nineteenth century. Before 1800 the Highland land market was not inactive, as the work of Allan Macinnes on Argyll has shown. The buying and selling of estates did not start in the nineteenth century, but in the 1820s and 1830s there was an unprecedented acceleration in the scale of property transfer and at least 55 estates, several of them of very substantial acreage, were exposed to sale in the western Highlands and Islands between 1810 and the 1850s. The final figure is likely to be significantly higher than this since a number of properties, such as Arisaig, Glenelg, Glengarry, Lochalsh on the mainland, and insular properties in Mull and Morvern, changed hands more than once during this period. For instance, in 1851 there were 21 separate estates in Mull and all, with the exception of five, had been acquired by purchase, between 1810 and 1850. Several had been sold once and some twice or more during this time, with the year of transfer of 48 of the 55 properties mentioned is known. Only three were sold between 1810 and 1819, but thereafter the rate of transfer quickened. Six were sold between 1820–9, 15 from 1830–9, 8 from 1840–9; and a further 8 from 1850–9.

Almost all of these estates were acquired by Lowland or English interests, though several purchasers had family ties with the Highlands. At least fourteen of the forty-five purchasers in the sample were either English landowners, merchants or financiers and several, such as the Bristol merchant James Baillie, who bought Glenelg, Glensheil and Letterfinlay, the London merchant, Edward Ellice, owner of Glenquoich and Glengarry, and James Morrison of Morrison, Dillon and Co. of London, who acquired Islay on the insolvency of Walter Campbell, soon became among the largest landowners in the Western Highlands and Islands. Of the twenty-nine non-Highland purchasers whose occupational and social background can be identified, at least in general terms, thirteen were landowners from the Lowlands or England, ten were merchants and financiers, four were professionals (three lawyers and a university professor) and two were industrialists.

This inward movement temporarily reversed the trend towards concentration of ownership which had been occurring in the seventeenth and eighteenth centuries. The spate of land sales which ended the territorial dominion of the MacDonalds of Clanranald between 1813 and 1838 resulted in the emergence of nine separate owners in an area where there had previously been one. Similarly, while the Lewis estate of the McKenzies of Seaforth was preserved intact when it passed to James Matheson, the family's mainland property in Kintail and Lochalsh was subdivided among several newcomers. One purchaser bought the Islay estate but quickly began to carve other properties out of it, and the Duke of Argyll's lands in Morvern were put up for sale in 1819 in five separate lots and were further subdivided thereafter. In the later seventeenth century there were six proprietors in Mull; by the middle decades of the nineteenth century, the number had risen to twenty-one. Yet this argument ought not to be pushed too far as the penetration of newcomers did not necessarily accelerate the fragmentation of ownership in all areas. Sutherland remained broadly inviolate, with only James Matheson's purchases of Achany and Gruids in that county marginally affecting the pattern of ownership. But the hegemony of the dukes of Sutherland was secure and their territorial predominance was further consolidated by the acquisition of the Reay lands on the west coast. More important, however, was the emergence of new proprietors, who in certain districts sought to build up great landed possessions which eventually equalled or surpassed even those of some of the ducal grandees whose estates had long dominated the Highland region. The most remarkable examples of this pattern were the two Matheson baronets, Sir James, the owner of Lewis and parts of Sutherland and Wester Ross, and Sir Alexander, proprietor of a number of estates in Ross-shire.

The main significance, however, of these massive land sales in the western Highlands only becomes apparent when they are compared with the condition of the land market elsewhere in Britain at this time. There seem to have been two key differences. First, there was a contrast in the phasing of sales. In both the western Highlands and in other regions the volume of transfers was relatively high in the 1820s and this was to be expected as deflationary pressures after the Napoleonic Wars forced those with high fixed charges based on wartime values to unload some parts of their property on to the market. But in England the velocity of land sales diminished in the 1830s and the years from then until the 1850s were a period of relative stagnation. The main factor seems to have been the abatement of the flood of forced sales in the immediate post-war period. It was a quite different pattern in the western Highlands where there were more than twice as many transfers between 1830 and 1839 as in the period 1820 to 1829. Furthermore, at least eight major properties changed hands between 1840 and 1849 and a further eight in the following decade. There are obvious indications here that the land market in the western Highlands was subject to a series of specific regional influences which maintained sales at a high level despite the reduction in transfer which was occurring in many other areas of Britain.

Second, the scale of land sales, especially of large, self-contained estates, the ebbing of the control of hereditary owners in some parts of the region and their entire disappearance in others, together with the unprecedented influx of new proprietors, had few parallels anywhere else in Britain. Indeed, recent research on the structure of the British landed class and the purchase of landed estates by successful businessmen has tended to show that the number of *arrivistes* who achieved landed status actually declined after *c*.1820. It is asserted that even in the most rapidly growing economy in the world, few of the mercantile and manufacturing classes had the resources to acquire large landed estates, especially when the availability of marketable properties was effectively limited by the legal devices of trusts, entail and strict settlement and by the stability of the agrarian economy. One calculation, for instance, by W. D. Rubinstein, suggests that in Britain as a whole only 15 of the 200 landlords owning 25,000 acres or more in the mid-nineteenth century were first-generation merchants or industrialists. Interestingly, three of the five greatest such 'new' landowners, Sir Alexander Matheson, James Morrison and James Baird, were west Highland proprietors. The key problem for the historian, therefore, is not simply to offer a general explanation for the pattern of land sales in this region but to explore the particular and specific reasons why the volume of transfers and the numerical increase in the number of 'new' proprietors was much greater than most other areas of Britain in this period. Current interpretations suggest that it was only from the 1870s and 1880s, with the onset of the Agricultural Depression, followed soon afterwards by the introduction of death duties in 1894, that the selling off of lands by hereditary owners became common elsewhere in the country. In the western Highlands and Islands, however, the power and position of most of the old elite had already been eclipsed by the middle decades of the nineteenth century. It was the era after the Napoleonic Wars which saw the end of the old order there and it is the particular factors which became significant in that period which now require close examination.

II

The first point to stress is that from the 1820s large areas of land in the western Highlands became available for sale to an unprecedented extent and that most of these sales were forced, in the sense that hereditary owners parted with territory because of the threat or the reality of financial disaster. One student of the British landed class has noted that it was only when a family's predicament became 'exceedingly grave' that landowners would 'sell parts of the family lands big enough to mutilate or destroy the historic character of the estate'.[2] This apparently happened over and over again in the Highlands from the second decade of the nineteenth century. Lord Reay sold off his ancestral estates in the west of Sutherland and retired to a villa in Ealing; Walter Campbell's bankruptcy forced the sale of his Islay estate; a similar fate overtook McNeill of Barra and MacDonald of Clanranald had had to sell a number of his hereditary properties in Moidart, Arisaig and the Small Isles between 1813 and 1827 until he was left with only the family lands in South Uist and Benbecula. But the financial pressures were still inexorable, and despite the fact that Clanranald opposed the alienation of his last remaining possession and showed considerable tenacity in trying to retain it, his Hebridean estate was eventually put on the market by his trustees in 1839. So too were the lands of the McKenzie earls of Seaforth in Lewis and the western mainland and the family patrimony of the MacDonnels of Glengarry, the last remnant of which, Knoydart, was brought to market in the 1850s.

Forced sales on the scale which has been described were quite unusual in the British context at this time. The volume of land transfers did rise elsewhere in the 1820s, but there is little evidence in any other region of Britain of a financial catastrophe on the scale which overwhelmed the west Highland landed elite in the post-war period. As one writer has put it: 'The demise of Highland families in the period 1770–1850 suggests that, in financial terms, the class committed suicide'.[3] In nineteenth century Britain, however, it was exceptional for great landed families to be completely ruined or so be so severely embarrassed by the accumulation of debt as to be stripped of most of their inheritance. Examples such as the Duke of Buckingham, who went bankrupt in 1848, the Duke of Newcastle, the Earl of Winchilsea and Lord de Marley, who were all before bankruptcy courts in 1870, were untypical. Acute financial difficulty, on the other hand, was the characteristic pattern in the western Highlands and Islands in the 1820s, 1830s and 1840s and actual insolvency was far from being an unusual occurrence.

The reasons why the Highland elite should be so much more vulnerable to financial embarrassment than their peers in other regions of Britain are still imperfectly understood. They were partly responsible for their own sorry plight because their indulgence in wasteful expenditure led to dissipation of the windfall gains of the good years of the Napoleonic Wars in conspicuous consumption (often in the southern capitals) and careless mismanagement of their inheritance. They did not live within their means. Sir James Riddell of Ardnamurchan had debts of £50,000 in 1848; Lord MacDonald owed over £140,000; Clanranald's debts totalled over £100,000 as early as 1812 and the Earl of Seaforth was burdened with debt in 1815 to the extent of £205,999; and when Norman MacLeod of MacLeod finally became insolvent in 1849 his assets totalled £100,027 and his debts £106,851. There were examples of reckless overspending, and in such cases a family's fortune and position in society could be irreparably damaged by the behaviour of a few irresponsible individuals. Two classic instances of this type were Charles McLean of Drimnin in Morvern, 'a careless, imprudent and extravagant man', who sold the family property in bankruptcy in 1797–9, and the sixth Duke of Argyll, 'a notorious rake and outrageous spendthrift', who managed single-handedly to reduce the family fortune by £2 million.[4] But, large debts in themselves were not new, as indebtedness was very common among most west Highland proprietors in the seventeenth and eighteenth centuries. It was debt, for example, which led to the downfall of the McLeans of Duart in 1674 and the notorious transfer of their lands to the Campbell earls of Argyll. Nor were the sums owed negligible. To cite but one example, an account of Clanranald's debts to MacDonald of Sleat in 1700 indicates that they stood at £64,000 and such amounts were by no means exceptional. What requires explanation in the nineteenth century, therefore, is not so much the extent of debt in itself but why (unlike the pattern in previous periods) it apparently precipitated such a massive increase in sales of land. Nor can it necessarily be assumed that the incidence of debt in itself necessarily implied overspending or financial weakness. As F. M. L. Thompson has put it, 'Debts require careful handling as evidence: they may as easily indicate increasing prosperity as increasing adversity, intelligent use of available resources as wayward appropriation'.[5] A survey of the estate papers of Lord MacDonald, MacLeod of MacLeod and Sir James Riddell reveals that some debt was incurred for reasons of conspicuous consumption, such as the improvement of estate mansions, the building of town houses and the purchasing of fine furniture. But it is equally clear that much also derived from unsuccessful investments in the infrastructure of the estate and the provision of relief for destitute tenants during bad seasons. The Riddell family, for instance, sunk more than £52,000 in their Ardnamurchan and Sunart estates in 'buildings, roads, enclosure, drainage' between 1818 and 1848 which then failed to bring the expected returns.

The key factor, therefore, in the survival of financially embarrassed families was not so much the level of debt alone but the balance between debt and income and disaster loomed only when the cost of servicing annual interest charges became equal to or even greater than annual income and it was here that west Highland landowners were most at risk. Historians of the British landed classes argue that it was exceedingly difficult for landowners to reduce absolute debt levels even through the imposition of strict measures of economy. This was because a good deal of debt was inherited and a considerable amount of income was tied up in servicing the interest charges associated with earlier loans and mortgages. Furthermore, each estate was burdened with an array of annuities, life-rents, and portions for different members of the landed family other than the life-tenant. The convention of primogeniture meant that it became customary to make allowances to younger sons and daughters which became fixed and unavoidable charges on estate income. The composition of Lord MacDonald's debt of over £140,000 in 1846 was typical of those other Highland proprietors, £84,489, or 60 per cent of the total sum, was inherited from his father and grandfather and £56,187 was incurred during his lifetime. He had a gross annual income of £11,269 but only £3,298 of this was 'free', the rest being absorbed in interest payments and other charges. Similarly, in 1826, 83 per cent of the Earl of Seaforth's annual rental of £7,087 from his Lewis estate was absorbed in the payment of interest. It followed, therefore, that without spectacular increases in revenue from land sales or significant increases in estate income it was difficult, if not impossible, substantially to reduce levels of inherited debt. There were several instances of land being sold to increase revenue and, in some cases, these actions did stabilise the situation, but the pressures were so inexorable and insidious that the respite, especially for smaller landowners, was often only temporary. Thus MacLeod of MacLeod cleared off all his father's debts and also obtained a 'revision' of about £30,000 after selling off Glenelg in 1810 for £100,000 and by 1820 he had 'a clear, unencumbered estate' which yielded £9,000 a year. Less than three decades later, however, the family's properties were being run by trustees for the family's creditors. Only a combination of stable or increasing levels of income, lower annual costs and sound estate management could have saved the Highland landed class. In the event, however, the first two of these factors were missing, and some would argue that even the third was also absent. The hereditary elite of the society was therefore doomed.

The economic cycle which precipitated bankruptcies and land sales in the aftermath of the Napoleonic Wars has been documented in chapter 3. In the period 1790 to 1812 money flooded into the Highlands as a result of the spectacular increases in cattle prices, the windfall gains from kelping, and additional income from sheep-farming, fishing and illicit distillation. Rent rolls on all west Highland estates swelled as proprietors creamed off the increasing returns from these varied economic activities. but then, just as dramatically, prosperity ebbed away in the 1820s with the collapse of kelp manufacture, the slump in cattle prices and the malaise in the fisheries. The great land sales of this period were one result of this economic crisis as deflationary pressures forced those with high fixed charges based on wartime levels of income to unload their properties on to the market. The story is a familiar one but it does not in itself entirely explain the unique and unprecedented scale of land transfers in the western Highlands or why debt should have had a more devastating effect in the region in this period than in previous centuries.

The majority of British landowners had to contend with a more difficult economic environment by the 1820s but the position of west Highland proprietors was probably more critical and insecure than most. Increased income, ephemeral though it was, was not sufficient to overcome the central problem of the old west Highland elite: the difficulty, or perhaps even the impossibility, of maintaining the material standards now necessary to ensure full participation in the life of the British landed class on the relatively paltry returns from a poor land, an insecure economy and an impoverished peasantry. Highland proprietors socialised with southern landlords, many of whom increasingly depended on the fruits of urban expansion and mineral royalties to sustain a higher standard of living. These were not available to most Highland landowners and they could not compete. But in trying to do so they destroyed themselves and their territorial inheritance.

The post-war recession in the western Highlands was also more devastating in its effects than the contemporaneous fall in agricultural prices which occurred in Lowland Scotland. There the depression caused difficulty and lowered income as rents fell and abatements were awarded to hard-pressed tenant farmers, but it did not produce a crisis. Mixed farming in the Lowlands allowed for adjustment to a different market structure; the price of oats and barley, staples in the Scottish countryside, fell only moderately compared to wheat, which was cultivated widely only in some parts, and continued industrial and urban expansion allowed many proprietors to tap non-agricultural sources of income. It was a quite different story in the western Highlands where, as prices fell, marginal economic areas invariably suffered most. The vital point is that *all* sectors of this regional economy including sheep-farming, were in difficulty and hence, there was little opportunity for manoeuvre or for the implementation of policies which might temper the worst effects of the recession. Each one of the wartime supports of the economy crumbled in the years after Waterloo, but the most serious crisis was caused by the collapse of kelping which sank to unprofitable levels in most areas by the later 1820s. It was, therefore, no coincidence that it was the two greatest kelp lords, MacDonald of Clanranald and McKenzie of Seaforth, who were among the first to lose their lands in the post-war era. The manufacture of kelp had come to dominate the economy of their estates and they inevitably suffered the consequences of such risky over-specialisation when the bottom fell out of the market in the 1820s. As late as 1826, for example, by which time the proceeds of kelp had already declined considerably, they still made up 53 per cent of the total Seaforth rental on Lewis of £7,953.

The immediate consequence of the price collapse was a dramatic surge in rent arrears and hence a sharp fall in the disposable income required to service debt charges. Because rentals had been raised to cream off most of the peasant income in return for the possession of land, arrears inevitably began to accumulate as soon as prices faltered. The proprietor had often to bear the full brunt of the contraction because in the kelping estates the population 'paid' rent in the form of labouring in the industry while the wage consisted of meal supplies and land provided by the landowners. Yet, while income from kelp was depressed several proprietors had still to maintain the traditional obligation to supply meal which became even more pressing in such years of harvest failure as 1816–17, 1821–2, 1825, 1836–7 and, above all, during the great potato famine of 1846 to 1856. At these times, in particular, arrears spiralled as relief costs rose and several proprietors were therefore caught in a seemingly inescapable vice between contraction in income and stubbornly high, or even on occasion, rising costs. Evidence from estate papers demonstrates both the pain inflicted by this crisis and the desperate measures which were taken to try and retrieve the situation. Land sales, financial retrenchment, negotiations of fresh loans, changes in land use (particularly conversion of croft lands to sheep-farming), were all attempted. In many cases, however, they merely postponed the inevitable.

One reason why they were generally ineffective was that the financial and market environment in which nineteenth century Highland landowners had to live was radically different from that of their predecessors of the seventeenth century. Then, too, as has been seen, indebtedness was common, but despite the heavy debts of many of the landowners in the Western Isles, very few large estates changed hands or were broken up before 1700. Two factors possibly help to explain the different consequences of indebtedness in the two periods. The first of these was the changing sources of credit. In the seventeenth century, the overwhelming majority of loans were obtained from kinsmen, vassals or close associates usually in the form of a *wadset*, a pledge of lands in security for a debt, and it would appear that these arrangements rarely resulted in legal forfeiture or annexation of lands from the debtor even when he was in dire financial straits. This can be explained in terms of the strong sense of kin-loyalty which existed between debtor and creditor, a relationship cemented by hereditary attachment to the family lands and the influence of the ancient Celtic kin-based social structure which ensured that the loyalty of the kindred group focused on its ruling family.

However, the social and economic context of borrowing and lending had fundamentally altered by the early nineteenth century. The expansion of landed debt which occurred in the later eighteenth century Highlands was simply a regional variant of a British phenomenon. It now became much easier to borrow as a result of the growth of the banking system, the advent of the insurance companies, secular decline in the rate of interest and legal changes which rendered it easier for landowners to obtain credit. From the 1770s, for instance, landed estates became acceptable security for bankers' advances in Scotland. The wartime prosperity of agriculture boosted the attraction of providing mortgages on landed property while the post-war slump in the yield of consols stimulated insurance companies in particular to lend vast sums on the security of land. One could even speculate that the huge debts of Highland proprietors may have been due as much to the ease with which money could now be borrowed from a wide range of sources as to their own individual patterns of consumption and expenditure.

An analysis of the long-term loans owed by Lord MacDonald in 1846 illustrates the changes which had occurred since the seventeenth century. Only £19,542, or about 14 per cent of the sums owed, were due to creditors with Highland surnames and a mere 2 per cent were owed to individuals with the surname MacDonald, whereas Lord MacDonald's grandfather had owed 15 per cent of his debt to creditors of that name. On the other hand, of the total debt in 1846 of £140,676, over £37,600 were owed to trust funds and a further £20,637 to banks and insurance companies. In the short term, this flow of credit from the savings of the Lowland upper and middle classes and institutions helped to raise the standard of living of Highland proprietors and was an important (if rarely acknowledged) source of subsidy to the west Highland economy as a whole. But in the long term, its results were more ambiguous because the formalised and impersonal credit structure made it more probable that default on annual interest payments would not easily be permitted. Creditors were likely to appoint trustees to supervise the administration of properties in difficulty and, when deemed necessary, sell off lands to protect the value of their securities.

The second factor facilitating land sales in this period was the changing nature of the market for Highland property. In the seventeenth century, the purchase of west Highland land outside Argyll by outsiders was not common and the weakness of demand therefore doubtless also helps to explain the slow turnover of estates in that period. Creditors were perhaps less inclined to foreclose when the 'market' value of the asset against which their loan was secured was in doubt, but by the middle decades of the nineteenth century, however, this artificial insulation of debtors from the rigours of the market had come to an end. Highland estates were in great demand from social groups outside the Highlands who often had the resources to pay considerably more for them than the asking price and creditors were now therefore more likely to be keener to force sales. The great transfers of Highland property which occurred in this period were, therefore, not simply due to an increase in the supply of estates to the market but of augmented demand which itself accelerated the release of much territory for sale.

III

The new interest which developed in the acquisition of Highland property from the 1820s is in one sense paradoxical and ironic. Despite the economic and social crisis land prices rose as never before and the west Highland region began to attract very wealthy purchasers, not only from the Scottish Lowlands but from further afield. As one commentator observed in 1848: 'Look at the whole stretch of country from Fort Augustus to Fort William and Arisaig in the possession of rich English capitalists . . .'.[6] There can be little doubt of the new market potential of Highland estates and when property was put up for sale, the final price was frequently significantly higher than the original sale price. Glentronie in Badenoch was sold in 1835 to Henry Baillie, a wealthy Bristol West India merchant, for £7,350, over £2,000 above the advertised price; the Cromartie lands of Fannich and Lochbroom in Ross-shire were put for sale at £13,150 in 1835, but fetched £17,700; and Barra was advertised for £36,000 in 1839 but eventually purchased by James Menzies for over £42,000. When an estate was placed on the market, considerable competition from prospective purchasers could be anticipated. Glengarry, for example, attracted many offers and the sale price rose as a result from £88,000 until the property was finally acquired in 1840 for £91,000 by Lord Ward.

Even in periods of acute crisis in the western Highlands, there was little indication that the land market was adversely affected. A clutch of estates was released for sale in 1838–9 in the aftermath of the serious harvest failures of 1836–7, but they all quickly obtained ready purchasers. During the potato famine of 1846 to 1856, when the population of entire districts was plunged into destitution, it still proved possible to successfully market property in the stricken region. The estate of Lynedale in Skye, in the very heart of the famine zone, was acquired for £9,000 by Alexander MacDonald of Thornbank near Falkirk in the summer of 1849 at an advance of 10 per cent higher than the price it fetched when sold in 1838. Larger properties did prove more difficult to sell but even they eventually found purchasers. The Islay estate was advertised in 1848 for £540,000 but had to be lowered to £451,000 before it was bought four years later by James Morrison of Basildon Park. But the trustees did not have to split up the estate into separate lots to facilitate a sale and, in the event, Morrison only acquired Islay after the intervention of James Baird (a member of the greatest Scottish coal and iron manufacturing dynasty) which pushed up the sale price from £440,000 to £450,000. Indeed, what is especially interesting about this pattern of demand for Highland property is that it did not apparently fluctuate in accordance either with trends in the national land market or with the vicissitudes of the national economy. The exchange of Highland estates increased between c.1820 and c.1860 and did not suffer the temporary recession in the 1830s and 1840s which seems to have occurred elsewhere. This suggests that there were peculiar factors influencing demand and supply of Highland land which did not operate to the same extent in other parts of the country.

In the very broadest sense, the development can be seen as one important manifestation of the evolution of pronounced regional economic specialisation within the British economy in the nineteenth century. The economic plight of the Highlands in the generation or two after Waterloo derived to a large extent from the adverse impact of competition and demand from the dynamic industrial economy of the rest of Britain. It was the advanced manufacturing centres and improved agricultural regions to the south and east which undercut the marginal producers of the western Highlands and islands, destroyed the infant industrial growth points of the wartime era and converted the region into a source of wool, mutton and cheap labour for the rest of Britain. The process of economic growth itself, therefore, created a chronic regional imbalance which in simple terms can be viewed as the development of an impoverished north and west and a relatively prosperous Lowland economy. In the latter zone, enormous surpluses emerged, concentrated in the possession of the wealthy entre- preneurial and rentier classes, which were then redeployed in the purchase of land which was now in plentiful supply in the north because of the economic disasters which had overwhelmed the Highland region. The emergence of a new elite was therefore one further inevitable consequence of the dependent and weakened position of Highland society, and was a confirmation of its satellite status. Highland estates served the needs of the affluent of the south in the same way that the region's pastoral farms and teeming populations served the economic requirements of southern cities and industries. The result was '. . . a remarkable juxtaposition of some of the most successful entrepreneurs of the Victorian age with the least modernised agrarian margin'.

But straightforward economic analysis does not adequately explain the extraordinary surge in demand for Highland property. Even when the general economic context was far from propitious landed estates still sold well. It is interesting to note, for example, that while Walter Campbell's trustees managed to sell Islay in 1852, they were still attempting to get rid of Woodhall, his other estate in Lanarkshire, as late as 1854 and despite the fact that this mineral rich property lay in the very centre of the booming industrial area of west-central Scotland. It was apparently the Highland estate, with its famine-stricken popu- lation and uncertain rental, which proved more attractive to buyers than the lands in Lanarkshire which were richly endowed with coal and iron-ore measures and situated close to manufacturing industry. Indeed, the purchase of land in the Highlands in the nineteenth century hardly seems to reflect rational economic self-interest. Agricultural land, even in rich farming counties, yielded little more than an annual return of 2.5 to 3.5 per cent which was substantially less than the dividends which could be earned in other forms of investment.

The great value of landed property was not its profitability but rather its permanence as it was not only a secure investment but also provided a passive source of income. Philip Gaskell has shown that in Morvern in Argyllshire several small estates were acquired in the nineteenth century by owners who rarely if ever visited them and simply extracted rental as a secure and dependable income. The value of Highland property for these purposes had increased with the clearance of small tenants, the massive growth in sheep-farming and the expansion of deer forests. In Inverness-shire, the total number of sheep rose from 154,000 in 1811 to 542,000 in 1854; in Ross-shire from 50,946 to 251,619 and in Sutherland from 37,130 to 162,103. Sheep farms not only yielded regular rentals but they were also more easily collected by local factors for the owner and these increased on trend as prices for wool and mutton rose from the later 1840s to the early 1870s.

Others saw land purchase in the Highlands as a way of making quick, speculative profits and as demand for estates developed, speculators exploited the opportunity of buying land in a rising market and selling later at a handsome advance. The island of Harris was sold for 60,000 in 1831; half of it was converted to deer and in 1871 it fetched £155,000. Lord Hill bought part of Applecross in 1860 for £76,000 and after spending £14,000 on it he was able to resell it for £191,000. There were also those incorrigible optimists who imagined that they could make a fortune by purchasing debt-encumbered Highland estates and transforming them into highly profitable assets by investing in them and assiduously applying the techniques of Lowland improvement to their administration. This was a basic reason why the acquisition of some Highland estates by outsiders was sometimes followed very quickly by the clearance and forced emigration of the small tenantry who were viewed as one of the major economic obstacles to profitability. This was the predictable outcome when the Stirling lawyer, Francis Clark, bought Ulva; after the purchase of Raasay by George Rainy; when several estates in Mull and Morvern were acquired by new owners;

Raasay House, Raasay, off Skye

and above all, when John Gordon of Cluny bought Barra, South Uist and Benbecula.

The very cheapness of Highland land, relative to other areas of Scotland and England, posed both a challenge and an opportunity to these adventurers. They bought partly *because* rentals were low and the land was poor in the hope of transforming its prospects and so making huge gains in the long term. Gordon of Cluny is a classic case. He died possessed of property worth £2 to £3 millions and was acknowledged as the richest commoner in Scotland. Gordon was an extremely hard-headed businessman who undertook very careful supervision of his properties; it was said that nearly every receipt of rent was signed by his own hand. He was far from being a naive visionary who rashly hoped to transform barren acres into fertile soil and his acquisition of the Uists was part of a much wider programme of estate purchase and improvement which was completed when he became the owner of vast properties in Aberdeenshire, Banff, Nairn and Midlothian as well as in the Hebrides. However, his speculation in the Uists was spectacularly unsuccessful. By 1848, he had obtained less than ⅔ per cent return on his capital and had had to lay out nearly £8,000 on famine relief for the people on his estates. In 1847 arrears stood at £14,500 and the annual rental of £8,223 at the time of purchase had to be reduced to £4,894.

III

It would be quite wrong, on the other hand, to give the impression that the majority of new estate owners acquired Highland property to maximise economic returns or to obtain secure and permanent assets. These elements were relevant in several cases, but they were not generally decisive nor do they adequately explain why Highland land became so much more marketable in the nineteenth century than it had ever been in the past. To deal effectively with this question it is necessary to take a wider view. In essence, it seems to have been a direct consequence of the revolutionary change in the perception of the western Highlands and islands on the part of the affluent and leisured classes of British society in Victorian times described in the next chapter. Before the middle of the eighteenth century, the region was viewed by external observers as a barren and sterile wilderness, inhabited by a barbarous population, many of whom were disaffected to the British crown, but by the early decades of the century, a transformation had taken place. The revolution in taste associated with the Romantic Movement, the new interest in Nature and the rise of the ideas of the sublime and the picturesque, all served to create a wholly new response to the physical features of the Highlands. Truly 'modern' attitudes to scenic beauty were born; the wilderness became invested with qualities of romance and

imbued with historical, legendary and traditional associations. The western
Highlands became an area (like the Lake District) where it was now possible to
commune with nature and achieve spiritual renewal and restful solitude in an
atmosphere of other-worldly isolation. The former disadvantages of the region,
its relative inaccessibility and wild character, became points of positive attraction rather than features which repelled and disgusted.

It is difficult wholly to appreciate the enormous appeal which the
'romantic' Highlands had for the British upper and middle classes by the 1840s.
In 1853, for instance, the *Illustrated London News* described how

> The desolate grandeur of the scenery of Skye annually attracts to it crowds of
> tourists. Every phase of our society is duly represented in the course of each
> season, at the Stor, Quirang, Coruisk, and the Cuchuillin or Coollen Hills. They
> returned delighted as well they may with the wildest and most impressive scenery
> in the kingdom.[7]

Another observer around the same time pointed to the irresistible attraction of
the Highlands for the rich and famous:

> Within the last forty years scarcely one of any note in the world of letters that has
> not left footprints in Benledie, Benlomand, Benevis, and Cairn Gorum, and
> wandered by the lakes and scenes rendered dear to heart and eye by the songs and
> stories of Ossian and Scott; while the most celebrated of these classic scenes have
> been transferred to canvas by the pencils of Williams, Landseer, MacCulloch and
> others the first artists of the age.
>
> Instead of wandering on the banks of the Rhine, the Med., the Missilonghi, the
> Tiber, the Po and the Seine, which formerly formed the grand tour . . . a visit of
> some weeks' duration to the mountains and rivers of the Tay, the Dee, the Avon,
> the Spey, the Caledonian Canal and the Western Islands now constitutes the grand
> tour of fashionable life.[8]

It was in this period, too, that the region developed as a major centre for
the physical sports of hunting, shooting and fishing. The *Inverness Courier*
concluded as early as 1835 that 'Even unconquerable barrenness is now turned
to good account. At the present moment, we believe, many Highland proprietors
derive a greater revenue from their moors alone, for grouse shooting, than their
whole rental amounted to sixty years since'.[9] Twenty-eight deer forests were
formed before 1839; a further sixteen were established in the 1840s, ten in the
early 1850s and a further eighteen between 1855 and 1860. The greatest
expansion only came after 1880 but already by the middle decades of the
nineteenth century there had been substantial development. The comment
made in 1892 that '. . . as soon as a man has amassed a fortune in any way his first
desire seems to be to buy or hire a deer forest in Scotland and there to gather his

Stornoway Castle, Lewis

The interior of Stornoway Castle, Lewis

friends to enjoy his hospitality and sport' also has much relevance for earlier decades.[10]

The precondition both for the vast expansion in Highland tourism and the rise of the sporting economy was the revolution in communications. The western Highlands throughout this period possessed the unique qualities of 'remoteness' and isolation which were an integral part of its magical appeal for Victorians, but the region was no longer inaccessible and new transport facilities guaranteed reasonably quick and comfortable connections from the great urban centres in the south. The pathbreaking development was the invention of the ocean-going paddle steamer which for the first time brought a reliable and regular transport system to the Western Isles and the lochs of the western mainland. Equally significant in other areas was the revolution in road transport. Coach services radically improved and in 1836 it was said, with some astonishment, that 'a person might now dine in Edinburgh one day, and breakfast in Inverness the next',[11] whereas twenty years before the journey had taken four days. In the later 1830s the Caledonian coach left Edinburgh three times a week, '. . . crowded with tourists, and their baggage, a motley catalogue of guns, fishing rods, pointers, creels and baskets'.[12]

The transport revolution was both cause and effect of the new importance assumed by the western Highlands in the recreational pursuits of the Victorian middle and upper classes. The *Inverness Courier* reported that

> The passion entertained by English gentlemen for field sports has been fostered by increased means of communication northward and up and down the country, from the highest hill to the deepest and most distant glen. The sportsman throws himself into a steamer at London and in 48 hours or less he is in Edinburgh or Aberdeen. Another day and he is in the heart of moor and mountain, where he may shoot, saunter or angle to his heart's content.[13]

But the appeal of the region was not simply confined to those who sought to kill for pleasure. All the leisure interests of the affluent classes were catered for, and the new tourists not only consisted of 'sportsmen with dogs and guns' but also 'the geologist with his bag and hammer, the botanist with his book of specimens, the scene hunter with his pencil and numerous groups intent only on picnicking among wild hills, stream or waterfalls'.[14]

Only a handful of those who swarmed into the Highlands, carried by the steamships and faster coaches in the middle decades of the nineteenth century aspired to estate ownership. But the attractions which now enticed the many into the region were also those which stimulated the few to purchase land. It was the 'glamour' of the western Highlands which encouraged Octavius Smith, the wealthy London distiller, to buy the estate which was eventually named

Ardtornish in Morvern and to erect an elaborate mansion on it as a 'holiday home'. In 1845, the Marquis of Salisbury purchased the island of Rhum for £24,000 to develop it as a deer forest, and Sir Dudley Marjoribanks, later Lord Tweedsmouth, acquired Guisachan in Strathglass in 1854 for £52,000 for the same reason. Duncan Darroch's purchase of Torridon in 1872 was stimulated by his desire to 'enjoy the sport I love so well, the noblest sport of all, deer stalking'.[15]

But the exceptional availability of Highland estates also helped to satisfy other more powerful psychological drives and needs among the wealthy. Recent research by W. D. Rubinstein has demonstrated how it was difficult even for the most affluent members of the new merchant and industrialist classes to buy a great deal of land in Victorian times. This was not because they did not wish to do so but because few large estates ever came to market. In the western Highlands, however, extensive areas of land were not only available for purchase from the 1820s but, in relative terms at least, they were reasonably cheap. In the 1870s the owners of the Arisaig estate in Inverness-shire also possessed property in Cheshire and whereas the Arisaig lands had a gross annual value of only £0.07 per acre the Cheshire property was valued at £3.7 per acre. The Marquis of Northampton's Mull estate was reckoned to be worth £0.15 per acre while his estates in Warwick were valued at £1 per acre. It was possible, therefore, for successful businessmen to buy up many thousands of acres of wild and beautiful country in the north west for an outlay which would have afforded them only a small country estate in most other regions of Britain and it mattered not that much of the land was useless because its main function was primarily to satisfy the urge for territorial possession. It became a form of conspicuous consumption, a means by which material success could be demonstrated, status and place in society assured and a family line established. In this sense, buying a Highland estate and 'improving' it gratified the same passion for possession as the collection of fine art or the acquisition of expensive and elaborate furniture.

Those who obtained Highland land in great quantities could afford to indulge themselves because they were among the very wealthiest men in Britain. James Morrison, who acquired Islay, for example, was possibly the richest British commoner in the nineteenth century. Alexander (later Sir Alexander) Matheson and his kinsman, Sir James Matheson, had amassed huge fortunes in the lucrative China trade and returned to Britain in their middle years to establish landed families and each was drawn to the country of his ancestors. James was the son of an officer in the Earl of Sutherland's fencible regiments. Alexander's family were from Lochalsh and his father had owned the estate of Attadale but had had to sell it because of financial difficulties in 1825. On his return from the east, James Matheson purchased two small estates in his native Sutherland in 1840 and then obtained the island of Lewis in 1844 from the bankrupt earls of Seaforth. Over the following two decades he spent substantially more than a quarter of a million pounds on a wide range of land improvements, additions to the island's infrastructure and support for the fisheries. Alexander indulged in an even more spectacular spending spree. He acquired six separate estates in Lochalsh and Kintail, including the former lands of his family, at a total cost of £238,020 and a further outlay of over £185,000 was used to purchase property in Easter Ross. By 1870, he owned territory of more than £220,000 acres in extent, an area which yielded only just over £23,000 in annual rent but made him a greater Highland landowner in terms of territory possessed than such aristocrats as the Duke of Atholl or the Duke of Argyll. During his lifetime, £400,000 were spent on purchase, improvement to his properties and on the building and elaborate furnishing of mansion houses.

Matheson was the apotheosis of one type of new landowner in the Highlands, an individual of colossal wealth who lavished expenditure on his estates and in the process helped to subsidise the local economy from the profits of trade earned in distant and exotic parts of the world. The activities of men like him ensured that the drain of rental income from the Highlands, which had occurred when the old elite expended much of the surplus of their estates in the fashionable capitals of the south, was now reversed. Instead, the new landed class spent much of the profit derived from their world-wide commercial and professional success in the Highlands and the economic power of the new landowners helped to bring relief to the people of many estates during the famine crisis. But the negative aspects of the revolution in landownership should also be recognised. It completed the process of the disintegration of social cohesion between the elites of the Highlands and the people of the society which began with the anglicisation and commercialisation of the native aristocracy. In some areas, though by no means all, new owners with less sentimental regard for older ways, carried out some of the most brutal, notorious and extensive clearances. The most infamous examples were those pursued by the Stirlingshire lawyer, Francis Clark, on the island of Ulva in the 1840s and John Gordon of Cluny in Barra and South Uist. Other proprietors viewed their lands as sporting playgrounds or as sources of revenue which were rarely visited and often neglected. But generalisation in this area is not easy. For one thing, the distinction between 'old' and 'new' landowners is very blurred, and ancient Highland families also evicted without impunity or compunction. They, like many of the new possessors, were effective exponents of the ethic of commercial landlordism. In addition, the wealth of some of those acquiring Highland property in the nineteenth century gave them more freedom of action than the impoverished lairds of an earlier time. A few used this to play the role of feudal patriarchs among the inhabitants of their estates by dispensing charity, attempting economic improvements and building schools and churches and this was a position which afforded even more psychological satisfaction for some than mere territorial aggrandisement, the most extraordinary example of such benevolent despotism in the western Highlands being that of Lord Leverhulme in Harris and Lewis after the First World War. The impact, therefore, of new landlordism was complex as its effects varied between different owners and estates.

NOTES

1 J. Mitchell, *Reminiscences of My Life in the Highlands*, London, 1883–4, II, p. 114.
2 D. Spring, 'The English landed estate in the age of coal and iron: 1830–80', *Journal of Economic History*, XI, 1951, p. 16.
3 E. Richards, *A History of the Highland Clearances*, London, 1985, II, p. 417.
4 *Ibid.*, II, p. 418.
5 F. M. L. Thompson, 'English great estates in the nineteenth century, 1790–1914', *Contributions to the First International Conference of Economic History*, Paris, 1960.
6 Scottish Record Office, HG7/47, W. Skene to Sir Charles Trevelyan, 23 February 1848.
7 *Illustrated London News*, 15 January 1853.
8 W. G. Stewart, *Lectures on the Mountains*, London, 1860, pp. 309–10.
9 *Inverness Courier*, 28 October 1853.
10 W. Orr, *Deer Forests, Landlords and Crofters*, Edinburgh, 1982, p. 40.
11 *Inverness Courier*, 13 July 1836.
12 *Ibid.*,
13 *Ibid.*, 28 October 1835.
14 *Ibid.*, 28 August 1833.
15 Orr, *Deer Forests*, p. 40.

FURTHER READING

T. M. Devine, *The Great Highland Famine*, Edinburgh, 1988.
P. Gaskell, *Morvern Transformed*, Cambridge, 1968.
W. Orr, *Deer Forests, Landlords and Crofters*, Edinburgh, 1982.
W. D. Rubinstein, 'New men of wealth and the purchase of land in nineteenth century England', *Past and Present*, 92, 1981.
T. C. Smout, 'Tours in the Scottish Highlands from the eighteenth to the twentieth centuries', *Northern Scotland*, 5, 1983.
F. M. L. Thompson, 'The land market in the nineteenth century', *Oxford Economic Paper*, 2nd ser., 9, 1957.
F. M. L. Thompson, *British Landed Society in the Nineteenth Century*, London, 1983.

6

THE MAKING OF HIGHLANDISM, 1746–1822

I

To the rest of the world in the late twentieth century Scotland seems a Highland country. The 'land of the mountain and the flood' adorns countless tourist posters and the familiar and distinctive symbols of Scottish identity, the kilt, tartan and bagpipes, are all of Highland origin, but this curious image is bizarre and puzzling at several levels. For one thing it hardly reflects the modern pattern of life in Scotland, as from the later eighteenth century the country had experienced such a revolutionary expansion in towns and industry that by the 1850s it was second only to England in the rate of urbanisation. By the later nineteenth century Scotland had become an industrialised society with the vast majority of its citizens engaged in manufacturing and commercial activities and living in the central Lowlands, and most rural areas by that time were losing population rapidly through migration to the big cities of the Forth and Clyde valley. Yet, ironically, it was one of these regions, the Highlands, the poorest and most underdeveloped of all, which provided the main emblems of cultural identity for the rest of the country. An urban society had adopted a rural face.

This was especially surprising in the light of the attitudes towards the Highlands which prevailed among most of the Lowland political, religious and social establishment until well into the second half of the eighteenth century. The concept of the 'Highlands' does not appear in the written evidence for the period before 1300 despite the geographical division between the north and south of Scotland. When the Highlands did become part of the vocabulary in the medieval period it was in response to a need to isolate and distinguish a part of Scotland which differed in cultural and social terms from the rest. A crucial difference was linguistic, for, as Gaelic retreated from the Lowlands, the 'Highlands' became culturally distinctive and linguistically separate from other parts of the kingdom. Very quickly, too, it became regarded by the state as a problem region. In the early modern period, Highland instability was seen as a major obstacle to the effective unification of the country. After the Reformation the Highlands were not properly evangelised for the new faith and were regarded as irreligious, popish and pagan for generations thereafter; for the Scottish political elites and the protestant church before 1700 the Highlands were alien and hostile, in need of more state control and both moral and religious 'improvement'. The consensus was that the society had to be assimilated to the social and cultural norms which prevailed in the rest of Scotland because it was both inferior and dangerous.

At the more popular level attitudes towards the Highlanders were equally hostile. There was a long tradition of anti-Highland satire in both Lowland poetry and song which can be traced back into the Middle Ages and references in satiric works by such poets as William Dunbar and Sir Richard Holland caricatured the Gael as stupid, violent, comic, feckless and filthy. A short poem dating from around 1560 was entitled 'How the first helandman of God was maid of Ane horse turd in Argylle as is said'. The Highlander also inhabited a physical world of desolation, barrenness and ugliness and to the Lowland mind before the revolution in aesthetic taste of the later eighteenth century the north of Scotland was both inhospitable and threatening. As late as 1800, when perceptions were already changing, the author of *The General Gazetteer or Compendions Geographical Directory* (London, 1800, 11th edn.) noted how: 'the North division of the country is chiefly an assembly of vast dreary mountains'.[1] Dr Johnson was also repelled and astonished by the 'wide extent of hopeless sterility' during his celebrated journey to the Western Isles in 1773,[2] and when the English army officer, Edward Burt, described the mountains near Inverness in 1730 he saw them a 'a dismal gloomy Brown . . . and most of all disagreeable, when the Heath is in Bloom'.[3] Heather-covered bens were neither romantic nor attractive – as they were later to become – but merely ugly and sinister.

There can be little doubt that for protestant Whigs in the Lowlands, and that in essence meant the political and economic ascendancy in most areas south of the Tay, the support of many Highland clans for successive Jacobite rebellions instilled an even more intense suspicion of Gaelic society. The Highlanders were no longer figures of fun and ethnic contempt but in the '45 had threatened to overthrow the protestant succession itself and this elicited an almost hysterical reaction. One commentator, 'Scoto-Britannus', depicted the Highlanders as men beyond the pale of civilisation. The Young Pretender had secretly landed in the remote parts of the kingdom 'amidst dens of barbarous and lawless ruffians' and a 'crew of ungrateful villains, savages and traitors'.[4] For Lowland presbyterians, the Highland Jacobites posed a dreadful threat because

of their association with popery, and thus, in one Whig poem of the '45, the
Jacobite army is described in the following terms:

> From Rome a Limb of Antichrist
> Join d with a Hellish Band of Highland Thieves, came here in haste,
> God's Laws for to withstand.[5]

The Young Pretender was identified with the Antichrist, the Pope, and his
followers were tainted with the same satanic origin and therefore it is scarcely
surprising that the response to the rebellion took the form not only of military
and judicial repression but also resulted in an attempt to transform Highland
society and culture through legislation designed to encourage economic
improvement, the expansion of presbyterianism and the removal of cultural
differences with the rest of Britain.

The strategy of assimilation, which had been pursued by southern governments since the reign of James VI, reached its climax with the Disarming Act of
1746. In addition to proscribing the carrying of weapons, it forbade anyone not
in the army to wear Highland clothes or even to use 'plaid, philibeg, trews,
shoulder-belts . . . tartans or parti-coloured plaid'.[6] A government minister
described the bill as one for 'disarming and undressing those savages'.[7]
Disobedience warranted six months in prison and transportation for seven years
for a second offence, and this law remained in force for thirty-five years. Its
impact may be questioned, especially in districts far from government garrisons,
and, in the early 1760s, enforcement seems to have been relaxed in general
terms until final repeal in 1781. However, during this period the wearing of the
Highland garb does seem to have become less common in some areas, and when
Johnson and Boswell made their tour of the Western Isles in 1773 in search of a
'people of peculiar appearance' they were disappointed. Johnson stated they had
never seen the tartan worn during their wanderings. One scholar has even
concluded, albeit with considerable exaggeration, that, 'By 1780 the Highland
dress seemed extinct, and no rational man would have speculated on its revival'.[8]
Yet is was precisely at this time that tartan and plaid started to become widely
popular among the Lowland upper and middle classes of Scotland. This strange
development was part of a wider process, which was all but complete by the end
of the Napoleonic Wars through which (mostly) imagined and false Highland
'traditions' were absorbed freely by Lowland elites to form the symbolic basis of a
new Scottish identity. This 'Highlandism' was quite literally the invention of a
tradition. What made it deeply ironic was not simply the actual historic Lowland
contempt for ancient Gaelic culture which existed well into the eighteenth
century but the fact that Highlandism took off precisely at the same time as
commercial landlordism, market pressures and clearances were breaking up the

old social order in northern Scotland. Indeed, as will be seen, some of the main protagonists of the new traditionalism were themselves Highland proprietors who had long ceased to be clan chiefs and had instead become rapacious improving landowners.

The roots of Highlandism can be traced back to the '45 and before, but an important institutional step in its development was first taken in 1778 with the foundation of the Highland Society in London. Its avowed intention was the preservation of ancient Highland tradition and the repeal of the law forbidding the wearing of the Highland dress in Scotland, an objective achieved in 1782 when the Marquis of Graham, at the Society's behest, successfully carried the legislation through Parliament. The tartan was not only quickly rehabilitated, but it also swiftly became extraordinarily fashionable. In 1789, the year that Charles Edward Stewart, the Young Pretender, died in Rome, three of the king's sons, the Prince of Wales (later George IV), and his brothers, William Henry and Frederick, were provided with complete Highland dresses. They were instructed by Colonel John Small in the wearing of 'tartan plaid, philabeg, purse and other appendages', and the future king even wore the kilt to a masquerade in London. Some years before this bizarre event tartan seems already to have started imprinting itself on the British consciousness as the dress of the Scots rather than simply of the Gaels. In Allan Ramsay's poem *Tartana*, which was written to promote native textiles, the warriors and shepherds of old Caledonia are all rigged out in plaid, and in 1773 there was the first production of *Macbeth* with the hero dressed in tartan, an innovation which quickly became established as a stage tradition.

The reputation of the Highland regiments, especially during the Napoleonic Wars, lent a new prestige and glamour to the wearing of tartan. These battalions had been specifically exempted from the ban on Highland dress in the Disarming Act of 1746 and thereafter the kilt was forever associated with the heroic deeds of the Scottish soldier. During the phase of intense patriotism during the wars with France many of the Scottish volunteer corps and fencible regiments which flourished for a short time all over the country adopted tartan and the kilt as their uniforms. The martial tradition had long been an important part of the Scottish identity, and now that was being decked out in Highland colours and the kilted battalions were depicted as the direct descendants of the clans. Importantly, however, they now represented the martial spirit of the Scottish nation as a whole rather than a formerly despised part of it.

The zenith of this development came in 1822 with the remarkable celebration of the visit of George IV to Edinburgh in August 1822. No monarch had set foot in Scotland since Charles II in 1651. The king spent two weeks in the Scottish capital and a series of extraordinary pageants, all with a Celtic and

Highland flavour, were stage-managed by Sir Walter Scott. What ensued was a 'plaided panorama' based on fake Highland regalia and the mythical customs and traditions of the clans. Scott had determined that Highlanders were what George would most like to see and he therefore urged clan chiefs to bring followers to Edinburgh suitably dressed for the occasion. Seven bodies of 'clansmen' including MacGregors, Glengarry MacDonnels, Sutherlands and Campbells paraded during the visit and His Majesty himself was clad in kilt, plaid, bonnet and tartan coat. The climax came with the procession from Holyroodhouse to Edinburgh Castle when the Honours of Scotland – crown, sceptre and sword of state – were solemnly paraded before the monarch with an escort led by the once-outlawed Clan Gregor. At the banquet in Parliament Hall, the king called for a toast to the clans and chieftains of Scotland to which Sir Evan MacGregor replied with one to 'The Chief of Chiefs – the King'.

Scott had wished the royal visit to be 'a gathering of the Gael', but what his Celtic fantasy had in fact produced was a distortion of the Highland past and present and the projection of a national image in which the Lowlands had no part. The great ball during the royal visit where full Highland regalia were worn has been seen as a seminal event in the acceptance of the kilt as the national dress of Scotland. After all, the head of state had himself given it a bogus legitimacy and the ruling class of the society was addressed as 'the chieftains and clans of Scotland' during the public events. However, more realistic voices at the time were less impressed than the 'enthusiasts for the philabeg'. J. G. Lockhart, Scott's son-in-law and biographer, regarded the pageantry as a 'hallucination' in which the glorious traditions of Scotland were identified with a people which 'always constituted a small and always an unimportant part of the Scottish population'.[9] Even more appalled was Lord Macaulay. Looking back from the 1850s he found it incredible that the monarch should show his respect for the historic Scottish nation 'by disguising himself in what, before the Union, was considered by nine Scotchmen out of ten as the dress of a chief'.[10] It was especially astonishing that this mania for tartanry coincided in time with the breaking up of the real Highland society and indeed, several of the leading participants in the events of 1822, such as MacDonnel of Glengarry, had themselves been to the fore in the ruthless transformation of their estates into profitable assets. Nothing of this disturbed the pageantry of the royal visit. The realities of the Highland present and recent past were quite separate and distinct from the cult of Highlandism.

II

Much of the new awareness of the Highlands in the eighteenth century throughout Britain can be traced to Jacobitism in general and the '45 in particular. The rebellion ensured that the Highlands were well and truly put on the map and there was an immediate fascination with the personalities and events of the rising. Histories of the rebellion, such as *Young Juba or the History of the Young Chevalier*, were published in significant numbers, and of special interest was the story of the Young Pretender's escape and his months of hiding in the heather protected by loyal and heroic figures such as Flora MacDonald. The most popular account was the frequently reprinted *Ascanius or the Young Adventurer, containing a particular account of all that happened to a certain person during his wanderings in the North from his memorable defeat in April 1746 to his final escape on the 19th of September in the same year.* This seminal text was subsequently available in French, Spanish and Italian versions.

Even during the rebellion itself Jacobitism had developed a certain glamour. Jacobite songwriters portrayed Prince Charles as a gallant, charming and courageous Highlander clad in colourful plaid and, as William Donaldson has shown, this celebration of the Young Pretender was partly derived from the tradition of the 'Bonny Highland Laddie', a youthful figure of considerable personal beauty and sexual energy who had featured in Scottish popular song since the later seventeenth century. By borrowing from this *genre* the Young Pretender was transformed from 'statesman and conqueror' to lover and galant'.[11] Charles Edward Stewart became 'Bonny Prince Charlie'.

But this stereotype could not achieve wide appeal until Jacobitism itself was finally crushed and the threat of a Stewart counter-revolution permanently removed. Indeed, it was the decisive nature of the Hanoverian military victory which made possible the sentimentalisation of the Jacobite cause. Any lingering menace from the Highlands would have prevented this. The rebels were, however, effectively tamed and their martial power destroyed, and the scene was set for their metamorphosis from faithless traitors to national heroes. The rehabilitation of Jacobitism was enhanced when William Pitt's strategy of channelling the military prowess of the clans into the imperial service during the Seven Years Wars (1756–63) proved such a stunning success. The anti-Union element in Jacobitism also appealed to those Scots of the later eighteenth century who wished for a symbol of Scottish political and cultural distinctiveness without in any way seeking to threaten the relationship with England which was so vital to Scottish prosperity. The outbreak of revolution in France was also influential because, 'the spectre of Republicanism rendered the traditional opposition of Hanoverian and Stuart obsolete at a stroke'.[12] The famed military song 'The Gathering of the Clans', a reinterpretation of 'The Campbells are Coming' set out a detailed list of Highland clans ready to take the field against Napoleon. This and other similar songs of the time expressed in popular form the transfer of loyalty from the Stewarts in the '45 to the Hanoverians in the later eighteenth century. In this way Jacobitism was redefined as an ideology committed to monarchy in the abstract sense at a time when the institution in Britain was under attack from radical enemies both within and without. As such it became politically acceptable, and wide dissemination of the Jacobite myth, with its potent mixture of themes of love, loyalty, exile and loss, was now possible. Jacobitism came to be regarded as representing the heroic Scottish past, the more seductive because it was so recent, and was seen as synonymous with the Highlands. The fact that only a minority of clans had 'come out' in the '45 and that many others had supported the Whig cause was historically accurate but nevertheless irrelevant.

Jacobitism and hence Highland 'tradition' entered the national consciousness through both song and literature and a powerful force in the latter process was Robert Burns who was a prolific writer of Jacobite songs including such familiar tunes as 'Charlie he's my darling', 'Strathallan's Lament' and 'The White Cockade'. The fact that Burns himself was a poet of Jacobite sympathy who hailed from one of the strongholds of Scottish Whiggism in south-west Scotland was itself a significant confirmation of the new perceptions. Burns sympathised with Jacobitism for patriotic reasons, seeing it as a movement which had fought for Scottish independence rather than for the restoration of an absolute monarchy, and his songs therefore associate the Jacobite rebellion with the heroic struggles of the Scottish past from the Wars of Independence onwards. It has been suggested that that great expression of nationalism, 'Scots wha hae', was itself inspired by the Jacobite rebellion and that Burns' role was therefore vital in placing Jacobitism, and so the Highlands, at the centre of the new national consciousness which was emerging in Scotland after the Union.

He was followed by James Hogg who, in his *Jacobite Relics of Scotland*, published many examples of genuine early eighteenth century Jacobite verse which, much to the chagrin of the Highland Society, which had commissioned the work, did not contain enough of the sentiment, pathos and nostalgia deemed essential in 'authentic' Jacobite verse. Much more acceptable were the songs of Carolina Oliphant, Lady Nairne, who composed, 'Will ye no come back again?'. This nostalgic lament for the exiled Prince was written by the scion of an old Jacobite family who was only born twenty years after Charles left Scotland for ever! Subsequently three major new collections appeared, *Songs of Scotland* (1825), *The Scottish Minstrel* (1824–8) and *The Scottish Songs* (1829). By the 1820s songs with a Jacobite theme were second only to love songs in number and quality in the popular Scottish canon, and became an enormously influential factor in disseminating widely the association between Jacobitism, the Highlands and Scottish national consciousness.

The prose writers added to this cultural momentum. David Stewart of Garth, Anne Grant of Laggan, Patrick Graham and, above all, Sir Walter Scott, presented idealised images of heroic Highlanders who, despite following an unfortunate cause, had remained true and loyal. Scott's work, in particular *Waverley*, more than any other single influence, made Jacobitism acceptable and even more it made it romantic and seductive, skilfully embeddeding the Jacobite movement firmly within a Highland context of chieftains, clans and tartans. With only some exaggeration one Victorian writer asserted that as a result of Scott's novels 'the whole nation . . . went over the water to Charlie'.[13] If the '45 put the Highlands on the map within the United Kingdom, Scott was mainly responsible for publicising it widely throughout the world.

III

The '45 was the fourth and last occasion when a Highland army under a Jacobite leader threatened the revolutionary settlement of 1688–9. Not surprisingly therefore, as Peter Womack notes, 'the Highlanders impressed themselves on British consciousness first of all as warriors and their society as one where the martial virtues of courage, daring and loyalty predominated',[14] and in the short run after Culloden the valour of the Highlanders in fighting against all odds for what was eventually a lost cause was a feature which appealed mainly to Jacobite sympathisers. However, as the martial energies of the Gael were successfully channelled into service in the imperial armies, the exploits of the Highland regiments rapidly became the stuff of legend and romance and a basic factor in the development of the Highland myth.

As early as 1739, one prophetic commentator had observed:

> They [the Highlanders] are a numerous and prolifick People; and, if reformed in their Principles and Manners, and usefully employ'd, might be made a consider-able Accession of Power and Wealth to Great Britain. Some Clans of Highlanders, well instructed in the Arts of War, and well affected to the Government, would make as able and formidable a body for their Country's Defence, as Great Britain, or Switzerland, or any Part of Europe, are able to produce.[15]

Even before the '45 the state had started to exploit this military potential. In 1739 the Independent Companies of the Highland Watch were regimented as the 43rd and later the 42nd of foot 'destined for renown in many a song and story under their more familiar names: the Black Watch, the Royal Highland Regiment, "The Gallant Forty-Twa" '.[16] But it was in the years 1757–60 that the elder Pitt for the first time on a systematic basis diverted the martial spirit of the Highlanders to the service of the imperial state, and in subsequent eighteenth

century conflicts over fifty battalions of Highland troops were raised, distinguishing themselves at Quebec, Seringapatam, Waterloo and a host of other
battles in many parts of the world. The Highlanders having been seen as lawless
barbarians were now perceived as vital assets when Britain was engaged in a
great struggle for most of the later eighteenth century with France for world
domination and had much need of loyal troops. Whether rightly or wrongly the
loyalty of the Highland soldier was deemed his most important virtue and this
was linked with the steadfastness of the Jacobite army during the '45 and with
the hierarchical structure of the clans which bound followers to chief. The fact
that clanship was disintegrating in this period was beside the point. The composition of the Highland regiments seemed to suggest that clan values and
structures lived on within the army. Fraser's Highlanders (the 71st Regiment)
had six chiefs of clans among its officers: Simon Fraser, Cluny MacPherson,
MacLeod, Cameron of Lochiel, Lamont and Colquhoun as well as the sons of
some others and several tacksmen. The Highland battalions were not therefore
simply daring in war but they were also politically reliable because of their
loyalty to their hereditary leaders and this rendered them an invaluable military
resource because as one state paper put it in 1797, the Highlanders are
'strangers to the levelling and dangerous principles of the present age' and
unlike the rest of the population at a time of radical unrest and republican
sentiment could be trusted to bear weapons.[17]

It was not therefore surprising that the Highland regiments became a
major factor in altering perceptions of Highland society after the '45. The speed
of the transformation from Jacobite traitors to imperial heroes is astonishing. It
can be seen clearly in the famous contemporary song 'The Garb of Old Gaul'
which celebrates the gallantry of the Highland soldier and in the version
published in the 1760s several of the main ingredients of later mythology are
present. There is first repeated the traditional claim that even the Romans had
failed to conquer Scotland because of the martial qualities of the Highlanders
and, in addition, the Highland regiments are depicted as defending Britain from
France and Spain, a remarkable reversal twenty years after Culloden. Finally in
the song Highland valour is incorporated in a *Scottish* tradition of heroism.
Before the Gael was alien and racially inferior; now the deeds of the Highland
soldier made him a standard bearer for long-held beliefs about the martial
virtues of the Scottish nation.

The Highland regiments were therefore crucial to the development of
Highlandism. They added to the glamour of the Highlands, perpetuating the
association with Jacobitism and clanship which were also being idealised at the
same time, they enhanced the contemporary image of a 'noble peasantry' uncon-
taminated by urban vice and displaying all the virtues of loyalty, courage and

endurance to heroic effect. Above all the kilted battalions, more than any other single factor, popularised Highland dress and made it the national symbol of Scotland. At the end of the Napoleonic Wars their prestige was never higher, the Highland regiments took pride of place in the allied march of triumph into Paris, returning home as heroes. The Black Watch entered Edinburgh to a tumultuous reception. As the regiment's quartermaster sergeant recalled, '. . . we entered the city amidst the loud cheering and congratulations of friends; while over our heads, from a thousand windows, waved as many banners, plaided scarfs or other symbols of courtly greetings'. Finally, they marched into the castle, 'proud of the most distinguished reception that ever a regiment had met with from a grateful country'.[18]

Over time the entire Scottish military establishment began to assume a dominant Highland flavour. By 1881, indeed, the connection between militarism and Highlandism was so strong that the War Office ordered all Lowland regiments to wear tartan trews and Highland-style doublets and this directive applied also to those who had won battle honours fighting against Highlanders. The victory of Highlandism was complete.

IV

At the same time as the Highlands were winning international fame as the home of kilted heroes, European intellectual and aesthetic developments were drastically altering older attitudes both to the society and physical configuration of the north of Scotland. Enlightenment thinkers became interested in the scientific study of man and human social evolution and the Scottish *literati* were to the fore in these enquiries. John Miller argued that there was a natural progression from 'rude' to 'civilised' manners while Adam Smith elaborated a schematic structure of evolution by which man moved from the age of hunters, through the age of shepherds to the ages of agriculture and commerce. These ideas impinged on perceptions of the Highlander at two levels. First, in a practical sense they served to give intellectual legitimacy to the varied programmes of 'improvement', ranging from the Annexed Forfeited Estates Commission to the British Fisheries Society which endeavoured to move the Highlands from backwardness to progress and secondly, the analysis placed considerable emphasis on the need to understand 'primitive' societies. As Withers has argued:

> Highlanders fitted this notion . . . rude savages in an uncultivated landscape. To the urbane *philosophe* of the late eighteenth century the Highlander was a contemporary ancestor, the Highlands the Scottish past on the doorstep.[19]

In this way, therefore, the Highlands were effectively incorporated as part of Scotland and were no longer an alien world beyond the pale but a living illustration of the social mores of the Scottish past. At the same time, the primitive and antique aspects of Highland society were given particular emphasis and this rendered the society interesting to the intellectually curious:

> The Scottish Gael fulfilled this role of the primitive albeit one quickly and savagely tamed, at a time when every thinking man was turning towards such subjects. The

A private soldier of the 42nd Regiment of Foot, 1742

Highlands of Scotland provided a location for this role that was distant enough to be exotic but close enough to be noticed; that was near enough to visit, but had not been drawn so far into the calm waters of civilisation to lose all its interests.[20]

It was these intellectual changes which were tapped and exploited so successfully by James MacPherson who published his alleged 'epic' *Fingal* in 1761. This work and associated others were supposed to have been composed by

Seaforth Highlanders

the blind old harper Oisein or Ossian about the heroic figure Finn, in the third century. The tales were complete forgeries and mainly amounted to the refashioning of poems which had long been available in Ireland and the High-lands, but when they appeared MacPherson enjoyed enormous success and the poems of Ossian were eventually translated into eleven languages. Throughout Europe they had a widespread impact. Napoleon was said to have been a fervent admirer and such figures as Victor Hugo, Alfred de Musset, Lamartine, Goethe, Herder and Schiller were influenced by them. They caught an intellectual and spiritual mood at a time of massive economic, social and political change which saw 'primitive' societies possessing virtues which modern societies had lost. This was a notion which could easily be transferred to the eighteenth century Highlands because there too, into the contemporary period, lived a 'primitive' people amid a landscape which seemed hardly to have altered since the time of Ossian.

The Ossianic impact was so great because it both influenced and coincided with parallel changes in attitudes to the Highland landscape. In the later eighteenth century the land ceased to be regarded as simply repellent and came to be viewed as beautiful, romantic and inspiring. Modern notions of 'scenery' and scenic beauty were born and resulted in a transformation of aesthetic responses to the Highlands. The Ossianic craze was deeply significant in this process because the fact that the northern landscape *was* rugged and untamed made it entirely suitable for the 'primitive' society depicted in MacPherson's best-selling epics. This was the view propounded by Hugh Blair, professor of rhetoric and *belles lettres* at Edinburgh University in his *Critical Dissertation on the poems of Ossian, the son of Fingal* of 1704. Blair's work built on the development of the idea of the sublime which was at that time gaining currency in intellectual circles in Europe. Its theoretical basis was laid out in Edmund Burke's *Philosophical Enquiry into the Origin of our Ideas of the Sublime and Beautiful*, but Blain separated out the 'beautiful' from the 'sublime' whereas Burke stimulated quite different emotions: 'the sublime is found to be rooted in the terrific, inspiring a fear which fills the mind with great ideas and stirs the soul . . . any menacing object may produce the sublime, but especially those associated with obscurity, power, privation, vastness, infirmity or difficulty'.[21] Equally influential was the idea of the picturesque propounded by William Gilpin in his two-volume work of 1792 entitled *Observations relative chiefly to picturesque beauty, made in the year 1776 on several parts of Great Britain, particularly the High-lands of Scotland.* Gilpin enunciated the notion that the picturesque landscape required discriminating and careful observation in order to see its diverse elements as a perfect composition and that the admirer of the picturesque required judgement. Not all nature was attractive; discernment required careful selection. It was a form of cultural elitism.

These new ideas transformed the Highlands from a barren wilderness to a place of compelling natural beauty, and by the early nineteenth century an upper class tourist trade was already established partly because European travelling was made more difficult during the French wars. As Sir Walter Scott remarked in 1810, 'Every London citizen makes Lochlomond his washpot and throws his shoe over Ben Nevis.'[21] Scott himself contributed enormously to the popularisation of Highland travel. Hitherto touring had been confined to the frontiers of the Highlands, with the fashionable 'Short Tour' entering the region at Dunkeld and leaving via Luss with Loch Lomond as the highlight and few penetrated the wild country to the far north and west. At first Scott's writings, and in particular the 'Lady of the Lake' of 1810, invested the Trossachs with further romance and ensured that Loch Lomond was soon eclipsed by Loch Katrine as the mecca for fashionable tourists. But his 'Lord of the Isles' put Skye on the map and extended the tourist trail to the Hebrides where those seeking the 'sublime' could come face to face with truly wild mountain scenery.

But these changes in attitudes to Highland landscape did not simply reflect alterations in aesthetic taste, they were also linked to practical economic developments in the eighteenth and early nineteenth centuries. People could get to the Highlands in greater numbers because of transport improvements and among these the invention of the sea-going paddle steamer was crucial with an intricate shipping network established up the west coast and the Inner Hebrides from the Clyde by the 1830s. Cook's tours using steamers and railways began from 1846, the year the potatoes failed in the Highlands. The wilderness seemed less daunting when seen from a comfortable and convenient mode of transport and, in addition, the Highlands had a seductive appeal in an era of profound economic transformation. Elsewhere in Britain by the early nineteenth century the 'natural' landscape had been permanently altered by enclosed fields, neat farm steadings and improved agriculture and only the remote areas of the north remained untouched. Despite the reality of large-scale commercial sheep-farming, as efficient as any in the country, which dominated the region, the Highlands seemed to exude 'the radiance of a disappearing authenticity' which gave it a special magic.[22] The 'archaic' nature of the landscape therefore became indissolubly linked with the romanticisation of the historic Highlands which was taking place at the same time. It was an essentially imaginary world in which the harsh realities of life for the contemporary common people rarely impinged.

V

The adoption of Highland emblems, costumes and associations as its national image by a modernising Scotland in the nineteenth century is curious but not entirely incomprehensible. Scottish society was in a contradictory position within the Union relationship with England. On the one hand the nation's rise to prosperity depended on the new connection with her southern neighbour, but on the other, the political and material superiority of England threatened the full-scale assimilation of Scotland. At the same time, from the later eighteenth century, romantic nationalism spread throughout Europe and it was difficult for Scotland to remain isolated from such a cultural and political trend. Any vigorous assertion of national identity would, however, threaten the English relationship on which material progress was seen to depend and Highlandism answered the emotional need for the maintenance of a distinctive Scottish identity without in any way compromising the Union. Indeed the indissoluble link between tartanry, the Highland soldier, patriotism and imperial service bestowed a new cultural and emotional cohesion on the Union relationship.

It was Sir John Sinclair, a leading agricultural improver and Caithness landowner, who composed the resolution passed by the Highland Society of London in 1804 to wear tartan at its meetings in order to recall 'the high character of our ancestors', and significantly he stressed the need to assert Scottish identity before 'Scotland becomes completely confounded in England'.[23] As Womack notes, 'As Lowland Scotland becomes more and more like England, it turns to the Highlands for symbols and beliefs to maximise its difference'.[24] Among these was the notion that the kilt had been the national dress of Scotland since time immemorial. Writers such as MacPherson, Scott, Stewart of Garth and others gave emotional depth to these attitudes because they portrayed eighteenth century Highland culture as the *Scottish* past surviving into the present. What had once been the customs and dress of *all* the nation had been lost in most parts but had been preserved in the 'archaic' world of the contemporary Highlands. It was an alluring myth for a society searching for an identity amid unprecedented economic and social change and under the threat of cultural conquest by its more powerful neighbour.

NOTES

1 Quoted in T. C. Smout, 'Tours in the Scottish Highlands from the eighteenth to the twentieth centuries', *Northern Scotland, 5*, 1983, p. 120.
2 S. Johnson, *A Journey to the Western Islands of Scotland in 1773*, London, 1876, p. 32.
3 Quoted in P. Womack, *Improvement and Romance*, London, 1989, p. 1.
4 Quoted in W. A. Speck, *The Butcher*, Oxford, 1981.
5 Quoted in W. Donaldson, *The Jacobite Song*, Aberdeen, 1988, p. 46.

6 21 Geo II c34.
7 Quoted in Speck, *The Butcher*. p. 174.
8 H. Trevor-Roper, 'The invention of tradition: the Highland tradition of Scotland' in E. J. Hobsbawm and T. O. Ranger, eds, *The Invention of Tradition*, Oxford, 1983, p. 24.
9 *Ibid.*, p. 30.
10 Quoted in *Ibid.*, p. 31.
11 Donaldson, *Jacobite Song*, p. 66.
12 *Ibid., p. 94.*
13 Quoted in *Ibid.*, p. 94.
14 Womack, *Improvement and Romance*, p. 27.
15 *Gentleman's Magazine*, IX, June 1739.
16 Donaldson, *Jacobite Song*, p. 71.
17 Quoted in Womack, *Improvement and Romance*, p. 50.
18 Quoted in Donaldson, *Jacobite Song*, p. 92.
19 C. W. J. Withers, 'The historical creation of the Scottish Highlands' in I. L. Donnachie and C. A. Whatley, eds, *The Manufacture of Scottish History*, Edinburgh, 1992, p. 147.
20 M. Chapman, *The Gaelic Vision in Scottish Culture* London, 1978, p. 19.
21 Smout, 'Tours in the Scottish Highlands', pp. 101–2.
22 Womack, *Improvement and Romance*. p. 80.
23 Quoted in *Ibid.*, p. 145.
24 *Ibid.*

FURTHER READING

M. Chapman, *The Gaelic Vision in Scottish Culture*, London, 1978.

W. Donaldson, *The Jacobite Song*, Aberdeen, 1988.

L. Leneman, 'A new role for a lost cause: Lowland romanticisation of the Jacobite high-lander' in L. Leneman, ed., *Perspectives in Scottish Social History*, Aberdeen, 1988.

M. Pittock, *The Invention of Scotland*, London, 1991.

J. Prebble, *The King's Jaunt*, London, 1988.

T. C. Smout, 'Tours in the Scottish Highlands from the eighteenth to the twentieth centuries', *Northern Scotland*, 5, 1983.

H. Trevor-Roper, 'The invention of tradition: the Highland tradition of Scotland' in E. J. Hobsbawm and T. O. Ranger, eds, *The Invention of Tradition*, Oxford, 1983.

C. W. J. Withers, 'The historical creation of the Scottish Highlands' in I. L. Donnachie and C. A. Whatley, eds, *The Manufacture of Scottish History*, Edinburgh, 1992.

P. Womack, *Improvement and Romance: Constructing the Myth of the Highlands*, London, 1989.

7

THE SOCIAL IMPACT OF
PROTESTANT EVANGELICALISM

In many parts of the early eighteenth century Highlands the established presbyterian church of Scotland had limited impact. Areas of catholic loyalty existed in
the islands of Barra and South Uist and in the western mainland districts of
Arisaig, Moidart and Morar and indeed, in the early 1700s, the presbyterians
thought that popery was intent on expanding from these districts into other
enclaves. In many other parts, episcopalianism was dominant and even,
although subjected to persecution by both church and state because of its
association with Jacobitism, was still strong in the eastern Highlands, Lochaber
and northern Argyll. Presbyterianism itself faced significant difficulties in the
region. It was based on the parish unit and an administrative structure of
sessions, ministers and elders, but many Highland parishes were too large to
ensure adequate contact with the people of remote areas. There were few
Highland parishes under 400 square miles in extent, a typical example being
Harris which was forty-eight miles by twenty-four and covered seven inhabited
islands. The geographical problems were immense but so too were the linguistic
and social obstacles to protestant proselytisation. The church had few Gaelic-
speaking clergy and had to rely to a significant extent on teacher catechists and
itinerant missionaries to serve widely dispersed communities.

But these problems were seen increasingly as a major challenge to
Lowland presbyterianism. The Highlands had to be brought within the domain
of the established church because catholicism and episcopalianism were the
twin ideological sources of Jacobitism. The irreligion of the Highlander in some
districts and the weakness of presbyterianism in many others had to be tackled
not only for religious reasons but in order to achieve vital political ends. In
addition, the perceived chronic instability of some areas could be eliminated by
the more effective establishment of the church which would impose civil order
through its strict supervision of individual behaviour by means of its system of

courts. From the early eighteenth century, therefore, the conversion of the Highlanders became a joint mission of both church and state, a partnership designed to civilise the inhabitants of the region by destroying clanship, eradicating popery and inculcating loyalty to the Hanoverian crown.

In 1724, George I provided an annuity of £1,000 through the royal bounty to support catechists and itinerant preachers and even more significant was the foundation in 1709 of the Scottish Society for the Propagation of Christian Knowledge (SSPCK). This organisation was intent on using schools to disseminate religious instruction and knowledge. The General Assembly gave moral and financial support but the impact of the SSPCK was limited for much of the eighteenth century because of its policy of forbidding the use of Gaelic in its schools until 1766. The language was seen as a major source of the very superstition and barbarity the Society was trying to destroy and only when Jacobitism was well and truly defeated was it willing to countenance the use of Gaelic as a medium of instruction. This problem was compounded by the relative poverty of the SSPCK as, despite legal backing from the state, it did not receive any direct funds, and as a result, for most of the eighteenth century its income was never more than £2,000 a year. Nevertheless, the Society made a major contribution in 1767 with the publication of the first Scottish Gaelic version of the New Testament and in 1801 the first Scottish Gaelic Bible appeared under its auspices. By the 1830s, when its resources had increased to £4–5,000, the SSPCK was maintaining ten missionaries, thirty-three catechists and 261 teachers.

It is difficult, however, to be certain about the effects of all this effort. Much of it was driven by political expediency rather than religious impulse and, for much of the eighteenth century at least, was part of a wider strategy to destroy the distinctiveness of Gaeldom and absorb it within the wider British polity. In addition, the policy was often based on an institutional approach with evangelisation taking a much lower priority. Thus between the 1740s and 1770s there was a vigorous government-backed drive to erect churches and manses, with the construction of buildings seeming to take precedence over the saving of souls and this strategy was maintained into the nineteenth century. In 1824 'parliamentary churches' were created with the intention of erecting forty new centres of worship throughout the Highlands and islands. Yet even in its own terms this approach had limited success, and the entries in the *Old Statistical Account* showed that whole districts were still devoid of religious provision and clerical visitation was intermittent at best.

There were basically two reasons for the limited impact of the established church. First, in the decades up to the 1750s, policy was driven mainly by considerations of *realpolitik* rather than by an abiding concern to induce

Christian conversion and the church could very easily be seen as an arm of the Hanoverian state and hence in many areas an alien and offensive presence. Second, the middle and later decades of the eighteenth century were the years of the 'Moderate' ascendancy in the General Assembly of the Church of Scotland and this regime was not committed to energetic missionary effort and the saving of souls. The Moderates have had a bad press, not least from the 'popular' or 'evangelical' wing of the church, and it is easy to caricature them. For instance, Hugh Millar, editor of the Free Church paper, *The Witness*, in the nineteenth century saw them as corrupt, with mainly secular rather than religious interests, and often slack in the performance of their duties. In large part this was a distortion, though doubtless some individual clerics could be found who conformed to the stereotype, and the Moderates were more likely to be distinguished by their toleration, their conviction that faith was acquired by the intellect rather than by the heart and their distaste for emotionalism. The Moderates were not in the majority among Scottish presbyterians, even in their heyday, but they did have a significant influence in the governing councils of the church in the second half of the eighteenth century. Their dominance ensured that for much of that time protestantism in the Highlands was developed through institutional channels as the Moderates were innately suspicious of missionary activity.

In the nineteenth century the religious tradition which was to have the most fundamental impact on the society and culture of Gaeldom was protestant evangelicalism. Evangelicals took the view that faith was a matter of the heart rather than the mind and that it was a gift from God through revelation and conversion. Learning and knowledge in themselves were not enough, and mere church membership and ritual reception of the sacraments were also by themselves inadequate. Assurance of salvation in this Calvinist tradition rested only on the election by God of the repentant sinner. Christ alone could do this but a visible symbol of election could be found in participation in the sacrament of communion where God publicly affirmed His covenant with the chosen few. Observance of the sabbath reinforced by fast days were also essential disciplines to atone for sin.

Evangelicals, deriving their heritage from the covenanting tradition of the seventeenth century, saw religion in much more personal and emotional terms than the Moderates. Moderates took the view that 'enlightenment' and 'civilisation' were necessary prerequisites for acceptance of the Christian gospel, and this explains why the SSPCK for much of the eighteenth century regarded instruction in the English language and culture as fundamental to the spread of protestantism. As one leading Moderate cleric put it: 'Men must be enlightened and polished in their manners before they can be properly enlightened in religious truths. Philosophy and learning must, in the nature of things, take the precedence'.[1] The Rev. Hamilton went on to suggest that it would be just as absurd to expose the unlettered to the Christian revelation as to introduce a child to Newton's *Principia Mathematica* before he or she knew the alphabet. From this standpoint, missionary effort was not simply suspicious but wrong because the development of 'civilisation' had to come first. On the other hand, the evangelicals were committed to mission as the route to conversion, accepting Jesus's exhortation to preach the gospel to all men as their guidance. Since the Highlands were seen as spiritually destitute in the later eighteenth century they posed a huge and compelling challenge to evangelicals who were already trying to undertake foreign missions to the heathen in overseas territories. Gaelic society with its different customs, culture and language was literally a foreign mission at home, which drew increasing interest from the pious as the evangelical reaction gathered pace throughout Britain in the 1780s and 1790s.

But in large part the success of evangelicalism in the Highlands was that it was an indigenous growth, using the language of vernacular Gaelic and spreading the Word through popular symbolism, and even missionaries from outside addressed the people in their mother tongue as the surest and quickest way to their hearts. It was not therefore seen as an obviously alien force, an implant from a foreign culture. Spiritual poetry was of considerable influence which first developed an evangelical flavour in Argyll and the Highland parishes of Perthshire from the mid-eighteenth century and later it became common in the north and west where the poets emphasised the need for each individual to be born again in Christ in order to obtain eternal salvation. This verse was meant to be delivered to large audiences and its emotional appeal was enhanced by the development of the singing of metrical psalms designed to bring the community together in collective praise.

An even more significance indigenous force were the 'Men' or *Na Daoine*, lay preachers so called to distinguish them from the ordained ministers of the church. They were a spiritual elite, successors to the tacksmen of the clan society in terms of their eventual social influence and a major factor in converting entire communities to evangelical protestantism in the first half of the nineteenth century. It must be remembered, however, that their impact was relatively limited in many areas, such as the Inner Hebrides below Skye and most of the central and southern Highlands. Elsewhere, however, their dominance by the 1840s was undeniable. The power of the Men first became obvious in Easter Ross in the 1740s and spread to the west and north in the following fifty years. They were as much a social as a religious elite providing the communal leadership which was vanishing in the traditional society as a result of the emergence of commercial landlordism and the growing pressures on the tacksman class. For the most part they were drawn from the better-off crofters and tradesmen rather than the underclass of cottars and squatters, but their standing and influence depended above all on their personal qualities of intense spiritual commitment, deep knowledge of scripture and capacity to blend and adapt traditional Gaelic culture and speech with the Christian message to maximum effect. Some were reputed to have the gift of prophecy, the second sight, which indicated their close relationship with the deity and many employed folk tales and popular symbolism adapted to Christian purposes. Though they did not necessarily have a formal education, the Men were clearly individuals of great natural ability with the personal charisma to project the Word of God in a way which helped to stimulate the series of revivals which became an important facet of Highland religious life in the first half of the nineteenth century.

Their early prominence can be traced to the role they played in the huge public communions which became common in many parts of Gaeldom. Because of the long distances involved, public communions were held only inter- mittently but normally attracted large crowds. In the days before the actual ceremonies, fellowship meetings were held to prepare the godly and at these the Men emerged as lay catechists, interpreting scripture and addressing matters of spiritual concern and in this function they could be seen, especially by parish ministers of Moderate inclination, to be a divisive influence, implicitly at least the leaders of a church within a church. They were indeed a threat to the Moderate ascendancy, because they branded ministers of the persuasion as ungodly, eulogised those of evangelical tendency and in a few localities developed a robust tradition of organised dissent. When the final split between Moderatism and evangelicalism came with the emergence of the Free Church from the Church of Scotland in 1843, the Men were a crucial influence in winning most of the western Highlands and islands for the new order.

The dynamism of Lowland evangelicalism also brought a new vibrancy to the age-old attempt to convert the Highlands to protestant Christianity. In 1796 one of the secession churches, the Relief Church, sent several ministers and probationers into Argyllshire and elicited an enthusiastic response, but much more significant was the establishment the following year of the Society for Propagating the Gospel at Home founded by James Haldane and other laymen from different denominations. Here the link between the organisation of mission to the Highlands and the contemporary vogue of foreign mission was direct. Haldane and his brother had earlier attempted to set up a missionary society for Bengal or Sierra Leone but had encountered the opposition of the East India Company, a mission to the Highland people was their alternative option. The initiative was financed by the sale of the Haldane family estates and it set out to provide itinerant preachers and sabbath schools. Between 1797 and 1808 the Society sent missionaries all over the Highlands and stimulated a spirit of religious restlessness in many districts. On his first tour alone, James Haldane and two companions were reckoned to have delivered 308 sermons and distributed more than 20,000 tracts. What Haldane's efforts demonstrated was the enormous hunger for evangelical preaching which existed in many districts and which other organisations were later to exploit to great effect. Among these were Baptist Missionary Society, the Highland Missionary Society and the Paisley Society for Gaelic Missions, all of which had several features in common. Their preachers were itinerant and so were able to have a wide geographical impact, they conveyed their message in Gaelic and made a direct appeal to the emotions, and the distribution of tracts then allowed the spiritual interest to be maintained when the preachers had moved on.

The impetus was reinforced by the emergence of the Gaelic Schools Societies in the 1810s and 1820s in Edinburgh, Dundee, Glasgow and Inverness. By the end of the second decade of the nineteenth century they had penetrated into the remotest corners of the Highlands and islands by establishing circulating schools teaching Gaelic literacy. The intention was to allow the people to read the word of God in their mother tongue, the teachers were supposed to move on as soon as these skills had been inculcated. However, the influence of the schools was not simply educational. Some of the teachers were the Men and itinerant instructors who were mainly responsible for revivalist outbreaks in Skye and the Outer Hebrides at the time of the Disruption in 1843.

This enormous expansion in missionary effort produced nothing less than a religious revolution in the Highlands. The dramatic peaks of the new spiritual awakening were the religious revivals which occurred with increasing frequency after 1790, which took place in Moulin in 1799, Arran and Skye in 1812, Breadalbane in Perthshire in 1816, on several occasions in Lewis from 1824 to 1833, and in Skye and parts of the Outer Hebrides in the early 1840s. At such times whole communities were seized with religious frenzy, manifested in convulsions, wailing and fits, but these were simply the more extreme manifestations of the new forces that had been unleashed in the Highlands by the sustained impact of evangelicalism. Religious intensity, albeit at a lower level, increased in many districts and there was a discernable rise in popular spiritual enthusiasm. This was being channelled into a movement of religious dissent by the 1830s and during the Ten Years Conflict which preceded the Disruption of 1843, the campaign of the Evangelical Party was well received in the Highlands by communities which had been schooled by itinerant preachers and teachers. Not surprisingly most of the region was carried for the Free Church when the great division eventually came. In the immediate aftermath of the Disruption the scarcity of Gaelic-speaking ministers meant that the Church had to rely on the lay religious elite, the Men and the itinerant teachers, to ensure the continued loyalty of the people.

This extraordinary transformation in religious attitude and commitment necessarily begs the question of the extent to which the spiritual revolution was ultimately a response to the contemporaneous upheaval in social and economic life. It is highly likely indeed that, while the missionary effort provided the direct stimulus, the structural changes in the society may have established the cultural context for a heightening of religious enthusiasm. Direct linkages between revivalism and clearance, famine and privation are certainly hard to find. The major revivals in Easter Ross in the eighteenth century do not seem to have been directly rooted in economic changes and there was also little evidence of much religious intensity during the potato famines of the 1840s. Revivals could occur in better times, such as the later 1850s, as well as in bad. One evangelical minister, Lachlan Mackenzie of Lochcarron, noted that religious commitment in his parish in the early nineteenth century was greatest among those tenants with some means and he also reported how a good herring fishing in the lochs of the district in the early 1790s had inspired new levels of religious enthusiasm. It would be unconvincing, therefore, to see the triumph of protestant evangelicalism as predetermined by the material changes in Highland society in the nineteenth century. Equally, however, the anxieties, insecurities, fears and despairs generated by the devastating impact of clearance and economic crisis could be assuaged by the evangelical message as it provided hope, consolation and spiritual comfort to a people racked by enormous psychological pressures as the old world they had known disintegrated with alarming speed over a few decades from the later eighteenth century.

In one ironic sense, indeed, the evangelical ministers and missionaries and their institutional successor, the Free Church, were themselves the scourge of traditional popular culture. Music and dancing were discouraged and recreations actively opposed on the sabbath and in the later nineteenth century there was a systematic campaign to impose strict temperance in many communities, most notably in Lewis, and energetic efforts made to reduce the number of licensed premises. But this repression of traditional culture was combined with the inculcation of a deeper spirituality which had potent appeal.

This had a number of facets. First Christian conversion was only possible, through complete submission to the Divine Will. Things of the world were of much less relevance and, in particular, a refusal to accept suffering was tantamount to questioning the Will of God. Acceptance of suffering was nothing less than the submission to God's plan. During the potato famine, the

Edinburgh Gaelic Schools Society stated '. . . for He hath said I will never leave thee nor forsake thee. It is this word that your teachers are, day and night, occupied in dispensing to the starving families of the Highlands and Islands'.[2] Second, the proper response to suffering was the examination of conscience as the preliminary to repentance, and tragedy in this world could be interpreted as the result of personal wickedness and those who were the victims of disaster were themselves the causes of their own misfortune. This was the reaction, for example, of the people of Glencalvie in Strathconan who were obliged to seek refuge in the church at Croick in 1845 after being cleared from their lands. They left a message on the window sill of the kirk that their plight was a dreadful punishment for sin. Third, the mighty who had behaved in an unjust fashion would not go unpunished. But retribution belonged to God not man, and in one sermon the Rev. John Sinclair, minister of Bruan in Caithness made the point explicit: 'It is true that we often see the wicked enjoy much comfort and worldly ease, and the Godly chastened every morning; but this is a dreadful rest to the former and a blessed chastisement to the latter'.[3] Fourth, the doctrines of Calvinism gave a spiritual certainty amid the social havoc of the transition from clanship to clearance, when the evangelicals concentrated the minds and emotions of the people on a highly personal struggle for grace and election. The miseries of this life were not therefore simply to be endured but were in themselves a necessary agony for those who wished to attain eternal salvation in the next.

This compelling set of beliefs had important implications for the response of the Highland population to the impact of clearance and dispossession. As chapter 14 shows there was some sporadic resistance to eviction and the Highlands were not entirely peaceful during the great removals. But physical resistance was still very limited in relation to the sheer scale of dislocation and not all or even the greater part of this essentially passive response can be explained in terms of protestant evangelicalism. The catholic districts in the southern Long Island and in western Inverness were hardly more proactive and many clearances occurred in the central, eastern and northern Highlands before evangelicalism had taken root. In addition, there were powerful constraints on protest which had nothing to do with religious attitudes. But the new beliefs inculcated with such emotional fervour by the missionaries and the Men must have buttressed the forces making for stability and further diluted influences making for resistance. The evangelical gospel was not a theology of social justice but a faith designed to promote personal spiritual growth and commitment. It offered solace and the certainty of punishment for the oppressor, not by man but by God and so deflected opposition in this life to the other side of the grave. The vision that suffering had to be endured as a necessary preparation for salvation was an obvious constraint on insurrection and it was hardly surprising that the poet, Mary MacPherson of Skye, eloquently condemned evangelical preachers for their indifference to the poor conditions in which the people lived. This was simply not their concern.

At first sight it might appear that the triumphant Free Church was a more powerful force for radicalism. It had emerged in 1843 in the Highlands as the church of the crofters with only the landed and gentry families, big farmers and professional men in most areas remaining within the Church of Scotland. Implicitly, therefore, it seemed to be anti-landlord, a perception which was strengthened by the struggle which took place for several years after the Disruption over the opposition of some proprietors to grant church sites to the new congregations and 1843 has been seen as the most popular and effective challenge to landlordism in the Highlands before the crofting agitation of the 1880s. The 'radical' line of the Free Church seemed confirmed by the activities of Hugh Miller, editor of the newspaper, *The Witness*, who achieved fame as an articulate critic of landlordism and who argued that the new church would end the political isolation of the crofters.

Doubtless the Free Church did imbue the people with a new sense of confidence and collective identity. But it has to be remembered that its foundation was followed a few years later by the trauma of the potato famine and an associated wave of clearances which were unprecedented in their scale and extent and it is hard to believe that these crises did not cause widespread demoralisation. Nor was the Free Church as an institution opposed to landlordism in the long run. It was in the last resort dependent on the evangelically-minded urban middle class of the Lowlands and so was unlikely to risk any substained or overt criticism of the rights of private property. Acts of resistance or violence were also inherently wrong and merited condemnation rather than approbation. At the time of the crofting agitation in the 1880s the Free Church articulated this view in its official response to the Napier Commission set up to investigate the disturbances. Suffering could not be relieved or removed by sinning, that is by illegal action against public order or private property whatever the scale of the injustice. Political meetings during the disturbances of the 1880s began and ended with prayers and activists in the crofting interest exploited the appeal of biblical texts to give legitimacy to the struggle for land rights. Yet the ethos of evangelical protestantism and its institutional vehicle, the Free Church, was in conflict with radicalism, not because of an overt conspiracy of co-operation with the political and social establishment but because of its evangelical commitment to the *spiritual* values of Christian awakening, conversion and salvation.

NOTES

1 Quoted in V. E. Durkacz, *The Decline of the Celtic Languages*, Edinburgh, 1983, p. 99.
2 *Ibid.*, p. 129.
3 Quoted in A. Auld, *Ministers and Men in the Far North*, Wick, 1868.

FURTHER READING

C. G. Brown, *The Social History of Religion in Scotland since 1730*, London, 1987.
V. E. Durkacz, *The Decline of the Celtic Languages*, Edinburgh, 1983.
A. L. Drummond and J. Bulloch, *The Church in Victorian Scotland* 1843–1874, Edinburgh, 1975.
J. Hunter, 'The emergence of the crofting community: the religious contribution 1798–1843', *Scottish Studies*, 18, 1974.
J. Macinnes, *The Evangelical Movement in the Highlands of Scotland, 1688 to 1800*, Aberdeen, 1951.
A. I. Macinnes, 'Evangelical protestantism in the nineteenth century Highlands' in G. Walker and T. Gallagher, eds, *Sermons and Battle Hymns*, Edinburgh, 1990.
A. Mearns, 'The minister and the bailiff: a study of presbyterian clergy in the northern Highlands during the clearances', *Records of the Scottish Church History Society*, 1990.

8

THE LANGUAGE OF THE GAEL

At one time much of Scotland spoke Gaelic except the northern isles. Today, after centuries of continuous decline, the *Gaidhealtachd* is confined mainly to isolated areas of the north and west mainland and the outer islands, although growing pockets of Gaelic speakers also exist in some of the Lowland towns and cities. As late as the 1880s there were around 200,000 monoglot Gaelic speakers in Scotland; a century later that figure had shrunk to about 80,000, the majority of whom were bilingual. The decline in Scotland was paralleled to some extent in nineteenth century Ireland and Wales, but the collapse in Gaelic-speaking in northern Scotland was much greater and more rapid than in either Wales or Ireland. Between 1891 and 1901, for instance, the bilingual population as a proportion of the entire population fell by 5.3 per cent in Wales, remained stable in Ireland but declined by over 18 per cent in Scotland, and this pattern was maintained throughout the first half of the twentieth century. Between 1931 and 1951, the proportion of the bilingual population was reduced by no less than 66 per cent in Scotland but by only 18 per cent and 10.5 per cent in Wales and Ireland respectively. Doubtless these figures in large part reflect the very heavy rate of migration from the Gaelic-speaking Highlands, but this is not the whole story.

It is sometimes argued that the victory of English speech and literacy was a result of modern educational policy. The fundamental Act of 1872 ignored Gaelic entirely in its plan for a national system of compulsory education and even in the more sympathetic legislation of 1918 there was still no requirement to teach the language. The schools system in the Highlands therefore used English as the medium of instruction and state education became a means of anglicisation.

The Act of 1872 and subsequent legislation were clearly significant, but the historical realities were much more complicated than this plausible version of events suggests. While the Act was going through Parliament the vocal Gaelic lobby in Scotland, the Free Church and the Gaelic Societies who had become much more active in this period, remained unusually silent. This reticence was apparently because the Lord Advocate, in responding to arguments that Gaelic should be given a statutory place in the forthcoming legislation, had stated that the position of the language could be better safeguarded in the Education Codes issued by the Scottish Education Department. When the Act of 1872 became law the Gaelic Society of Inverness in particular lobbied hard for a place for Gaelic in the Code and as a result, in the first Code issued following the Act, the Committee of Council agreed that in districts where Gaelic was spoken children in standards II and III could be tested by requiring them to explain in Gaelic the meaning of the passage read. This directive therefore accepted that Gaelic could have educational value. and in subsequent years more and more concessions were granted. One recent researcher has concluded that as a result, 'By 1918 the S.E.D. had granted everything asked of it by the friends of Gaelic, short of a rigid compulsion'.[1] The obstacles to the widespread dissemination of Gaelic education in the later nineteenth and early twentieth centuries were not so much the result of anti-Gaelic prejudice in the Scottish Education Department but were to be found in the attitudes of those who dominated the Highland school boards who were themselves the product of a process of anglicisation which had been going on for centuries and who therefore did not regard Gaelic of sufficient value to merit inclusion in the curriculum to any significant extent. Indeed, it would be fair to say that the landowners, big farmers and professional men who sat on the boards saw Gaelic as a barrier to the progress and advancement of the Highland population. It might have a place in the home or in church but not in the vital business of education which prepared young people for jobs and careers.

The decline of Gaelic had begun, however, long before the 1872 Act. A longer historical perspective reveals a process of attrition dating back to medieval times and around the later fourteenth century the language had already retreated into the Highland region and became synonymous thereafter with the culture and society of the Highlander. This was deeply significant in the subsequent two centuries as the state extended its grip in the north and west and the people of the region were seen to be 'different' from the Lowlander in the basic element of speech. Not only were the population in some areas dangerously subversive, especially when Jacobitism became significant from the later seventeenth century, but their language was alien and 'Irish'. Just as the people had to be pacified and integrated, so Gaelic, the great symbol of their different culture, had to be subordinated and removed. The rationale for anglicisation was in place.

Nevertheless, the returns made to the General Assembly's Committee anent (concerning) Highland Libraries in 1705–6 show that Gaelic preaching was still needed in Perthshire parishes on the fringes of the Highlands and that in the eastern Highlands Gaelic was the dominant language in the presbyteries of Abernethy and Aberlour and still prevailed in many parts of the Presbytery of Nairn. Thereafter, Charles Withers's careful work reveals the patterns of Gaelic's retreat in the eighteenth and nineteenth centuries. By the 1790s, Gaelic was still widely spoken in Caithness and did not give ground to English in any significant way in that county until the middle decades of the nineteenth century. By 1881, however, Gaelic was spoken by more than half the population only in the westerly parish of Reay, and in Sutherland by 1901 monoglot Gaelic speakers were mainly elderly and confined to the western parishes of Assynt, Durness and Eddrachillis. There was a marked decline in the numbers speaking Gaelic in the eastern parishes of Ross and Cromarty and south eastern parishes of Inverness from 1881. In Argyll Gaelic was in rapid retreat in the mainland parishes but managed to retain its strength in insular areas, although the pattern of decline in Perthshire was more rapid and widespread and since the early twentieth century Gaelic has fallen out of use in most parts of that county.

The general process of change was to some extent complicated by local town development, such as at Fort William and Inverness, where English made a faster impact. Similarly, migration from inland to coast and from west to east, as on the Sutherland estate in the early nineteenth century, could transplant Gaelic speakers into localities where English was on the increase. But the general trend is clear. In the century and a half before 1872 Gaelic was being displaced by English all along the Highland line and by the 1840s Gaelic was in rapid retreat throughout virtually all the mainland parishes of north and west Scotland. The axis of decline was from the south and east towards the west and north and only the Western Isles remained a bastion of Gaelic strength, but even here, and especially in the southern Hebrides, English was gaining currency as the new steamship networks brought insular towns and villages into even closer contact with the cities of the western Lowlands. The Act of 1872 and subsequent educational policies and practices may well have accelerated these trends but the general process of linguistic decline was apparent in the *Gaidhealtachd* long before the educational legislation of the later nineteenth century.

From at least the early seventeenth century state policy in the Highlands until after the last Jacobite rebellion was directed to the repression and eradication of 'the Irische language'. Not only was Gaelic associated with the instability of the region, it was also seen as one of its basic causes. In 1616, the Privy Council proclaimed that schools teaching English should be established so that 'the Irische language, whilk is one of the cheif and principall causes of the continewance of barbaritie and incivilitie amongis the inhabitantis of the Ilis and Heylandis, may be abolishet and removeit'.[2] Earlier the Statutes of Iona had directed that the eldest child of Highland landowners be sent to schools in the Lowlands for instruction in the English language and although the immediate practical impact of these pronouncements was minimal both ideas became quickly enshrined in state policy. The achievement of a unitary state and the absorption of the aberrant Gaelic society within the body politic demanded a single language and that had to be English. English was also equated with protestantism and Gaelic with catholicism, which meant that the language of superstitious error had to be removed as Gaelic was linked with 'barbarity and ignorance'. In order to 'improve and civilise' the Highlands, anglicisation was essential.

In the eighteenth century, these attitudes became even stronger as the Jacobite rebellions demonstrated the threat posed by Gaelic society and the vital need to subjugate it. The linguistic attack on Gaelic became fiercer. While military force might bring stability in the short term, only cultural transformation could bring final pacification in the Highlands and thus in 1716, immediately following the failure of the Jacobite rebellion of 1715, the committee of the Society in Scotland for the Propagation of Christian Knowledge (SSPCK), met to consider what could be done for civilising and reforming the Highlands. Their solution was to seek funds to establish more schools to teach the English language and later in 1723 they petitioned the king and asserted that anglicisation should be at the root of any policy of subjugation. Ignorance of English rather than any basic enmity to the established church and state was the reason for Gaelic disloyalty, but the SSPCK also urged that English schools were necessary to teach the protestant religion because Jacobitism derived from catholicism as well as political disloyalty. At this time the General Assembly of the Church of Scotland feared an apparently resurgent popery in several parts of the Highlands.

Not surprisingly, therefore, the General Assembly gave the SSPCK support and funding and, despite the failure of the state to provide direct finances, this body became one of the best-known institutions for the inculcation of the English language as part of a more general ideological assault on Gaelic. There were five schools by 1771, twenty-five by 1715 and 176 by 1758, teaching nearly 6,500 pupils. From the start, the Society was resolutely anti-Gaelic and at first teaching to Gaelic-speaking children was entirely in English. Only gradually was it agreed that teaching pupils to read the English Bible was entirely fruitless as long as they could not understand what they were reading. However, in 1723 teachers were directed to allow the translation of English words from the Bible into Gaelic in order to increase comprehension, but this was only a necessary practical adjustment and the repressive attitude to Gaelic was still in place. Schoolmasters were always to speak in English and talk between pupils was confined to the same language. 'Clandestine censors' were appointed to chide those who dared to speak Gaelic!

It is difficult to be certain about the precise impact of the activities of the SSPCK on Gaelic. The Society itself was bold in its claims and in 1781 its Directors concluded that the teaching of the English New Testament had not only opened up the minds of the people but it had also given them 'a greater desire to learn the English language than they had ever before discovered'.[3] There remains the suspicion, however, that whatever its significant effects in particular places, the SSPCK has been depicted as an important agency of anglicisation because it possessed a high profile in the eighteenth century and has left to posterity detailed records for historians to ponder. Many pupils were educated in its schools and by 1808 the figure had reached no less than 13,000. Yet not all of these were Highlanders. The Society was also active in several Lowland counties and most of the SSPCK schools were concentrated along the borders of the Highlands where the cultural and economic attractions of English were inevitably strong anyway. Above all, schooling was by no means confined to the SSPCK. Donald Withrington has recently shown that there were many more non-SSPCK schools in the Highlands than previously thought and that apart from the Outer Hebrides and a few mainland parishes instruction was often widely available to a greater or lesser extent. The important point, however, is that whether through the SSPCK's foundations, the adventure schools or the parish schools, formal learning had come to be associated with English and even without the political and religious attack, this would have pushed Gaelic into a position of inferior status and value. The heritage of the language was also mainly transmitted by oral means and it was therefore at a grave disadvantage against the language of formal education, metropolitan culture and economic progress which was advancing on all fronts.

At first sight the coming of evangelicalism might seem to have arrested this apparently irresistible tide of anglicisation because the evangelicals were interested primarily in saving souls rather than ensuring linguistic conformity. Evangelicalism was also a faith of the heart rather than the mind and effective means had to be found for conveying the Word of God in a manner which had deep emotional appeal. Like their counterparts in the colonies, the itinerant evangelical missionaries in the Highlands took the view that the people should be capable of reading the scripture in their mother tongue and thus evangelicalism was much more sympathetic to Gaelic as a necessary means to an end than had been either the Church of Scotland or the SSPCK in the eighteenth century. There was lavish distribution of religious literature in Gaelic. In 1798 the Society for Propagating the Gospel at Home had four tracts translated into Gaelic and 5,000 of each printed. The Edinburgh Religious Tract Society printed several thousand tracts in Gaelic which were then distributed in 1819 by two boys who tramped across the western Highlands and islands leaving bundles of them with local ministers and teachers. In addition to a flood of Gaelic bibles, tracts and catechisms, an indigenous Gaelic periodical literature, not all of it religious in orientation, flourished in the first half of the nineteenth century, and one estimate suggests that thirteen short-lived periodicals were published between 1803 and 1874.

All of this afforded Gaelic a new legitimacy and respectability and, indeed, Lowland evangelists quickly grasped the fact that Gaelic gave the spiritual message a greater emotional potency and raw appeal. Gaelic became the language of God and church, of the intense revivals of the period and the great open-air prayer gatherings. Dugald Sinclair, a preacher for the Baptist Itinerant Society in Mull noted in 1814:

> The peculiarly impressive and energetic manner in which divine truth may be conveyed and applied to the conscience in the Gaelic language, as well as the uncommon attachment of the Highlanders to their native tongue, to say nothing of its being the only language in which divine things can be conveyed with any probable prospect of success to nine-tenths of the people renders this object truly desirable.[4]

Numerous evangelical organisations were active in the Highlands in this period, but it was the Gaelic schools societies' promotion of circulating schools, teaching Gaelic literacy, which were to have the most important impact on the language itself. The biggest and the most enduring was the Edinburgh Society founded in 1811, followed by others established at Dundee, Glasgow and Inverness, which were less successful. Their only objective was to teach the people to read the Bible in their mother tongue and its teachers travelled throughout each district, moving on when the people had learned to read. In most cases the average sojourn was no more than eight months, thus having a much wider impact than the SSPCK especially since the Edinburgh Gaelic Schools Society concentrated its efforts on parishes north and west of the Great Glen and in the islands. The effects were far-reaching because adults as well as children attended the schools and children also gave instruction to their parents in the evenings. One estimate suggests that around 300,000 people gained some basic literacy in the nineteenth century throughout the Highlands as a result of these efforts and those of the Church of Scotland and the Free Church after 1843. Gaelic schools societies alone taught the reading of the Bible to over 100,000 people.

These figures were a remarkable demonstration of the depth of moral and spiritual commitment of the missionaries and of the appetite of the Gaels for the evangelical message. The drive towards literacy in Gaelic also bound the language inextricably with the protestant religion, but the policy of Gaelic instruction failed to slow down the trend towards bilingualism. On the contrary, Gaelic education actually accelerated anglicisation and, as several observers stressed throughout the nineteenth century, the Gaelic schools stimulated the desire to learn English because knowledge of Gaelic alone meant a man was only half-educated. For those who read Gaelic a necessary next stop was the acquisition of skills in reading English. As the Rev. Alexander Stewart commented in 1812:

> By learning to read and to understand that he [the pupil] reads in his native tongue, an appetite is generated for those stores of science which are accessible to him only through the medium of the English language. Hence an acquaintance with the English is found to be necessary, for enabling him to gratify his desire after further attainments . . . These premises appear to warrant a conclusion, which might at first appear paradoxical; that, by cultivating the Gaelic, you effectually, though indirectly, promote the study and diffuse the knowledge of English.[5]

Already in 1814 the Edinburgh Gaelic Schools Society claimed that its work was stimulating the Highlanders' appetite for English through the indirect means of promoting Gaelic education. In addition, for all its importance in encouraging Gaelic literacy for religious purposes, the Gaelic Schools Society contributed to the basic linguistic division where Gaelic was seen as the language of church and home and English the language of education and improvement.

The secular attractions of English were immense and increasing over time. The institutional channels of the SSPCK, the churches, the Annexed Forfeited Estates Commissioners and evangelical agencies facilitated the penetration of English into Gaeldom. But there were more subtle forces at work and, above all, temporary migration was deeply significant. In the middle decades of the eighteenth century temporary migration had been mainly confined to those parishes adjacent to the Lowlands, but by the 1850s it was occurring on a very significant scale even in the Outer Hebrides and increasingly older men, as well as young adult males and females, were travelling for work to the Lowlands. In addition, seasonal migration for a few weeks was being replaced by temporary movement for several months or longer. These trends must have had powerful effects on the diffusion of bilingualism and parish ministers both in the *Old Statistical Account* of the 1790s and the *New Statistical Account* of the 1840s repeatedly commented how these periods of work in the Lowland farms and cities spread familiarity with English speech. Seasonal migrants brought back English words and phrases and diluted Gaelic monolingualism in their native parishes. More subtly, the same process created an association between English on the one hand and prosperity and employment on the other. Expanding towns and villages on the fringes of the Highlands in the eighteenth century were probably also forces for anglicisation as, for example, Inverness in 1704 was mainly English-speaking but the countryside around almost totally Gaelic. Also important was the communications (especially the steamship) revolution of the nineteenth century which established fast and regular links between the western Lowlands and the heart of the *Gaidhealtachd.*

But these factors were essentially the *channels* of anglicisation rather than its basic cause. That lay in the simple fact that the majority of Highlanders by the nineteenth century were keen to learn English and the pattern was similar in Ireland and Wales. It was not so much the Celtic peoples who wished to preserve Gaelic as the Celtic societies in the cities and professors of Celtic from the universities. English was hugely popular and in fact the SSPCK found in the 1820s a considerable prejudice against Gaelic among the people, so much so that it was impossible to attract pupils without providing English instruction in the first instance. The Annual Report of the Edinburgh Gaelic Schools Society for 1829 also noted that, 'so ignorant are the parents that it is difficult to convince them that it can be any benefit to their children to learn Gaelic, though they are all anxious . . . to have them taught English'.[6] Fifty years later the Rev. James Grant of Kilmuir in Skye demonstrated to the Napier Commission the religious and secular attractions of Gaelic: 'Highlanders would like their children to be better scholars than themselves, to be able to read the Scriptures in Gaelic, but to be also able to speak English and carve their way through the world'.[7] Grant captured the ambiguities of the linguistic attitude. Gaelic attracted as the language of everyday life, religion, poetry and song, and the mother tongue was therefore not easily abandoned; indeed it was fostered in the western Highlands even as parents encouraged their children in their English schooling. But English possessed both prestige and status. The contempt in which Gaelic had been held by the lowland world for centuries doubtless contributed to this attitude, but English was also the language of the future, of education, economic opportunity and social progress and its triumph was therefore assured. As one sympathetic observer concluded in 1863:

> I have no prejudice against the Gaelic language . . . but the most ardent lover of Gaelic cannot fail to admit that the possession of a knowledge of English is indispensable to any poor islander who wishes to learn a trade or to earn his bread beyond the limits of his native Isle.[8]

NOTES

1 V. E. Durkacz, *The Decline of the Celtic Languages*, Edinburgh, 1983, p. 179.

2 Quoted in C. W. J. Withers, *Gaelic Scotland*, London, 1988, p. 113.
3 Quoted in C. W. J. Withers, *Gaelic in Scotland, 1698–1981*, Edinburgh, 1984.
4 D. Sinclair, *Journal of Itinerating Exertions in Some of the more Destitute Parts of Scotland*, Edinburgh, 1814, p. 8.
5 Quoted in Durkacz, *Decline of the Celtic Languages*, p. 221.
6 Quoted in ibid., p. 224.
7 Parliamentary Papers, XXXII, *Report of H.M. Commissioners of Inquiry into the Conditions of the Crofters and Cottars in the Highlands and Islands of Scotland*, Appendix A, p. 7.
8 J. Ramsay, *A Letter to the Right Hon. the Lord Advocate of Scotland on the State of Education in the Outer Hebrides in 1862* Glasgow, 1863, p. 4.

FURTHER READING

J. L. Campbell, *Gaelic in Scottish Education and Life*, Edinburgh, 1950.

V. E. Durkacz, *The Decline of the Celtic Languages*, Edinburgh, 1983.

K. Mackinnon, *The Lion's Tongue*, Inverness, 1974.

K. Mackinnon, *Language, Education and Social Process in a Gaelic Community*, London, 1977.

C. W. J. Withers, *Gaelic in Scotland, 1698–1981*, Edinburgh, 1984.

D. J. Withrington, 'The SSPCK and Highland schools in the mid-eighteenth century', Scottish Historical Review, XLI, 1962.

D.J. Withrington, 'Schooling, literacy and society' in T. M. Devine and R. Mitchison, eds, *People and Society in Scotland, I, 1760–1830*, Edinburgh, 1988.

9

PEASANT ENTERPRISE: ILLICIT WHISKY-MAKING, 1760–1840

In the nineteenth century, it was common for Victorian commentators to explain the poverty and underdevelopment of the Highlands in terms of the indolence, inertia and conservatism of the population. The people of the region had brought the misery of famine and clearance upon themselves because of their own ineptitude and failure to exploit economic opportunities in the way that had occurred so successfully elsewhere in Britain. Such condemnation, however, was grossly exaggerated at best and largely mistaken at worst. For a start Highland society was confronted by immense constraints of geography, climate, terrain and poverty which inhibited the easy development of capitalism from below. Moreover in the historical record, there is plenty of evidence of peasant enterprise which is in conflict with the Victorian racial stereotype of an apathetic Celtic population and the effective organisation of the droving trade and the large-scale emigration schemes of the eighteenth and early nineteenth centuries are only two examples of such successful initiatives. Another and equally remarkable one was the story of the manufacture and distribution of illicit whisky in the period between the 1760s and 1830s. The rapid expansion of illicit production in several parts of the Highlands during this period is a telling illustration of the capacity of peasant society to respond to market opportunity when it possessed a real if ephemeral competitive advantage over the Lowland economy.

I

In the later eighteenth century and for several decades thereafter the law was defied on a remarkable scale in the Highlands. In 1782 over 1,000 illicit stills were seized in the Highland zone, a figure which represented only a fraction of the total number in operation, and the flow of illicit liquor was so great that, according to some observers, it threatened to engulf the market of the Lowland licensed producers. John Stein of Kilbagie, the greatest distiller in Scotland at the time, asserted that over half the whisky consumed in Scotland was illicitly manufactured and that illegal spirits had cornered the lion's share of the market in Perth, Stirling, Glasgow and other Clydeside towns. Certainly, Lowland distillers had a vested interest in exaggerating the extent of Highland competition, but this does not deny the reality of the problem. Indeed, two decades later the extent of illicit manufacture had, if anything, intensified:

> The illicit distillers have lately extended themselves so widely and have assumed a character so alarming, that the further interference of the legislature has become a matter of immediate necessity; . . . in Scotland these evils are of comparatively recent growth but they exhibit a melancholy change in the Highland districts, and lead to the conclusion that from the fatal prevalence of illicit distillation their moral condition is rapidly approaching to the lawless and disorganised state existing in parts of Ireland.[1]

It was alleged that magistrates, themselves in receipt of illicit spirits, refused to deal effectively with culprits; respectable farmers in Ross, Aberdeen, Banff and Kintyre acquiesced in and profited from smuggling; most excisemen, it was rumoured, were susceptible to corruption, and collusion between officers and smugglers was commonplace.

The manufacture of illicit whisky took place at a time when demand for the spirit in Scotland was on the increase. Traditionally beer and wine had been favourite drinks but the consumption of plain malt spirit was becoming more popular in the second half of the eighteenth century. During the Napoleonic Wars, imports of French brandy and claret were threatened by rising tariff duties and interrupted trade and, at the same time, urbanisation and an increasing population stimulated an expansion in demand for all food and drinks, including spirits. Industrialisation accelerated the movement of young migrants to the growing towns and cities. Money wages, the loosening of traditional sanctions on conduct within the urban areas and the absence of alternative mass entertainments to group drinking were some of the factors behind the wave of intoxication which seemed to many contemporary observers to engulf several Lowland towns. It was now popular to take a 'dram' or one third of a pint at 60 per cent alcohol by volume of plain malt spirit; this was a much more formidable measure than that generally consumed today!

Both legal and illegal manufacturers were able to exploit this growing demand, but the illicit advantage was dependent ultimately on the development of government revenue legislation. In the eighteenth century, the government levied duties on malt, on the distilling of the spirit and on the finished product and the vastly inflated revenue demands of the Napoleonic Wars produced a marked rise in all of these taxes. Thus the incentive to cheat the revenue by avoiding payment of duty became most pressing precisely at the same time as the consumption of whisky was on the increase. The malt tax, standing at 7⅜d per bushel in the early 1790s, had risen to 3s 8d by 1804, and, despite fluctuations, had reached 5s 6d by 1822. As a result, licensed producers, now determined to reduce their malt tax assessments, began to employ large amounts of unmalted raw grain in the production process but the consequent fall in costs, however, necessarily led also to a sharp deterioration in quality. Thus the way was open for the illicit distiller, who could use as much malted grain as he desired, to exploit the selective market at the more affluent end of the social scale. Surviving data suggest that, in the nineteenth century, Highland illicit spirits, when marketed in the Lowlands, fetched a substantially higher price than the product of the licensed distilleries. Certain consuming groups were clearly willing to pay for quality. 'Corn spirits' (that is, spirit produced from raw grain) were, in the 1790s, 'chiefly drunk by the dram drinkers, who wish to get drunk at the cheapest rate, and whose corrupted stomachs prefer the hardest spirits'.[2]

The sustained rises in the malt tax, culminating in the rapid increases of the early nineteenth century, had always encouraged illegal production; it was not, however, until the 1780s that government regulation provided the vital stimulus. In 1786 the system of still licensing was adapted throughout Scotland with a differential which favoured the Highland zone because of its poorer natural endowment and higher fuel and transport costs. Still duty in the north was fixed at 20s per gallon of capacity and in the Lowlands at 30s. However, in order not to give the Highland producer any unfair advantage over his Lowland counterpart, it was forbidden to transport Highland whisky across a 'Highland line' from the Sound of Jura to the Moray Firth and in subsequent years licence duties rose dramatically. Finally, in order to facilitate collection of annual licence fees, stills below forty gallons still-content were declared illegal.

This legislation constituted the basic precondition for illicit distillation because it was broadly unsuited to the nature of the legal manufacture as practised in northern Scotland and the outlawing of small stills drove private household and family production underground. Previously, every person who had a still whose contents were limited to twelve gallons might by law distil for his own use and this prohibition of private stills thus represented a wholly novel form of state interference. It was small surprise therefore that for many years afterwards illicit whisky-making was not considered a crime in many parts of the north. Again, licence fees for forty-gallon stills, which rose from £40 in 1786 to £100 a decade later, effectively prohibited legal peasant manufacture for the market and, at the same time, sharply-rising licence fees improved the comparative advantage of illicit distillers over their licensed rivals. The latter, mainly operating larger units concentrated in the Lowlands, responded to the perennial increases by more rapid working of the distillation process in an effort to extract from their plant as much spirit as possible and in as short a time, but quality deteriorated, since, as has been noted, many of these distilleries were also using unmalted grain. One Perthshire innkeeper pointed out in 1798 that his customers would pay double for illicit spirit rather than imbibe the increasingly unpalatable legal product which did not agree with their stomachs: 'it gave them a great head ach [sic] if they took the quantity that they could take of Highland spirits without that effect'.[3]

The substantial fall in the number of licensed units, their owners squeezed by inflated duties on the one hand and illicit competition on the other, further encouraged the illegal industry. In a period of only slowly improving communications there was often no alternative supplier in certain localities to the illicit whisky-maker. In Campbeltown, for instance, no still licences were issued between 1797 and 1817, although there were hundreds of illicit stills in the Kintyre region.

Subsequent legislation down to the 1810s merely confirmed and strengthened the trend towards illegality. Because of very high grain prices during the Napoleonic Wars distillation was forbidden in 1800–1, 1804–8, 1809–10 and then occasionally to 1813. From 1814 stills of less than 500 gallons (later reduced to 200 gallons) were banned in the Highland area and this was to outlaw all but a tiny minority of licensed distillers in the north.

Furthermore, the 'Highland line' which existed until 1816 was simply an additional incentive for even the small group of licensed distillers to participate in the smuggling trade to southern towns. For the north-eastern farmer and landowner, like his Kintyre counterpart, conversion of surplus bear (a rough kind of barley) into whisky was a lucrative and efficient method of disposing of a bulk product. Prohibition of the sale of Highland spirits in lowland towns deprived them of an important market and it was, thus, scarcely surprising that they acquiesced in illegal practices.

The influential report in 1816 of Woodbine Parrish, chairman of the Board of Excise in Scotland, which described the extent of illicit production, did encourage some adjustment of government revenue policy. The 'Highland line' was abolished, revenue was raised from spirits duty rather than from annual licence fees and penalties against smaller stills revoked. The volume of spirits paying tax rose from 1,030,772 gallons in 1816 to 2,336,998 in 1818 and here was clear proof of the close relationship between official regulation and the incidence of illicit distillation. The resurgence in the fortunes of the legal sector, however, was short-lived. In 1819 English and Scottish duties on barley were equalised and in reality this represented a tax increase and an incentive for farmers to dispose of their grain to the illicit whisky-makers, a trend encouraged by the general malaise in grain markets at the time.

Thus between c. 1780 and 1820 demand for whisky was rising and government regulation ensured that much of the market would be supplied by illegal producers, but several other stimuli helped to boost production. Throughout most of the Highlands, rising population, less rapidly growing employment opportunities and substantial increases in rent produced a search for alternative sources of income in addition to indigenous agriculture. An expansion in the rate of temporary migration to the Lowlands described in chapter 11 was one response to these pressures, but this was often complemented in the north-eastern and southern Highlands by increases in the manufacture of whisky. Indeed, the fact that illicit distillation was a clandestine activity was all to the good because earnings from it were less readily estimated and appropriated by avaricious landlords, and some argued that the element of risk involved in illegal practices lent a certain colour to drab lives:

> It presents all the fascination of the gaming table; . . . in smuggling, as in poaching, there is a spirit of adventure and hazard, which has a charm for the minds of the peasantry. An escape or a successful resistance is remembered, and related as an heroic achievement; men encourage each other and a fraternity of feeling is produced among them by a sense of common danger.[4]

Yet it is plain that in eastern Sutherland, Ross, Banffshire and highland Aberdeenshire, necessity and expected cash return rather than 'love of adventure' drove the tenantry to illicit distillation, and in parts of Sutherland 'they have no other means except the smuggling to carry them through'.[5] It was alleged that in Highland Aberdeenshire in the 1820s, 'the lower orders almost breed their children to it as a sort of profession . . . they must do it or starve'.[6] In addition, illicit distillation was peculiarly well adapted to existing financial and technical limitations as, unlike commercial fishing and large-scale sheep-farming, the capital required was not an effective barrier to involvement, and on the contrary, the illegal nature of the manufacture ensured that it remain one of small units in order to avoid detection. The records of Robert Armour, an early nineteenth century Campbeltown still-maker, show that the complete apparatus for pot-still distillation could be purchased for less than £4. Armour was providing equipment for a series of kinship and friendship groups in the Kintyre area who thus pooled capital and spread risk. Distillation was therefore well suited to the socio-economic communalism of the Highlands where social links at local level preserved that 'fellow feeling' against the law so vital to the success of the illicit trade. It was not unknown for communities to share in the payment of fines and for individual distillers to take it in turn to appear in court. The only other major cost to the producer, apart from equipment, was outlay on raw materials, because professional smugglers from outside the Highlands conveyed the whisky to market and labour costs were reduced by the employment of the family in the production process. In the north-east hill country grain was purchased from farmers on credit and repayment made by instalments as returns from sales accrued. In parts of Argyll, a period of seasonal work in the Lowlands could provide the necessary cash to begin operation:

> Sons of the small farmers will go during the summer and harvest months, to the low country, and earn by their industry and sober and frugal habits of living, a few pounds, with which they come back and purchase an illegal still, about which two or more join. Then they bargain with the local farmers, 'if you will give me a given number of bolls of barley I will give you so much money'[7]

Distilling, as a seasonal activity which did not require full-time concentrated attention, was also well suited to an agrarian society with prolonged periods of idleness and which functioned on the basis of a mixture of occupations. Operations took place most commonly in late autumn when the harvest was gathered, burns were in spate and the men had returned from seasonal labour elsewhere. Finally, the process of manufacture blended well with the traditional pastoral economy – spent grain or draff, together with the dregs from stills, provided valuable additional food for cattle, particularly during the autumn and winter months when demands on hay were likely to be high and pasture was close-cropped.

Only vigorous enforcement of the law could have restrained the boom in illicit whisky-making. Government regulation had systematically outlawed whisky manufacture by traditional methods at a time when peasant communities increasingly depended on it as a source of income and employment and in such a situation popular acceptance of new revenue legislation was inherently unlikely. The burden on the courts and the excise establishment became greater.

In this respect, the attitude of the landed class was of vital consequence. Not only were the gentry the basis of law enforcement in their capacity as justices of the peace, but a landlord's control over tenancies and his power to evict delinquent persons could effectively discourage illicit practices and almost certainly, therefore, illegal production could not have developed as it did if the majority of the landowning class in the relevant regions had not acquiesced in it and indeed abetted it. In fact magistrates were often most lenient in those counties where illicit distillation was most endemic.

Economic self-interest partly dictated their policy. MacLeod of Geanies, sheriff of Ross for thirty years, when questioned on the lenient attitude of his fellow magistrates, replied rhetorically, 'How then are we to sell our grain?'[8] The fall in bear and barley prices after the Napoleonic Wars had exposed the vulnerability of farmers in the north east and south west, and in these circumstances there was scope for commercial linkages to develop between zones of arable surplus and adjacent regions with more limited natural endowment where increased income was desirable and where distilling traditions existed. As a result of this interrelationship it was rumoured that the Morayshire farmer was able to gain 20 per cent more for his bear by selling it to illicit distillers in the upland districts than he obtained in the ordinary grain market.

For the landlord, distillation of whisky was one means of raising the rental yield of inferior land out of all proportion to its real value and estimates suggest that on some estates the rental could be tripled if the owner turned a blind eye to illegal practices. When demand for grain was stagnant or where transport difficulties inhibited easy access to markets, there was an incentive to convert a bulky, low-value commodity (bear or barley) into a less bulky, higher-value product (whisky). Until the Excise Act of 1823, successful landlord initiative against illicit whisky-making was rare; only untypical proprietors, such as the 5th Duke of Argyll, whose aim was to build up licensed production on Tiree, seem to have had an enthusiastic interest in eradicating it at this time.

By the second decade of the nineteenth century, therefore, illicit distillation had become so deep-rooted that even the most zealous magistracy was largely reduced to impotence. The dilemma of the justices was put most forcibly by Sir George Mackenzie of Coul:

> When we sit in judgment, we see before us our own and our neighbour's tenants; we know and we feel, that when we inflict even the lowest penalty directed by law, if the tenant be able to pay he will not pay his rent; and if he be no able to pay it we must send him to prison, where he can do nothing to help his affairs; while, in the meantime, his family may be starving on account of being deprived of his help, or attempting to find relief by conduct far worse than that of defrauding the revenue; . . . it cannot therefore be expected that under such circumstances, we can feel hearty for the cause of the revenue; . . . if our tenants fall we must fall along with them.[9]

In Scotland, failure to implement the law at the local level could not easily be put right by more vigorous intervention from the centre, for there was no superintending jurisdiction over JPs in revenue matters. In England, however, the court of king's bench did exercise such powers and regularly prosecuted magistrates for refusing to act in accordance with the law.

Given this tacit approval of the smuggler on the part of many landlords, the role of the exciseman was an unenviable one because he operated in communities where 'the illicit spirit is on every person's table' . . . from that of the lords lieutenants of the counties to that of the lowest individual'.[10] Several prominent centres of illicit distillation in the north-east (such as Glenlivet) were areas of lingering Jacobite sentiment where the distillery benefited from distrust of southern government and antagonism to legislation which taxed a basic essential of life. The nature of the terrain and the scale of illegal operations made detection difficult in some regions and in others, the armed strength of the smuggling communities rendered them immune from excise interference.

Allegations also proliferated in the first two decades of the nineteenth century concerning the wholesale corruption of the revenue service. It was said in Ross in the early 1820s that smugglers' wives sent presents of veal, poultry, whisky, butter and cheese to the wives of officers in return for information about a visit from the excise, and on the island of Lewis the local revenue official was allocated a proportion of the smugglers' earnings as a reward for his co-operation. However, the number of illicit stills actually seized throughout our period and the evidence of the prosecutions against illicit distillers (running at over 4,000 per annum in the Aberdeenshire district in the early 1820s) do not suggest a complete collapse in the morale of the officers. Rather, what can be said is that some excisemen were perhaps less than zealous in the execution of their duty because of the very size and nature of the problem which confronted them. It seems, for instance, that when illicit activity was discovered the still itself was only rarely seized, because by doing so the officer would lose the opportunity of making any more seizures of spirits and so of accumulating gains from fines. His perquisites came not from the money fine levied in court but from the judicial sale of the contents of a detected still. Moreover, in areas of widespread illicit production common sense and instincts of self-preservation dictated that the excisemen were not too obtrusive, and only when army and naval assistance was guaranteed in the later 1820s would more energetic enforcement of the law by the local excisemen become possible in such regions.

II

Perhaps the most common form of illicit distillation was household manu-facture for family and local consumption, a continuation of a tradition long established before the days of costly licences and heavy duties. Again, in certain districts there was large-scale manufacture of illicit whisky for sale at a distance and often outside the Highland zone. These centres were likely to be located in that broad, crescent-shaped belt of country which runs from Kintyre in the extreme south west via Highland Perthshire to Banff, Aberdeen, Ross and Sutherland in the north east because there is little evidence that the Outer Isles, north-west coastlands or central Highlands participated to any great extent in the large-scale marketing of illicit liquor. Indeed, in the early nineteenth century this region was itself in receipt of smuggled whisky from the south and east. The establishment of specialised centres of production suggests that access to cheap and abundant supplies of grain was an additional important determinant in the industry's location and that illicit distillation flourished most strongly in deprived areas fringing regions of grain surplus. The relative inaccessibility of such localities made them natural fortresses secure against all but the most determined forays of the excise but also open to the intrepid groups of smugglers who transported the illicit production. Typical of such areas in the north east was the Cabrach in Highland Aberdeenshire:

> The land is very poor; it is a very high table-land, and at the same time boggy to a great extent . . . There is in the lower part of the parish, a piece of land, a narrow valley that runs alongside the river . . . there is less smuggling, I believe, than in the other part. The people there are remarkably poor, it is a very cold district; the grain does not ripen there very well, and the breeding of black cattle, and the universal smuggling, forms the whole trade and occupation of the people.[11]

Similarly in Sutherland, the men of Kildonan, bordering the grain lands of Caithness, smuggled grain into the impoverished interior parishes of Lairg, Creich and Rogart, where it was converted into whisky. But not all centres of the illicit industry were poor and remote. Strathspey's success, for instance, was undoubtedly based on classic natural advantages – Morayshire grain, abundant water of exceptional purity flowing from the hard schists and granitic rocks of the Highland plateau and availability of plentiful supplies of peat.

The structure of production in these specialist regions of illicit manufacture was more elaborate than that of most parts of northern Scotland. In Strathglass malt-houses were sunk underground and operations conducted in hills and woods which afforded fuel and security. Customs officers rarely penetrated such regions for fear of assault and it was therefore not essential to conceal plant too carefully. One distillery in Ross had 'regularly built, low stone walls, water-tight heather thatch, iron pipes leading cold spring water to the still rooms, and such an array of casks, tubs etc. as told that gaugers never troubled their owners'.[12]

On the whole the process of manufacture seems to have been in the hands of those groups who had least to lose and most to gain from defying the law and so the producers tended to be small farmers, crofters and cottars. In Ross whisky-making was carried on 'chiefly by persons of little or no capital: sometimes holding very small farms' and, although in Perthshire there were instances of consortia of respectable farmers and distillers, the manufacturing process itself was always controlled by those of the 'lowest rank'.[13] Court records and a recent examination of the clientele of one Campbeltown still-maker by I. A. Glen suggests that women played a significant role in operations. Female servants were recruited as labour to act as 'cover' for more respectable individuals; for widows the returns from small-scale distillation would be an invaluable supplement to income and female participation would fit easily into family economics in which the menfolk were regularly working away from home.

The nature of the producing group had some important consequences for the fortunes of the industry. In the first place, it meant that fining was likely to be an ineffective method of reducing the incidence of activity as confiscation of property was not an efficient penalty when used against those who did not have the resources to pay the amounts defined by law. On the other hand, imprisonment was not practicable either, since jails in the Highlands were neither large nor numerous enough. One country gentleman suggested that the only solution was to bring the hulks to the Dornoch Firth! In their absence, convicted persons were given unlimited time for payment of fines and certificates of poverty were issued, signed by supervisors of excise with the effect of entirely discharging delinquents from responsibility for paying.

Again, given their financial weakness and dependence on credit from grain-supplies, illicit whisky-makers were unlikely to be able to gain the maximum monetary return for their efforts. They were generally unable to hold supplies until prices rose, were charged a higher price for grain than that sold in the ordinary market and distribution was controlled by professional smugglers who dealt directly with retailers and customers in the south. Significantly, the price to buyers of Highland whisky in Lowland towns could be as much 100 per cent higher than the selling price at the still mouth. But at the same time, generalisation in this area is fraught with difficulty, because as a black-market product illicit whisky could provide considerable gains in some years and disastrous losses in others, and certainly returns must have been sufficient to have made the effort worthwhile. In Kintyre, in the early nineteenth century, illicit distillers could clear 10s a week and this, it was said, was an important supplement to other sources of income. In this area, however, illicit distillers seem to have utilised their own homegrown grain and therefore did not incur the major cost borne by many of their north-eastern counterparts. Illicit whisky-making was not generally the route to easy riches, and successes were rare enough to merit specific mention by contemporaries. Ranald MacDonald, a man of wide experience of the practice in both the southern Highlands and the north east, did not know 'of one instance of the hundred I am acquainted with, where any man engaged as an illicit distiller has ever earned a comfortable competency'.[14] Rising rents and grasping middlemen ensured that for the majority of illicit distillers income would remain stubbornly low, even if at a slightly higher level than that of their neighbours.

Whatever doubt there may be as to the extent of profit accruing to the distillers, it seems plain that grain farmers, landlords and distributors of the illicit liquor did regard it as very lucrative. As a result, there evolved an elaborate system of grain supply to the manufacturing districts of the north east and a similarly clandestine network of distribution of the finished product. Around harvest time, supplies of bear and barley were sent from the south into Strathconan and Strathglass every eight to ten days and Lowland dealers brought vessels loaded with grain into the Beauly Firth which was then sold to the smugglers. Coastal farms in Aberdeenshire and Ross supplied illicit distillers up to forty miles inland, and in Highland Perthshire local barley was used along with supplies drawn from merchants in Stirling and Alloa.

After distillation, the product was conveyed to market by 'regularly trained smugglers', normally strangers from outside the district of manufacture and generally Irishmen or Lowlanders. Heavily-armed convoys, thirty to forty strong, carried the illicit liquor to Lowlands towns. 'Glenlivet' was brought across the mountains on horseback to the outskirts of Perth, 'where the carriers are met by parties of men, women and children, who conceal the spirit in small tin cans, and bring it into Perth with such secrecy as to render detection almost impracticable'.[15] The chief quantity of illicit spirits meant for the Glasgow market passed to the south between Stirling and Drymen and was distributed for sale to retailers in the Cowcaddens area of the city, but it is impossible to be too specific about the financial interests behind this secret commerce; only a few clues survive to indicate who controlled it. Thus some Glasgow publicans had direct links with illicit distillers in Breadalbane in Perthshire, while in the 1810s, the MacFarlanes from Loch Lomondside, who had connections with the cattle trade, were also extensively involved in the smuggling of illicit whisky to the Clyde towns.

Highland illicit spirits were produced for two main regional markets. The vast proportion of whisky consumed in the north by all social classes was the product of illicit stills, and the whisky of the north-eastern centres was distributed as widely as Skye and the island of Lewis in the west, while the dramshops and taverns of Tain, Aberdeen, Inverness and Dingwall were full of illicit stock. In the south, however, it catered in the main for a more select clientele. The very fact that it was smuggled perhaps lent Highland whisky a cachet which was one element in promoting sales among the elite, but its main attraction was that it was more palatable than the legal product. Illicit spirits selling in Ross for 5s a gallon in the early 1820s were marketed in Glasgow and Leith at 12s 6d, a price double the legal equivalent. North-eastern illicit spirit had also to face competition from the illegal industries of Kintyre and Perthshire, although illicit liquor produced within the urban areas and extracted from a variety of raw materials was designed for a quite different market. It was reckoned that there were more than two thousand private stills in Edinburgh in the later eighteenth century, producing a spirit known as 'molasses', which was much in demand by the common people of the city.

III

In its heyday, illicit whisky-making gave income and employment and made life more convivial, yet in the longer term its results were more ambiguous. As has been seen, grain farmers, landlords and distributors probably gained more than the distillers themselves, and moreover, like kelp manufacture in the north west, illicit distillation in the north east allowed a traditional economic and social structure to survive by creating temporary additional employment at a time of population increase. In doing so, however, the industry merely exacerbated the economic vulnerability of those regions by encouraging dependence on a source of income which was ephemeral and by immobilising a larger population than could be provided for by agriculture alone. Illicit distillation had a social and economic impact very similar to kelp manufacture and in parts of Sutherland, for instance, 'farms are reduced by subsets to mere patches, the occupiers of which live by smuggling'.[16] Paradoxically, however, the more extensive and elaborate that the manufacture of illicit spirits became, the more rapidly was it likely to invite destruction by concerted government action.

Undoubtedly it was the dramatic expansion of illicit distillation after the Napoleonic Wars which concentrated judicial and government attention. Two major investigations in 1821 and 1822 exposed the extent to which the law was being flouted and the revenue cheated but more insidious, some thought, were the social effects on the smuggling regions themselves. It was argued that in parts of Ross and Argyll a generation of *banditti* had been bred and decadence and intoxication were said to be rampant, while whole areas had become immune to the enforcement of the excise laws. It was suggested that the practices associated with illicit distillation often led to a *general* defiance of lawful authority. The famous Culrain riots of 1820 in Ross, when the local population violently resisted warrants of removal, were due, so it was said, to the truculent habits engendered by illicit distillation.

From 1822, then, the government began a radical alteration of its revenue policy with the explicit intention of destroying illicit whisky-making in Scotland. By the Illicit Distillation (Scotland) Act of that year, scales of fines were increased, new penalties laid on those who allowed the practice on their estates and the powers of the excise were extended to permit searches without prior warrant from JPs. This legislation, however, was in a sense merely an extension of a traditional faith in the value of a fining system which had proved completely ineffective in a Highland context, but more effective action came in the following year. In the Excise Act of 1823 duty was reduced by over 50 per cent to 2s 4¾d per gallon and payment of a uniform licence fee of £10 gave permission to distil. In addition, a drawback of 1s 2d per gallon was allowed on malt employed in the distillation process.

This Act substantially eroded the illicit producer's cost advantage over his licensed rival, but in practical terms it amounted to a drop in the malt tax and licensed distilleries would now be able to use malting barley more extensively in the production process. Thus the first few years after the Act witnessed a substantial expansion in the number of malt whisky plants licensed for distillation in the Highlands.

The uniform licence fee fixed at a low level meant that legal distillers had no further need to work their plant so intensively in order to save in costs. A wealth of evidence suggests that in the later 1820s, as a result, the product of the licensed Highland distilleries improved markedly in quality, a process doubtless encouraged by the absorption within the legal sector of the skills of the 'sma still' operators of illicit days.

The government's newly sharpened sword was double-edged. While vigorous attempts were made to minimise still duty and malt taxes, more effective punitive measures were developed to combat those who continued to break the law and the excise was encouraged to intervene in a more robust fashion by utilising the army and navy. In the later 1820s, for instance, specialised squads of sailors from the revenue cutter *Atalanta* helped to suppress smuggling in Ross and Cromarty, riding officers were employed to support local excisemen and, when desired, the aid of the military could be called upon. This was more often needed than might be expected. The decade after 1823 saw a series of violent incidents between the revenue service and groups of illicit distillers determined to brook no outside interference in their activities.

Changes in the attitude of the local magistrates occurred less speedily. For some time the average fines in the smuggling counties continued to be much lower than those levied elsewhere and the commissioners of excise complained bitterly that the new energy of their officers was not paralleled on the justices' bench. In time, however, as a result of the relaxation in the malt tax, the vested interest of owners of grain-producing land in protecting illicit distillers began to diminish. Further, the more sympathetic excise regulations of the post-1823 period were the basis for substantial expansion in licensed whisky manufacture and it was thus possible to preserve the value of lands where illicit distillation had flourished by sponsoring licensed production, a much more secure and larger-scale operation. Some landed gentlemen invested in these enterprises and so had an obvious economic interest in curtailing the activities of illicit rivals. The 'improvers' believed that illicit whisky manufacture bred lazy and improvident tenants who were less likely to co-operate in the grand design of economic progress. This antagonism had existed before the legislation of 1822–3, but vigorous practical action against illicit distillation had been inhibited by recognition of its cash value to impoverished estates. Now, however, the rise of licensed production in Islay, Kintyre, Glenlivet and Strathspey dictated a change in policy, and when alternative sources of land use became available, landlords had few qualms about removing whole communities of illicit distillers. So in Sutherland some of the great clearances of interior land displaced hundreds of illicit whisky-makers in the parishes of Rogart, Lairg and Creich, while Strathconan, a notorious smuggling district in Ross, had become a sporting estate by the 1830s after a series of large-scale removals.

The commissioners of excise were also determined that leniency on the part of the local judiciary would not damage their plans of quickly bringing illicit distillation to an end and the aim was quite simply to ensure that the tougher penalties enshrined in the 1822 Act would be put into effect in the magistrates' courts. Yet, even after the passage of this legislation, evidence continued to accumulate that convicted persons were still being fined derisory sums. Finally, in June 1823, at a JP court in Inverness, nearly 400 persons from the districts of Strathglass, Aird and Urquhart were found guilty of infringing the revenue laws and all were fined less than 20s. The low level of these penalties stung the excise into retaliation and at subsequent sessions, counsel for the crown appeared and justices dared not levy less than the statutory penalty of £20 or six months' imprisonment. In addition, some cases were transferred to the court of exchequer in Edinburgh and on each occasion heavy sentences were passed. Those who violently resisted the excise were sentenced to transportation.

By every measurement, the new policy would appear to have been spectacularly successful. The amount of duty-paid whisky almost doubled in one year from 2,232,000 gallons in 1823 to 4,350,000 in 1824. In Islay, Kintyre and Highland Perthshire illicit distillation was regarded as a thing of the past by the early 1830s in the professional opinion of excisemen and estate factors, and only a few of the former centres of production survived in the north east, albeit on a much diminished scale. Significantly, illicit activity remained prevalent in parts of the remote north-western mainland, where whisky-making had long been a part of the traditional economy and where it was geared to the needs of the family or locality rather than distant markets. Now cash incomes, inaccessibility and absence of licensed distilleries temporarily preserved it.

It is difficult to overstress the effects of the 1823 legislation on the fall of illicit distillation in northern Scotland. Yet government action in itself cannot fully explain why the industry collapsed so quickly as a similar policy of lowering of duties and more determined use of force was tried in Ireland with little short-term result.

In both countries the excise was confronted with a general indifference to revenue legislation. Yet in Scotland, illicit distillation was confined to specific and localised areas where lawlessness could be suppressed by skilful use of army and naval resources, whereas in Ireland poteen-making was endemic *through-out* the entire south and west of the country and less easily controlled. The grip of state power and landlord authority in Ireland was also much weaker than in northern Scotland and the economies of traditional smuggling regions of the two countries were different. In the deprived west of Ireland there was little investment in licensed distilleries because of poor economic circumstances. Such areas were incapable of producing an industry on any scale above that of the smuggler's hut and so no effective competition to the illicit product was likely to emerge. Though such localities existed too in northern Scotland, most were intimately connected with wealthier grain-producing lands on which they depended for raw material and finance and once government revenue regulations were reformed, these districts produced the capital resources and the entrepreneurship essential to the development of a successful legal industry. At that point, large-scale whisky-making outside the law was doomed.

NOTES

1 British Parliamentary Papers, VIII, 1816, p. 400.
2 British Parliamentary Papers, VI, 1803, *Two Reports (1798–9) from the Select Committee on the Distillery in Different Parts of Scotland*, Appendix 36, p. 60.
3 *Ibid.*, p. 61.
4 Major-General Stewart of Garth, 'Observations on the origins and cause of smuggling in the Highlands of Scotland', *Quarterly Journal of Agriculture*, i, 1829–30, p. 360.
5 British Parliamentary Papers, VII, 1823, *Fifth Report of the Commissioners . . . for inquiring into . . . certain Departments of the Public Revenue . . .*, p. 409.
6 *Ibid.*, p. 382.
7 *Ibid.*, p. 432.
8 *Ibid.*, p. 389.
9 *Ibid.*, p. 382.
10 *Ibid.*, p. 425.
11 *Ibid.*, p. 427.
12 Osgood Mackenzie, *A Hundred Years in the Highlands*, new edn, London, 1972, p. 215.
13 British Parliamentary Papers, VII, 1823, p. 397.
14 *Ibid.*, p. 432.
15 *Ibid.*, p. 524.
16 *Ibid.*, p. 391.

FURTHER READING

T. M. Devine, 'The rise and fall of illicit whisky making in Northern Scotland, *c.* 1780–1840' *Scottish Historical Revue*, LIV, 1975.

I. A. Glen, 'An economic history of the distilling industry in Scotland, 1750–1914', unpublished Ph.D. thesis, University of Strathclyde, 1969.

M. S. Moss and J. R. Hume, *The Making of Scotch Whisky*, Edinburgh, 1981.

S. W. Sillett, *Illicit Scotch*, Aberdeen, 1965.

10

THE MIGRANT TRADITION

I

The temporary or seasonal movement of Highlanders for work outside the region was of central importance in the later eighteenth and nineteenth centuries. Such was the scale of mobility that it deeply influenced all aspects of Highland life, from income levels to peasant culture, from social attitudes to language. What the evidence suggests is a regional pattern of huge migrant streams, generally, but not exclusively, consisting of the adult young, moving to jobs in the Lowlands and then, in time, back to the Highlands again. Especially during the busy months of summer and early autumn, the roads to the south and the steamers sailing for the Clyde would be full of young Highland men and women making their way to find work in Lowland farms and towns.

The type of employment they entered varied significantly. Perhaps the most famous temporary outlet was military and naval service though it did not conform to a seasonal pattern. From the Seven Years War of the eighteenth century to the Crimean War of the nineteenth the Highlands became a source of supply of soldiers and sailors of crucial importance to the British state. The peak period was probably the Revolutionary and Napoleonic Wars when one estimate suggests the Highlands furnished almost 75,000 men for the regiments of the line, Militia, Fencibles and Volunteers from a total regional population of about 300,000 at that time. These astonishing numbers ensured that military service had profound economic and demographic effects on Highland society. But this form of temporary migration, though deeply significant between 1760 and 1815, became much less important after the end of the French Wars. Of greater long-term consequence was the more mundane seasonal employment of Highlanders in Lowland agriculture, industry and construction works.

By the later eighteenth century temporary movement from the Highlands was already significant. The fairs of the towns of Doune, Gartmore and Drymen on the fringes of the Highlands had become important markets for the hiring of Highland harvest labour and one contemporary, John Knox, estimated that at least half the young females in the southern Highlands went south for the harvest. Although agricultural employment was dominant, Argyllshire migrants also obtained work in the herring fisheries of the Clyde estuary and the bleachfields of the booming textile areas of the western Lowlands. Though less well documented, it is also apparent that Highland girls were sought after as domestic servants in urban households and it was common for many of them to return home in the winter months. Before 1800, then, the pattern of temporary mobility had acquired four main characteristics: first, military employment was especially important for males and agricultural work for females; second, most Highland migrants employed in the Lowland economy came from Argyllshire, eastern Inverness-shire and easter Ross and fewer from the far north and the Outer Hebrides; third, domestic service, fishing and industrial work were already established as seasonal outlets; fourth, apart from military service, mobility was essentially seasonal in nature, related in particular to the busy times in Lowland agriculture and Lowland fisheries in the summer and early autumn months.

The most striking feature of temporary migration thereafter in the nineteenth century was its further dynamic growth and development. Military service may have became less significant in the decades of peace following the Napoleonic Wars but other sectors expanded rapidly. The key change was that most parts of the crofting region by the 1850s, including the Outer Hebrides, came to depend on the income of temporary migrants. Reliance on the earnings of seasonal workers spread from the southern and eastern areas bordering the Lowlands to encompass virtually the whole of the Highland region. Moreover, although seasonality remained significant, especially in agriculture and fishing, it was increasingly common in the second half of the nineteenth century for migrants to stay away for longer periods of several months and even years. This trend was strongly influenced by developments in the Lowland industrial economy which allowed migrants to dovetail casual employments which had different seasonal work peaks. Thus, in the 1840s, men from Avoch in Ross-shire spent the summer months building roads in Aberdeenshire followed by part of the winter digging farm ditches. Migrants from Ardnamurchan divided their time between field work in the country and general labouring in the dye-works of Glasgow. Highlanders hired as labourers in the later nineteenth century at the Glasgow gasworks in winter, spent the summer as deck-hands in the Clyde herring fisheries.

Over time, the social composition of the migrant group also altered. Until the 1830s and 1840s it mainly consisted of young single males and females.

When heads of household were active, they normally belonged to the poorest social strata, the semi-landless cottar class who eked out a living on potato cultivation and temporary migration. But the famines of the 1840s and 1850s helped to transform this traditional pattern. Youthful migrants remained dominant but now older married crofters and small tenants were trekking to the south and the east in the search for employment because of the failure of the potatoes and the collapse in cattle prices. This type of crisis migration from the Highlands had been taking place for generations, but the famines of the mid-nineteenth century were so devastating that they seem to have ushered in a new era. Income from temporary mobility was now a central priority for the crofting economy as the produce of the land and indigenous forms of employment had become much less secure.

Temporary migration was not unique to the Scottish Highlands. It was and is widespread in many parts of the world where a poor and underemployed population lives in close proximity to a neighbouring richer economy with much demand for seasonal and casual workers. The connection between highland and plain economies is especially common. Pastoral farming in the hill country requires little labour and the difficult terrain ensures that the return from the land is modest and uncertain. On the other hand, the adjacent lowland economy, based on arable and mixed farming, has much need of additional labour at the key times of sowing, harvesting and processing and these workers can easily be recruited from the 'surplus' population of the neighbouring highlands. The needs of each region are essentially complementary and relationships of this type existed in localities in several European countries in the nineteenth century. Highland temporary migration was, therefore, one variant in a common demographic pattern. Nevertheless, it had certain distinctive characteristics, not least of which was the scale of mobility and its dramatic increase over time, and these require some explanation.

II

The long-term expansion of migration was a result of the chronic problems of the Highland economy after the end of the Napoleonic Wars. A structural imbalance developed, especially in the crofting parishes, between a consistently rising population down to the 1840s and the collapse of several of the traditional activities which flourished in the later eighteenth century. Kelp manufacture, commercial fishing and whisky-making were all in difficulties in the 1820s and 1830s while military employment became a factor of much less consequence. At the same time, in the islands and the north west, numbers rose by about 53 per cent between 1801 and 1841 and this in a region where arable land, already limited, was further reduced by the relentless expansion of large-scale sheep-farming and highlanders increasingly resorted to temporary employment in the Lowlands because of this growing gap between the supply and demand for labour in the crofting counties. But the migrations were not simply conditioned by material needs. The scale of temporary mobility also demonstrated a cultural choice on the part of the Highland people. In a 'rational' sense more permanent movement might have been expected because of the growing difficulties of a society where demographic and economic pressures were becoming steadily more intense, but temporary migration reflected the strength of the continued attachment to land; it was a means of clinging to the old way of life, which however harsh, gave a degree of security in most years. Only during the miseries of the Great Famine were these social attitudes temporarily abandoned as severe destitution and the threat of starvation drove many thousands to leave the Highlands forever. Until the 1840s, however, the tolerance of subdivision of holdings by many proprietors allowed temporary migration to expand on an unprecedented scale as potato growing and income from seasonal work in the Lowlands gave the opportunity to eke out a living in the crofting parishes on tiny patches of marginal land. Temporary migration therefore helps to explain why clearance was not always followed by mass migration from the Highland region itself because often evicted families were able to scrape an uncertain existence in overcrowded townships and slum villages by relying on seasonal work else-where.

Both agriculture and industry in the south had an even greater need for temporary labour in the nineteenth century than even before. Industrialisation had produced a much more complex labour market with new occupations, changes in traditional jobs and growing specialisation of functions. Technology was advancing but most tasks, even in manufacturing, were still carried out by hand and, in addition, seasonality remained an important feature of the developing economy. Employers in most trades and occupations had to contend with the fact that the demand for workers would still fluctuate markedly throughout the year and there was a great advantage in having a reserve army of labour which could be hired and then laid off when necessary. The Scottish industrial economy of the nineteenth century was based on a few heavy staple manufactures producing simple products for world markets. Although some skilled men were required success depended primarily on secure access to a large pool of low-paid, unskilled labour and abundant supplies of coal and other raw materials. In this sense, the Irish and the Highland migrants were crucial factors in Scottish economic success in the Victorian era.

Closer examination of the migrant flows reveals a complex pattern. By the 1840s, agricultural employment no longer maintained the dominance of earlier periods though still providing a very important outlet for seasonal workers. There was a rough regional division of labour. Migrants from the Inner Hebrides, mainland Argyll and parts of western Inverness-shire tended by and large to seek rural employment in the central and south-eastern Lowlands and, indeed, for the inhabitants of Mull, Tiree, Coll, Islay and Colonsay, agricultural work in the south seems still to have been the main type of temporary employ- ment in the mid-nineteenth century. Skye presents a more varied pattern. Migration for the harvest and other agricultural tasks was still very significant, especially for young females, but in some parishes it was balanced by an additional flow of people to the fisheries of the east coast. Elsewhere, in the western Highlands and islands, notably in Lewis, Harris, Sutherland and most parishes in Wester Ross, temporary migration to the Caithness and Aberdeen- shire fisheries was most important. Even here, however, there was a subordinate movement for work in the farms of Easter Ross, Caithness and Moray and, in any case, agricultural and fishing employment were not mutually exclusive. One traveller met women on the roads leading from Wick who were returning from the herring fishery and then going to the corn harvest. On the east coast, the herring season lasted from July through to August, thus fitting neatly into the period immediately before the grain harvest itself.

Women gutting fish at Peterhead, 1910

The continued significance of agricultural employment reflected the labour requirements of the farming classes of Lowland Scotland. The Agricultural Revolution had massively increased the productivity of the land and one estimate by the contemporary expert on rural affairs, George Robertson, suggested that between 1740 and 1829 corn production had doubled while that of animal food had multiplied sixfold. But agriculture still remained an essentially labour-intensive activity, a matter of sweat and muscle rather than of new machinery. Despite some experimentation in mechanised reaping, new technology did not become significant until the 1850s and 1860s and, indeed, the major innovation before the 1840s in harvesting was a revolution in hand-tools, when the scythe became more popular at the expense of the sickle. At the same time the spread of green crops, a vital element in the new agriculture, ensured that the farmer's busy season, and hence his need for seasonal workers, extended for a longer period in the year. Clover and turnips required an almost gardenly care as, from May until harvest, turnip fields were subjected to dunging, a double hoeing and thinning.

While improved agriculture had more need of reliable seasonal workers, organisational changes from the later eighteenth century made it more difficult to recruit an adequate supply in some districts from local sources. Two factors were important. First, before c.1820, subtenancy was eliminated in most Lowland areas outside the north-east counties, whereas in the old world the families of the subtenants and cottars had been the main reservoir of seasonal labour for the bigger farmers of the neighbourhood. As the cottar system was crushed, many farmers looked to the Highlands, Ireland and local towns and villages to make up the supply as, by using seasonal workers from distant regions with a labour surplus, farmers effectively reduced their costs and were able to cut their permanent labour force to a minimum. There was less need to employ additional workers for long periods simply to ensure a reliable supply at critical times and, in addition, they saved on accommodation costs because seasonal migrants lived rough, in barns and farm outbuildings.

Secondly, by the middle decades of the nineteenth century, increased migration from country to town in the Lowland countryside was making recruitment of seasonal workers in parts of the eastern counties more difficult. The families of handloom weavers and linen spinners had in the past been key sources of harvest labour, but as industry gradually concentrated in the coalfields of the central Lowlands and factory organisation in the larger towns hastened the demise of many textile village communities it became more difficult to maintain this supply. The Highland and Irish migrants therefore became even more necessary.

The pattern in fishing was different. The ambitious plans to promote a prosperous and successful herring fishery in Hebridean waters in the eighteenth century developed by the British Fisheries Society, southern commercial interests and Highland landlords did not bear enduring fruit. By the 1820s it was apparent that such progress as had been achieved in the later eighteenth and early nineteenth centuries was likely to be short-lived. Fishing remained an integral part of the way of life in the western Highlands but in most areas it was carried on to satisfy local needs. The white fishery had a continuing importance, and from time to time the herring shoals did visit the northern sea lochs but the commercial sector remained a pale shadow of the flourishing industry of the early 1800s. Over time, the herring fishery became more concentrated than ever before along the lochs of the Clyde estuary and an even bigger and more successful enterprise developed in Caithness, Aberdeen and Moray. Yet, although the commercial centre of herring fishing was situated elsewhere, the communities of the western Highlands and islands were able to gain in some degree because they provided an essential supply of seasonal labour both for the north-east and south-west industries.

Even in the eighteenth century, there had been a significant connection between the Clyde fisheries and the population of the western Highlands and, on one estimate, some 89 per cent of the crew members of the herring 'busses' based at Greenock in the 1790s were Highland-born. In the nineteenth century, however, the herring fishery developed most rapidly and successfully among the coasts of the north-east counties of Caithness and Aberdeen. The industry concentrated on particular pots, such as Wick, Peterhead, Fraserburgh, Aberdeen itself and a number of smaller centres and the structure of fishing in these areas ensured that a partnership of mutual advantage could develop with the impoverished western Highlands and islands. The boats were operated through a system of owner-fishermen and the normal pattern was for five or six men, all belonging to the same town or village and often related, to furnish the capital and most of the labour. But they could not provide from their own resources all the extra hands required at the peak season in July and August and it became the custom, therefore, and one which was firmly established by the 1840s, for each crew to be strengthened by the addition of one or two 'strangers'. These were commonly men from the western Highlands and from Orkney, with Highlanders predominating. Again, the expansion in output forced up demand for workers in the highly labour-intensive tasks of gutting and packing and it was reckoned that on average three experienced females were required through-out the season to handle the catch of one boat, and this demand was again partially satisfied by the young women of the Hebrides.

This relationship between the north east and the north west was based on mutual needs. The latter region had a surplus of labour and a population with considerable maritime skills and the vast majority of the seasonal migrants to the north east were natives of Lewis, Wester Ross and some parts of Skye and west Sutherland, which were areas which possessed considerable fishing traditions in their own right. Temporary employment in Caithness or Aberdeen blended well with the customary cycle of fishing activity in the west as the high season in north-eastern waters took place between the earlier herring fishery in the Minch and the later white fishing in the western Highlands. At the busiest times there was a great migration to the ports of Aberdeenshire and the Caithness coast and one observer reckoned that the population of Wick rose from 6,700 to over 16,000 during the fishing season. Official figures revealed that 11,710 people were involved in the Wick fishery in 1846. Of this number 26 per cent (2,639) were female gutters and 62 per cent (7,269) fishermen and seamen, and even these totals may understate the true figures. In 1849, for instance, the *John O'Groats Journal* accused the Fishing Board of under-recording the numbers employed by between one-third to one-half. The Town Council of Wick itself estimated that during the seven weeks of the herring season the port attracted 'a surplus population' of 10,000, many of whom were migrants from the west. A year later, the Council reckoned that 5,000 to 6,000 of this seasonal population were 'young, strong and healthy persons from the Highlands of Scotland' and so great was the migration that the Free Church supplied Gaelic-speaking catechists to minister to the spiritual needs of the labourers.

The availability of seasonal jobs in agriculture and fishing indirectly reflected the rapid urban and industrial expansion which had taken place in Scotland since the later eighteenth century because it was the demand for foods and raw materials from the growing towns and manufacturing centres which created the greater opportunities in farming and fishing. Moreover, as industry concentrated in the central Lowlands, peripheral regions were rapidly denuded of those weak alternatives to subsistence agriculture which had flourished briefly in the later eighteenth century. One after another, linen manufacture, whisky-distilling and commercial fishing went into decline or virtually disappeared under the inexorable pressures of Lowland economic competition. In one sense, indeed, temporary migration simply reflected the fact that the comparative advantage of many districts in the Highlands by the 1840s had become confined to the supply of low-cost labour for the Lowland economy and grazing ground for sheep.

One of the basic features of this form of migration was that its range of diversity increased in the nineteenth century and a whole variety of tasks had a seasonal cycle. Construction work, dock labouring and textile manufacturing tended to expand in spring and summer but fall back in winter and at the same time, the new industrial and urban economy brought into being a series of additional occupations and extended the scope of others which were longer-established. Work on railway construction merged into harvesting and employment on the fisheries was often followed by labouring in the fields. Men from Kilmalie in Inverness divided their time between labouring on farms and in the Glasgow dye-works. This industry where, unusually, employment could be obtained throughout the winter months, was also favoured by the people of Tiree and Ardnamurchan and many of the seasonal migrants of Tiree were employed at the world's biggest chemical factory owned by the Tennant family at St Rollox in Glasgow. The Glasgow and Vale of Leven calico printing works in the early 1840s offered employment to between 4,000 and 5,000 children, and the local factory inspector observed in 1846 that 'very many' of these came annually from the Highlands and Ireland. It was common for the young men of Mull, Lochalsh, Gigha and Applecross to go to sea, sometimes for several years on end, while domestic service was probably the most rapidly growing occupation for single females. Between 1851 and 1891 about a quarter of all women engaged in private households in Greenock were of Highland origin and, in the principal migrant area of central Paisley, 62 per cent of employed single females of Highland parentage in 1851 worked as domestic servants.

For men, navvying on the railways had assumed great significance by the early 1840s and was to become even more important during the construction mania of 1846–7. Railway work had two particular attractions. First, it paid better than agricultural employment: for instance, in 1845 weekly earnings in railway construction in the south-east region averaged 30 per cent more than harvest rates in the same area. Second, and perhaps more crucially, the period of employment on the railways lasted longer and even during the winter months operations continued other than under the most inclement weather conditions. Thus during disturbances between Highland and Irish labourers in the Linlithgow area the legal authorities counted around 800 men from the Highlands in the district and at Cockburnspath on the Edinburgh to Berwick line, Irish strikers in 1845 were replaced by 300 Highlanders. More than half the 2,100 men employed in railway construction in the Lothians in the 1840s were from the Highlands, and in the same period they were also strongly represented among the navvy gangs on the Hawick branch of the North British and on the Caledonian line.

III

The most fascinating issue of all in this survey of the migrant economy is the question of its impact on Highland society. Temporary mobility must have slowed down the rate of permanent migration by making up part of the deficit in regional income which was emerging from the collapse of the indigenous crofting economy in the first few decades of the nineteenth century. The very fact that a large proportion of the adult young had eaten away from home between May and September, the peak months for seasonal movement, was itself of key significance as this was the time of maximum pressure on food resources, the period when the old grain and potato harvests were running out and the new had still to be gathered. The positive economic effects of migration were vividly demonstrated during the potato famines when there was a huge increase in the seasonal exodus from virtually all parts of the Highlands in 1846 and 1847. In the same years, the peak of the railway construction boom in the Lowlands created an immense demand for labour and contemporary observers, from relief officials to estate factors, noted that this produced a flow of income into the crofting region which had a crucial effect in preventing wholesale starvation during the potato blight. Equally, however, when the industrial recession in the south became serious in 1848–9, earnings from temporary migrants dried up and it was no coincidence that 1849 was widely regarded as one of the worst years of the entire famine period.

Temporary migration was not an economic panacea for the Highland problem and, indeed, it reflected the acute maldistribution of resources and the chronic imbalance between people and opportunities which lay at the heart of the crisis in the crofting districts. Economic necessity, the need to scrape a very basic subsistence living, lay behind these mass annual movements. Moreover, while migrant earnings were a fundamental support of countless households, they perpetuated rather than solved longer-term difficulties by enabling and encouraging further subdivision of land. Migrant workers were also insecure, as their prime advantage to the host economy was that they were removable. By hiring temporary migrants, Lowland employers saved on labour costs during times when business was slow, yet when workers might still have to be maintained, and paid in readiness for the busy season. Furthermore, Highland migrants were concentrated in the casual labour market where wages were at their lowest and demand for workers most prone to fluctuation and uncertainty. The migrant economy prospered in the 1850s and 1860s but was in deep crisis in the 1880s, a fact which goes a long way to explaining the emergence of the crofting agitation of that decade.

It is also evident that migrant labour could only prop up Highland society for a limited period. In a subtle fashion, increased dependence on migrant earnings, coupled with the transition from seasonal (or short-term mobility of a few weeks) to temporary movement (for several months or longer) must have had powerful effects on the social values of the young people of the crofting region. Almost certainly the barriers to permanent migration were silently being eroded and, as shown in chapter 8, Gaelic was not simply in decline because of the spread of formal schooling but because English speech was becoming more common among temporary migrants. The flow of income from the migrant economy was also breaking down the old dependency on land. Cheaper grain prices in the last quarter of the nineteenth century enabled the development of a more cash-based economy in the Highlands as increasingly meal was purchased from outside with the earnings from temporary migration. In the 1840s there were few Lowland imports into the Hebrides apart from such necessities as salt, grain and luxuries for the elite. A few decades later, however, meal, tea, tobacco and clothing were all widely available as the migrant economy was pushing more and more of the community into cash-based relationships. The Highland equivalent of the pawnbroker and small shopkeeper in the working-class districts of the southern cities of the late nineteenth century was the village meal dealer who gave credit on the security of the following year's seasonal earnings.

By the end of the nineteenth century the entire economic and social system in many areas in the north west and throughout the Hebrides had come to depend on the migrant labour economy. It followed that depopulation would accelerate if this central support were ever to crumble and it did so suddenly and extensively in the years after the First World War, when depression in the Lowland industrial economy, combined with long-term recession in the herring fishery and the final mechanisation of the southern grain harvest dramatically cut back the need for Highland labour.

FURTHER READING

E. J. T. Collins, 'Migrant labour in British agriculture in the nineteenth century', *Economic History Review*, 2nd ser., XXII, 1969.

T. M. Devine, 'Temporary migration and the Scottish Highlands in the nineteenth century', *Economic History Review*, 2nd ser. XXXII, 1979.

T. M. Devine, ed., *Farm Servants and Labour in Lowland Scotland*, 1770–1914, Edinburgh, 1984.

T. M. Devine, *The Great Highland Famine*, Edinburgh, 1988, ch. 6.

M. Gray, *The Fishing Industries of Scotland*, Aberdeen, 1978.

W. Howatson, 'The Scottish hairst and seasonal labour, 1600–1870', *Scottish Studies*, 26, 1982.

D. F. MacDonald, *Scotland's Shifting Population*, Glasgow, 1937.

11

THE GREAT HUNGER

I

Food shortage was a familiar and recurrent feature of Highland life in the eighteenth and early nineteenth centuries as grain cultivation was always problematic in a region of poor natural endowment and uncertain climate. In 1782–3, 1795–6, 1806–7, 1816–17, and 1836–7, to name but the most serious crises, emergency supplies of meal had had to be imported into the western Highlands to avert mass starvation. But the famine of the later 1840s was of a quite different order of magnitude from the scarcities of the past. For a start, the failure of the potatoes in 1846 was virtually complete in many districts, especially in the Hebrides and along the western mainland, and this effectively removed a major part of the food supply in these impoverished areas which had come to rely on the potato as a principal source of subsistence. In addition, the crisis was protracted. The grain crop usually failed partially for one or two seasons, but this time the potatoes in the western Highlands were affected by blight for over a decade. The disease was caused by the fungus *Phytophthora Infestans* which afflicted potato crops all over Europe and North America in the 1840s, but some areas were more vulnerable than others to its lethal effects and maritime regions, such as western Ireland and the Scottish Highlands, were especially at risk although the severity of the blight depended ultimately on local weather conditions. Cool, rainy nights and moderately warm cloudy days are most suitable for propagation and germination of the spores and they spread most rapidly in a moist environment during the spring and summer months, and these were exactly the climatic conditions of the western Highlands. Not surprisingly, therefore, the consequences of the deadly fungus on the region were catastrophic. In August and September 1846, the press described how the stench of rotting potatoes pervaded numerous crofting townships up and down the west coast and throughout the Hebrides.

The disaster was made worse by the fact that there was no contemporary scientific understanding or effective cure for the blight. As its ravages continued into a second year, evangelical ministers proclaimed that the tragedy was the judgement of God on a sinful people and one witness asserted at the end of 1846 that '. . . the present year certainly marks the most momentous calamity in the condition of the Highlands that has occurred for a century that has taken place since 1746'.[1] But the famine was not simply a biological disaster, it also had profound economic origins and ramifications. Potato dependency was one hallmark of the intrinsic poverty of the Highlands and, however extensive the blight, famine would not have occurred if the population had possessed the economic resources to acquire substitute food supplies from elsewhere. Acute shortages reflected the insecure foundations of the crofting economy which had been profoundly weakened by the difficulties of the period after 1815 surveyed in chapters 3 and 4. Moreover, economic pressures after 1846 reinforced the adverse impact of crop failure as cattle markets were in the doldrums between 1847 and 1857, and commercial herring fishing also suffered several bad years in the later 1840s. The migrant economy was very active in 1846 and 1847 and seasonal workers helped to secure vital cash resources in these years but, however, with the coming of the great industrial depression of 1848, the southern labour market became decidedly more difficult for some time. All these forces were pushing Highland society inexorably towards social catastrophe and some observers asserted that a tragedy on the scale of Ireland was inevitable unless emergency measures were taken swiftly.

The most telling illustration of the intense pressures unleashed on the population by the failure of the potatoes was the increase in mass migration as certain districts experienced enormous demographic losses during these terrible years. Uig in Lewis lost an estimated half of its total population between 1841 and 1861, Jura almost a third (1841–51), the Small Isles almost a half (1851–61), Kilfinichen (Mull) a third (1841–51) and a further quarter (1851–61) and Barra, one-third (1841–51). In several parishes, the scale of out-migration was so great that it eliminated the entire growth in population which had occurred from the early nineteenth century. Over the decade of the famine more than 16,000 people were assisted to emigrate to Canada and Australia through a combination of crop failure, clearance, coercion and landlord subsidy. But this figure represents only one documented part of a much greater diaspora. The potato famine can be seen as an epochal development in Highland emigration history as, though often enduring an existence of grinding poverty, the small crofter and cottar class only emigrated with great reluctance. However, the duration and intensity of the famine weakened for a time the grip of the people on the land and large numbers seemed to have changed their attitudes radically from an unwillingness to move to a desperate urge to get away. Only the great crisis in food supply could have quickly worked this revolution in heart and mind and, at the same time, made landlord, philanthropic and government funds available to support mass emigration.

The famine induced movement from all over the Highland region but it is important to recognise that its effects varied significantly between different areas and social groups. The epicentre of the disaster was the western mainland, and especially the Hebrides, the very heart of crofting society. The southern, central and eastern Highlands were badly hit in 1846 but relief operations were soon abandoned in subsequent years as these areas had much more resilience than the localities further west because their dependence on the potato was not as excessive. Higher levels of permanent mobility had reduced demographic pressures and more of the population in the south and east relied on wage labouring in farming and fishing than in the land-dependent west. Even in the stricken region itself there was diversity of experience. Crofting communities which had grown up as a result of the boom in kelping suffered most, whereas fishing townships were much less vulnerable. However, at the local level, factors such as landlord strategy, social structure and the extent of dependency on temporary migration also had fundamental effects and make easy generalisations difficult. It is plain, nevertheless, that the famine was an economic disaster for most areas and the records of the big landed estates are full of evidence of the rapid accumulation of crofter rent arrears. In 1851 a government enquiry into the region conducted by Sir John McNeill revealed that though many crofters still retained some stock at that date the famine had taken a grievous toll on the small tenantry. Cattle numbers, the essential capital of the people, had been run down in a desperate effort to buy meal in 1846–7 and also the value of stock was less than the total arrears owed landlords. In effect, most crofters were bankrupt. Middle-ranking tenants fared best; cottars, many of whom only possessed small lots of potato ground, were the main victims both from the blight and the subsequent economic collapse. The position of the landlord class was complex and some families went to the wall. The Ardnamurchan estate of Sir James Riddell was placed under the administration of trustees in 1852, and MacLeod of MacLeod was obliged to sell off part of his hereditary lands in Skye and seek employment as a clerk in London. There were a few other spectacular insolvencies but in general, however, the most striking feature of Highland landlordism in this, the gravest crisis in modern Highland history, was its resilience and the vast majority of proprietors survived with their estates intact. Partly this was because many of the old, impoverished elite had been swept away and their place had been taken by a new class drawn from the merchants, bankers, military officers and professional men of the south who did not depend on the meagre rentals of the crofter class and, in addition, crofting rents were a significant source of income on only a few west Highland estates by the famine period. Sheep-farming had already advanced far into the fastnesses of crofting society and only in Barra, South Uist, Tiree, the Ross of Mull and a few other areas was large-scale sheep farming still underdeveloped by the early 1840s. Elsewhere, however, it was the dominant source of estate income in most properties and rentals on these possessions accrued not from poverty-stricken crofters but mainly from prosperous farmers whose returns depended primarily on prevailing world prices for wool and mutton which, fortunately for many landlords, were buoyant over most of the famine years. As a class, landowners were hit in their pockets both by relief costs and rising poor law payments but the crisis did not generate widespread economic collapse among the elite.

II

That the failure of the potatoes deepened destitution and caused a mass exodus from the region is beyond dispute, but it did not lead to the horrendous crisis of mortality which befell Ireland and led to famine-induced deaths of around one million people by the 1850s in that country. The Highlands were eventually spared a calamity on this scale despite the fact that several observers at the time

Planting potatoes using the cas chrom or foot plough

were proclaiming that a human tragedy was inevitable and certainly in the early months of 1847 some of the classic signs of famine mortality were evident. Deaths were increasing rapidly among the very old and the very young, and the diseases of famine, diarrhoea, scurvy and typhus, were becoming more common. However, by the end of that first year the potential threat of mass starvation had been averted. The Highlands had to contend thereafter with hunger, misery and distress but not with the human carnage which the Irish had to endure.

One basic reason for the different scale of the disaster in each country was the size of the population directly affected by the blight. Several millions were at risk in Ireland while in the Highlands the numbers involved were rarely more than 150,000 and often many less, and because of this the Highland crisis was much more manageable and containable. However, this in itself could not avert a rise in mortality because the magnitude of the relief problem was still very considerable; in the event, the Highlands were saved in large part by the overall strength of the Scottish economy and the effective mobilisation of relief.

The Scottish famine took place in a society which had experienced a massive change in economic structure by the 1840s. Industrialisation and urbanisation produced a new order in which agriculture, though still significant, was no longer the central dynamic in the Scottish economy. It was a society with much greater *per capita* wealth than Ireland and offered a greater range of employments in general and casual labouring in Lowland centres not far distant from the distressed districts of the north. Through temporary migration for work on southern railways, fisheries, domestic service, building and agriculture the poorest classes of the Highlands could escape the threat of starvation and at the same relieve pressure on scarce food supplies in the crofting region and, as shown in chapter 10, there was a marked increase in temporary migration in 1846 and 1847 when the steamships from the Hebrides to the Clyde were full to overflowing in the summer months with crofters and cottars making their way to the Lowlands in search of jobs.

The Highland landed class also appear to have been more active in providing relief than their Irish counterparts and, in 1846, only about 14 per cent of west Highland landlords were censured by government officials for the inadequacy of their relief measures. However, while some landowners took early initiatives, others were much more laggard and only became active after they were threatened with government sanctions. Most expenditure came from the ducal houses of Sutherland and Argyll and the 'new' landed class, who were in a better position to offer relief than the old families with their burden of multiple trusts and historic indebtedness. But it was not only the offer of meal at reduced prices or in return for work which was important. Several landowners, such as the Duke of Argyll, John Gordon of Cluny and Sir James Matheson also carried out elaborate schemes of 'assisted' emigration by which the poorest and most destitute were literally exported abroad, and the implementation of these programmes, often by draconian means, led to some of the most notorious and controversial clearances of the time. These were justified in some quarters as a necessary evil in order to avoid even greater suffering.

The greater wealth and technological progress of the Victorian era were also the essential preconditions for the growth of a great philanthropic agency of relief. By the 1840s there had been a revolution in communications and the potato famine in the Highlands was successfully relieved partly because news of the disaster was spread rapidly outside the distressed areas and vital food supplies were transported into the region with commendable speed. It was primarily through the contemporary press that most of those who later contributed so handsomely to the relief funds were first informed of the crisis. Press coverage was intensive during the first two years of the famine, and *The Times* sent a 'commissioner' to the western Highlands in 1846 and again in 1851. His first dispatches appeared as early as September 1846 and alerted the nation to the real possibilities of an Irish-type disaster on British soil; the *Guardian* also provided sustained coverage and the *Morning Chronicle* sent a special correspondent. All these journals were published in England and had a mainly southern readership, and their interest was a telling illustration of the attraction which the Scottish Highlands now had for a very wide middle- and upper-class readership both at home and abroad.

Press coverage on this scale and the effective provision of relief would not have been possible without the transport revolution which took place in the western Highlands in the decades before the potato famine. It was modern technology in the form of steam propulsion for ships which helped to save the people of the region from the full horrors of a subsistence crisis. As a contemporary observer put it in graphic terms, 'a bridge of boats now unites the southern mainland with the northern coast and very specially with the Western Isles'.[2] One traveller took five weeks going and returning from Edinburgh to Tiree in the 1770s using the most expeditious route, but in 1846, however, the round trip from Glasgow to Mull by steamship took less than three days. The steamer for Portree in Skye also called at Mull, Glenelg and Lochalsh. Lewis had a regular service from 1845 and by that year there was also a link to Lochmaddy in North Uist.

Perhaps even more crucial than the regular services was the role of the powerful steam vessels of the Royal Navy which were used by government in early 1847 and were made available on request to the relief committees thereafter to convey vital supplies to the most destitute communities. Their particular advantage was their speed and the fact that they could carry out their function in virtually all climatic conditions. It was due mainly to them that the Outer Hebrides could be sure of relief supplies even during the stormy winter months. Again, the regular tours of inspection carried out by Sir Edward Pine Coffin, in charge of government relief measures, and his officers which were vital in obtaining information on those areas requiring emergency supplies, would not have been possible without the assistance of the naval steamers. The winter gales no longer isolated the islands as easily as they had done in the very recent past.

Nineteenth century society therefore possessed the technical expertise to overcome the natural obstacles which had plagued the efforts of those who in earlier times had tried to bring relief to the Hebrides in years of food scarcity and shortage. But it also had a much more fully developed tradition of philanthropic intervention and endeavour, although this is not to say that the provision of charitable aid was unique to the Victorian period. Private charity had also been a vital social cement in earlier centuries, and in the eighteenth century, for instance, it was common for both landlords and townspeople to subscribe funds for those in distress in time of harvest failure. However, by the 1840s, the formation of official charities, seeking to respond to virtually every social need, had expanded as never before. In Glasgow, for instance, two charitable societies were founded between 1801 and 1810, in the following decade the number rose to eleven and, from 1821 to 1830, to fifteen. Each industrial slump in the expanding city produced an array of philanthropic agencies to bring some assistance to the able-bodied unemployed who had no legal right to relief under the Scottish Poor Law. Relief committees were formed in the major towns in 1816–17, 1819–20, 1826–7 and again in 1829. In 1836 and 1837 the Highlands benefited from Lowland philanthropy when, in association with government, relief organisations in Glasgow dispensed meal and clothing in the distressed districts, and this was almost a rehearsal for the much greater intervention which took place after 1846. Individuals such as Charles Baird and the Rev. Dr Norman MacLeod, who were heavily involved in 1836, also played a leading role in the formation of the Glasgow Section of the Central Board during the famine of the following decade.

The reasons for the extraordinary expansion in all forms of official philanthropy are not the primary concern here. Among other factors it came about because of the powerful influence of the evangelical movement in the Church of Scotland, which stressed the Christian duty of charity to one's less fortunate neighbours, and the need to respond to the social problems crystallised and aggravated by urbanisation and industrialisation. Philanthropy also became recognised part of the lifestyles of the urban middle classes, where charities offered opportunities for mixing socially with the great, making one's mark in polite society and providing suitable and acceptable work for the underemployed wives of the well-to-do. Philanthropy was at once a response to urban unrest and social dislocation, an assertion of Christian values which were seen to be under challenge by the forces of economic and social change and an accepted and integral part of the Victorian code of respectability. By the 1840s, to be philanthropic and respond with due generosity to worthy causes was expected of all who could afford it. The potato famine therefore occurred in a society which had the wealth, the social attitudes and the experience to launch and organise a great philanthropic endeavour.

But the response to the crisis in the Highlands was unusually generous even by contemporary standards. By the end of 1847 the Central Board had at its disposal a massive £209,376 available for famine relief, probably the greatest single cash sum raised voluntarily in nineteenth century Scotland for the relief of distress. In 1846, for instance, the total amount paid out by the official Poor Law, *throughout* Scotland, was only £80,000 more than the funds available to the Central Board in the Highlands which were much greater than the amounts collected during periods of heavy unemployment and mass destitution in the towns. In Glasgow in 1816–17 nearly £10,000 was raised and distributed among 23,000 people; in 1826–7, £9,000 was contributed for relief. Even the sums collected during the great depression of 1841–2 in Paisley, which forced almost a quarter of the town's population on to relief schemes, did not match the resources of the Central Board during the potato famine and the General Relief Committee in Paisley finally disposed of £28,000 of charitable money.

Yet the official resources of the Highland relief fund were only part of the total volume and value of charitable resources which flowed into the north of Scotland in these years. Unrecorded, individual sums of cash were sent through private channels and distributed through the agency of ministers of the Free Church and the established church, and even more important was the arrival of relief in kind from the United States. In 1847, a series of vessels from Savannah, Charleston, New York and other ports in North America brought cargoes of wheat, rice and maize to help feed the hungry of the western Highlands. How is this unusual level of charitable response to be explained?

Three factors were probably important. First, the population of the Highlands probably indirectly gained from the great tragedy which engulfed the people of Ireland. The potato blight struck a year earlier there and very quickly produced serious social effects, so that by early 1847 the two disasters had become linked in charitable appeals. The British Association, for instance, which eventually raised the huge sum of £434,251 for relief, was established to bring succour to both Ireland and Scotland. Press reports also stressed that unless assistance was provided on a considerable scale the Highlanders would quickly suffer the same terrible fate as the Irish. So horrendous was the Irish tragedy that it achieved publicity on a world-wide scale and this also helped to awaken international interest in the Highland crisis. On 13 January 1847, Queen Victoria issued a personal letter of appeal on behalf of 'our brethren in many parts of this United Kingdom who are suffering extreme famine',[3] and this raised over £170,000 which, together with £263,000 collected under its own auspices, was distributed through the British Association. The total sum was divided in the proportion of five-sixths to Ireland and one-sixth to the Scottish Highlands. In the light of the great difference in the number seriously at risk and in danger of starvation in each society, it is patently clear that the population of the Highlands did rather well out of this distribution. The Edinburgh Section of the Central Board obtained £31,000 from the British Association, a sum which amounted to 26 per cent of all the funds at its disposal.

Secondly, the infant Free Church of Scotland was in an excellent position to both collect funds and guide them in appropriate directions as in its own right it represented an embryonic relief organisation which through its local parishes, synods and ministers could be activated to provide assistance and not surprisingly, therefore, as early as September 1848 it was the first agency in the field to gather funds. The Free Church had two advantages. A large number of its followers lived in the region where distress was most acute and it therefore had a powerful motivation to action. In addition, however, the Church also had a loyal following among middle-class congregations in the cities who could be expected to respond to the plight of their co-religionists in the north west. By the end of December 1846 the Free Church congregations in the Lowlands, after five successive Sunday collections, had already managed to raise over £10,400.

Third, the changed perception of Highland society which took place over the century between the Jacobite defeat at Culloden and the potato famine and was surveyed in chapter 6, also had a major impact on the collection of relief funds: 'Before 1745 the Highlanders had been despised as idle, predatory barbarians . . . but after 1746, when their distinct society crumbled so easily, they combined the romance of a primitive people with the charm of an endangered species'.[4] Between 1800 and 1846 a series of influences combined both to sentimentalise the Highlander and place the Highlands not simply in the consciousness of the middle and upper classes of Britain but also firmly on the world map. Scott's *Waverley Novels* and the heroic deeds of the Highland regiments captured the imagination of Europe. The most distinguished members of the Romantic Movement visited the southern Highlands and were both stunned and thrilled by their dramatic and picturesque scenery and the Highlanders were now represented in some quarters as 'a pure peasantry', noble rustics whose martial virtues had not been contaminated either by urban vices or mischievous radicalism. It was in this period, too, that the 'traditional' *Highland* culture, so recently despised, came to be regarded as the final remnant of ancient *Scottish* culture. By the 1830s, the sporting attractions of the Highlands were also coming to be highly regarded and their future role of providing outdoor recreation for the rich and titled was given even greater prominence when Queen Victoria herself decided to build her own castle at Balmoral on Deeside as a summer retreat.

Highland society therefore had a recognisable image, a renown and an appeal which was familiar across both Europe and America by the middle decades of the nineteenth century and it is, therefore, hardly surprising that there was a very lively international response to the requests for help which came after 1846. One basic reason why the relief fund for the Highlands raised so much more than similar efforts during industrial crises in the cities was that more money was collected for the victims of the potato famine *outside* Scotland as Scottish expatriates in Canada, India and the East Indies were very prominent and contributed a total of almost £25,000 for relief. The Celtic Society Ball in Edinburgh gathered £180. Edinburgh advocates and Writers to the Signet were well represented on the subscription lists, Highland regiments raised a total of £347, and collections in local parish churches produced substantial sums. Equally revealing, however, were the small amounts raised from working people: servants, Cramond House, £2; workmen at Cockpen, £2 7s; inmates of Crichton Institution, Dumfries (a lunatic asylum), £18; Dalkeith Colliery, £24; 'a few Scotchmen on the South-East Railway Company', £3. The Highland potato famine touched the hearts of all social classes.

The organisers of the relief funds were able to exploit public sympathy with considerable skill as they made their appeal to both the emotions and minds of potential subscribers. Highly emotive descriptions of the suffering poor of the Highlands were published in both newspapers and contemporary pamphlets, and the unprecedented nature of the calamity and its scale was constantly emphasised. Invariably the numbers affected by the potato failure were claimed to be between 400,000 and 600,000, and in the initial stages of the appeal at least both the Free Church and the Glasgow and Edinburgh Relief Committees persistently exaggerated the extent of the crisis. Letters to the Rev. Dr Norman MacLeod from Highland parish ministers in distressed districts were published which pleaded for aid and contained graphic descriptions of the ravages of hunger and disease in local communities, and a strong religious theme also ran through the campaign, with the disasters in both Ireland and the Highlands being depicted as the awful signs of God's wrath, 'The Chastisement of the Lord'. A National Day of Fasting was proclaimed by Queen Victoria and subscriptions to the relief funds were advertised as a necessary form of atonement to an angry Creator.

Much was made of the comparisons and contrasts with the crisis in Ireland. On the one hand, the Irish example was used to demonstrate the horrific consequences of famine on a poor, peasant population and vividly showed what might happen in the Highlands unless relief came swiftly and effectively. On the other hand, the 'virtuous' Highlanders were contrasted with the unregenerate Irish as a race who were far more deserving of assistance and the romantic associations of Highland society were fully exploited. The Scottish Highlanders, suggested one contemporary,

> instead of being rude and unprincipled depredators, were possessed of many accomplishments and virtues . . . and, in respect of poetry and music, and national literature, were equal, if not superior, as a community to any similar class of their fellow subjects.

He suggested that the people of the Highlands were not only brave and daring in war but also 'peaceful, patient and submissive' in the face of the great disaster which had overwhelmed them;[5] no mention was made of the increase in sheep stealing which was widely reported in the winter of 1846–7. In contrast, the Irish were 'unruly and turbulent' and did not have the same claim on the generous feelings of the philanthropic.

Such images, however, were unlikely in themselves to convince the hard-headed businessmen and professional classes of the cities of Britain who eventually not only contributed much to the relief funds but were among the dominant influences on the Central Board of Management for Highland Relief when it was formally constituted in February 1847. As late as December 1846, for instance, the Free Church approached the Lord Provost of Edinburgh to promote a joint church and civic effort to raise funds: 'Contrary to expectation they met with a somewhat cold reception. His Lordship seemed to think that the time for movement had not arrived; spoke of the necessity of complete statistics'. Again, from the earliest months of the crisis, The Scotsman, true to its Whig principles, systematically and scathingly criticised the 'Ossianic senti-mentality' which obscured the reality of the problem 'like a mist'.

The Free Church soon recognised the need for convincing information to support its claims and circulated a 'schedule of enquiries' to its parishes in the Highlands with detailed questions on the extent of food supply, crop failure, numbers at risk, and availability of employment, and the answers to these queries were then published in full. In addition, both the Church and the Central Board, which eventually took over its responsibilities, appealed to the dominant social philosophy of the Victorian middle classes and their hatred of the demoralising effects of gratuitous relief. From the very beginning of the operations of the Central Board in early 1847 it was established as a cardinal principle that relief should be given only in return for labour: 'The Local Committee shall hold it as a general rule, that work of some kind should be given in exchange for relief; and shall impress upon the people that food given is not a gratuitous gift, but is to be paid for in one way or another'.[6] Despite this commitment, however, the Board's regulation was persistently breached in the first year of its operations and these failures help to explain why even more uncompromising policies were eventually implemented in 1848 and thereafter.

III

During the Scottish harvest failures of the 1690s and again in 1782 and 1783 the state had been heavily involved in relief measures. 'Mercantilist' governments in the seventeenth century sought to regulate the economy in a variety of ways and intervention in times of dearth was an inevitable extension of general state functions in this period. It was also at a more practical level designed to minimise the dangers of political and social unrest which the threat of starvation or a rapid rise in the cost of meal might bring about, and thus between 1695 and 1699 the state introduced a series of measures designed to combat or alleviate the problems of food shortage. The duty-free import of victual was allowed and bounties were paid to encourage the meal trade. Government also moved against forestallers and regraters, introducing searches for hoards of corn held in private warehouses and directing burghal authorities to control prices. Again, almost a century later, in 1782–3, the government intervened by making funds available in the form of a grant of £10,000 for grain to be distributed by sheriffs and another sum to allow food to be sold 'at prime cost'. The relief supplies in most areas consisted of white peas, surplus naval stores which could be boiled into a heavy porridge. The year 1783 was accordingly long remembered in the Highlands as *bliadhna na peasrach*, the peasemeal year.

By the middle decades of the nineteenth century, however, the intellectual basis of this form of intervention had been destroyed and a new view of the role of the state had emerged. No government, of course, could entirely remove itself from the normal processes of civil and economic life, but the intellectual critique of the classical economists and the extraordinary growth in national wealth produced by industrialisation combined to bring about a new consensus: that an economy thrives best when left to the free play of market forces and any unnecessary interference with them is bound eventually to cause much more harm than good. This, then, was the conventional wisdom which governed the responses of the state to the potato famines in both Ireland and the western Highlands.

But government attitudes and the policies which were eventually put in place were far from simple. There was too much at stake and too serious a threat to the lives of thousands in the Highlands and millions in Ireland for the orthodoxies of political economy to be followed entirely to the letter. In Ireland, the state was quickly drawn into the administration of a huge famine relief operation and in the Highlands, too, government officials adhered to one fundamental line of policy throughout the crisis. This was expressed by Charles Trevelyan as early as September 1846: 'The people cannot, *under any circumstances*, be allowed to starve'.[7] Equally, however, there was a strong desire to limit involvement to the very minimum consistent with the saving of life and to evolve techniques of intervention which would do least damage to the functioning of the 'natural' economic system. There was also an eagerness to disengage government agencies from famine relief at the earliest possible opportunity.

This overall strategy was resolutely maintained despite the great stream of petitions which poured in from landlords, official bodies and the churches for increased government assistance in 1846 and 1847 to aid the distressed districts. Clearly, much influential opinion in Scotland was less concerned to preserve the purity of the axioms of political economy during a crisis of this magnitude than government ministers and their officials, but it is clear from the correspondence of the latter that the heavy claims made on the state during the first year of the Irish famine in 1845 and early 1846 had if anything hardened attitudes and made government even more reluctant to respond to requests for aid from the Highlands. There was a strong feeling that once intervention took place, at however modest a level, the sheer enormity of the problem would force further interference until the state was hopelessly embroiled in a disaster which it did not have the resources or expertise to handle and from which it might not be able to extricate itself without causing irreparable damage to the 'normal' social and economic fabric of northern Scotland. At the same time, however, there was the awareness of the responsibility to preserve life. Total detachment was never regarded as a serious option.

In September 1846, the very experienced relief officer, Commissary-General Sir Edward Pine Coffin (1784–1862), was sent to the Highlands to report on the extent of the potato failure and its social consequences. Coffin had seen active service during the Napoleonic Wars and had taken part in famine relief operations in China and Mexico, and more recently he had been responsible for the administration of relief at Limerick in the west of Ireland and had been knighted for his services there. In the same month as Coffin was ordered north, secret plans were also drafted to augment the food supply of the Highlands. Government had to be prepared to fulfil its fundamental responsibility of saving life but with as little damage to the market economy as possible. It was also necessary to avoid undue interference with the normal retail trade and a series of requests for immediate state support for a variety of famine relief measures were denied on the grounds that they would either involve the government in huge expense or distort the efficient operation of the 'natural' economic system.

Public works, such as the construction of a railway from Oban to Glasgow and the enlarging of the Crinan Canal, were suggested and another petition included the proposal that loans at low rates of interest should be made available to railway companies. Government assistance for a massive scheme of emigration was also sought. The Free Church tried to obtain Royal Navy vessels to help transport men from the Hebrides to the south as part of its scheme for encouraging temporary migration and placing Highlanders in the employment of Lowland railway construction companies. Finally, several proposals came from a number of quarters in Scotland that government should undertake an enquiry into the social and economic conditions of the Highlands in order to probe the reasons for the disaster which had overwhelmed its society. After due consideration, all these suggestions were rejected. For instance, much as they welcomed the Free Church scheme, government ministers and officials were loth to become involved as they feared that the state might be expected to maintain responsibility for the labourers when they arrived in the Lowlands and were alarmed above all that such an action would be deemed a gross interference in the workings of the southern labour market.

By the end of 1846 the main lines of the policy to be pursued by government during the potato famine had become clear. A prime element was the assertion of the landowner's obligation to provide for the subsistence of the people residing on his property as tenants; secondly, those who received assistance were either obliged to pay for it or carry out work of some kind in return; and finally, the role of government would be residual. Every effort was made to avoid any innovative measure which could be regarded as a precedent which might lead to an unacceptable extension of the field of government action.

Loans were indeed made available, but under *existing* legislation: the Drainage and Public Works Act and the measures which were already on the statute book to encourage fishing. Two government vessels were to be stationed as meal depots at Portree in Skye and Tobermory in Mull, but the grain made available from these shops, however, was only to be retailed for cash at 'market prices'. The decision to send storeships into the famine area created a dilemma for officials. The basic reason for establishing such an emergency grain supply was to avoid the danger of spiralling scarcity prices, but subsidised meal also manifestly offended against the canons of political economy. Government therefore tried to steer a middle course between necessary assistance on the one hand and on the other the grave danger of destroying the 'private trade' by forcing meal merchants out of business as demand concentrated on cheaper grain from the depot ships. The compromise was to charge purchases at the rates prevailing in the nearest large markets of Glasgow and Liverpool which, so the argument ran, would not be as vulnerable to massive price increases as the stricken districts of the north west. Finally, Royal Navy steamers would be made available to assist in the distribution of food and seed throughout the distressed areas.

The government function in the Highland famine was therefore that of a great enabling agency which left the direct administration of relief to others. Furthermore, official government involvement in the Highlands lasted for less than a year and the two storeships at Mull and Skye were withdrawn in August 1847. The role of the state in the Scottish famine was both more limited and transient than in the Irish crisis. This was noted at the time and various commentators complained bitterly that the turbulent Irish were receiving more aid than the 'peaceful' Highlanders. The reason, however, was probably the different scale and circumstances of the two crises. The regional focus of the Highland famine, the rapid response to the Lowland charities and the Free Church, both of whom were active in relief work by early 1847, the more energetic participation of Highland landowners and the buoyancy of the labour market for seasonal workers in the Lowlands, were all significant and also of importance was the fact that the grain trade was more highly developed in such areas as Sutherland, Wester Ross, Skye and several other of the Inner Hebrides than in the far west of Ireland. Relief officials estimated that most of these districts imported meal in 'normal' times and proprietors kept grain stores as did several large tenants. Fish merchants provided meal on credit and income from temporary migration was also used to buy grain from local meal merchants. There was therefore a commercial mechanism through which additional emergency supplies could flow as long as supply was maintained and cash resources remained available.

These factors not only allowed government to keep a relatively low profile but gave the state the opportunity to disengage itself, officially at least, from famine relief from the end of the summer of 1847. It must be stressed that it was as much these fortunate circumstances as ideological hostility to involvement as such that was crucial. Sir Charles Trevelyan at the Treasury informed Coffin that news was to be relayed promptly of any district which required immediate relief and steps would then have to be taken to provide it. The impression given throughout the correspondence of government officials is that in the last resort the free distribution of food might be necessary to preserve life, but every other option was to be exhausted before any such action was seriously contemplated.

Favourable circumstances ensured that in the event ideological commitment was not put fully to the test.

Between the autumn of 1846 and the summer of 1847, however, government was far from irrelevant to the relief effort. The provision of meal depots was important but not of critical significance. By August 1847, they had carried out sales to the value of £58,000; £22,000 was spent by the Free Church and then the Central Board, £12,000 by proprietors and £24,000 by consumers for their own use. Nevertheless, a much greater volume of meal was imported through established channels: of the 34,850 bolls of oatmeal imported into Tobermory between 1846 and 1850, only 14,027 were landed in 1846 and 1847, and not all of this came through the government depot ships. In addition, most landlords acquired their grain from the north-east ports in 1846 and 1847, because it was alleged that prices there were lower than those current in Glasgow and Liverpool which were the rates governing the sale price from the government ships. The main significance of the state's efforts lay rather in three other areas. First, the careful monitoring of landlord policies and the pressure brought to bear on inactive proprietors had significant effects. Second, in the long term, the relief works made possible under the Drainage Act introduced much employment to the distressed region and helped to complement the efforts of the Central Board as the Board's operations were mainly confined to the spring and summer months while drainage and land improvement schemes were usually concentrated in autumn and winter. Third, the availability of powerful naval steamships to convey grain and seed assisted in maintaining reliable communications throughout the Hebrides, ensuring that no community was prevented from receiving aid because of remoteness or the hazards of winter storms and this facility did help to save life in the Outer Hebrides in the winter of 1846–7.

IV

The formation of the Central Board of Management for Highland Relief in February 1847 gave the government the opportunity to surrender official responsibility for the distressed districts of the western Highlands. The Central Board was established to carry out the aims of the three existing relief committees, that of the Free Church, the Edinburgh Committee, founded at a public meeting on 18 December 1846, and the Glasgow Committee, formed on 6 January 1847, and almost certainly came about through government pressure. As early as 8 December 1846, Trevelyan had written to Sir Edward Pine Coffin, indicating that 'It is to be hoped the Free Kirk and the general subscription will come to our aid',[8] and detailed discussions took place in January and early

February 1847 between government officials and the Edinburgh Committee. Coffin, for instance, approvingly noted the appointment of William Skene, Secretary of the Edinburgh Committee, to the new position of Secretary of the Central Board and hoped for continued co-operation with him. Trevelyan praised the sound views of the leadership of the Edinburgh Committee and it will become clear later in this chapter that the most prominent members of the Edinburgh Committee shared the same principles about the general management of famine relief as government officials.

Not surprisingly, therefore, Trevelyan decided a mere twelve days after the first meeting of the new Central Board that '. . . we are to depend on the Edinburgh Committee and its affiliated bodies for carrying out the detail of relief in the cases not provided for by the exertions of the proprietors' and Skene and his colleagues were asked to prepare and submit a plan for the organisation of relief.[9] Yet while the charities were to actually administer the assistance, they were not to be allowed complete independence as their strategy was to be checked and vetted by Trevelyan and his colleagues. Government obviously hoped for the best of both worlds. The charitable organisation would bear the burden of responsibility and any adverse criticism of the relief operations; government meanwhile successfully extricated itself from a difficult situation but at the same time continued to exert considerable influence on an 'independent' body. It was an arrangement similar to that in the town of Paisley during the industrial depression of 1841–4 when relief was dispensed through a charity activated by government and administered by a civil servant, Edward Twistleton. In 1846–7, however, the problem in the Highlands was infinitely greater in scale; the charities had first emerged autonomously and then had their independence usurped by government. But the political and intellectual pressures in Paisley and the Highlands were identical: the distaste for intervention founded on a *laissez-faire* ideology but, at the same time, the compelling need to intervene to some extent because of the danger to life and the threat to stability caused by social crisis. Allowing the charities to run the operations, as long as they paid due attention to government views, allowed for a neat compromise between the constraints of political economy and the obligations of humanity.

It is plain that the government officials who were prominent in famine relief in 1846 and 1847 did not suddenly leave the centre of the stage at the end of that year. Trevelyan, Coffin and Sir John McNeill remained of vital significance throughout the period until the mid-1850s and all of them had a crucial effect on the policies adopted by the Central Board. Even when its operations came to an end in 1850, Trevelyan and McNeill retained a strong interest in the Highland problem, and it was McNeill's *Report to the Board of Supervision in Scotland* of 1851 which finally discredited charitable relief as a solution to Highland

malth's idea

destitution and made a powerful case for assisted emigration as the only remaining solution. McNeill's *Report* in turn led to the passage of the Emigration Advances Act which provided loans at low rates of interest to proprietors who wished to assist the emigration of the destitute population of their estates. Both McNeill and Trevelyan then became deeply involved in the formation and administration of the Highland and Island Emigration Society which between 1851 and 1856 supported the movement of almost 5,000 people to Australia. Trevelyan was the principal organising force in the Society and McNeill was his trusted Scottish lieutenant and so it is essential, therefore, to sketch in some of the background, attitudes and values of these men who were to have such a profound and enduring impact on the lives of the people of the western Highlands and islands during the whole of the potato famine and its immediate aftermath.

Sir John McNeill (1795–1883) was of Highland birth and ancestry. He was born at Colonsay, the third son of the laird of that island, John McNeill, studied medicine at Edinburgh University and between 1816 and 1835 saw service with the East India Company in both India and Persia. He later became a diplomat and was special envoy to the Shah of Persia until 1841. In 1845, he was appointed first chairman of the Board of Supervision of the Scottish Poor Law, a post which he held until 1868.

Charles Trevelyan (1807–86) had also served in the East Indies. He entered the employment of the East India Company service in 1826 as a writer, rising eventually to be assistant to Sir Charles Metcalfe, commissioner at Delhi. He was appointed Assistant Secretary to the Treasury in 1840, a position he held at the time of the potato famine but his official title, however, gives a false impression of his real authority. In essence, Trevelyan might be better described as the Permanent Head of the Treasury with a very considerable influence over policy as well as administration. He was also a member of the evangelical 'Clapham Sect', a man of intense religious beliefs, renowned for his iron integrity, strong principles and unswerving commitment to duty.

Both these men shared many similar attitudes to Highlanders and the Highland problem. Their values were firmly grounded in the teachings of classical political economy and the writings of Thomas Malthus, and they both gave tacit support to the contemporary individualist consensus: that poverty was a reflection of personal failure and economic success an achievement which merited moral approval. Misplaced charity would encourage the cancer of pauperism, the habit of the poor depending on the help of others rather than on their own efforts. Instead, McNeill stressed that rather than inflict such 'demoralisation', the charitable funds should be used to promote habits of industry and self-reliance. In other words, the crisis was to be used as an opportunity to teach the Highlands more industrious habits and bring about moral and material regeneration. It was a point of view which echoed the policies of James Loch, William Young and Patrick Sellar on the Sutherland estate a few decades before and derived from the same intellectual roots as their formulae for Highland improvement. Men like McNeill did not share the romantic notion of Highland society. To him the Highlanders to a very large extent had brought the calamity of the potato famine upon themselves.

Trevelyan was even more outspoken in his condemnation of the Highland population and viewed the inhabitants of the north as racially inferior. They were Celts exactly the same as the inferior Irish, and he believed that only through prolonged social and economic intercourse with Anglo-Saxon society might the indolent and feckless Celts become 'practical men'. He regarded himself as being the result of such a process of improvement because his family belonged to the class of reformed Cornish Celts who had benefited by close and long contact with Anglo-Saxon civilisation. The inferior and uncivilised Highlanders might also benefit if communications between their barbarous society and the rest of Britain were more fully developed. He believed also that both the Highland and Irish famines represented the judgement of God on an indolent people and that relief should not therefore be too lavish because the lazy had to learn their lesson so that eventually improvement could take place:

> Next to allowing the people to die of hunger, the greatest evil that could happen would be their being habituated to depend upon public charity. The object to be arrived at, therefore, is to prevent the assistance given from being productive in idleness and, if possible, to make it conducive to increased exertion.[10]

Both McNeill and Trevelyan regarded gratuitous relief as a curse, saw the Highland population as inadequate and shared the belief that they had to be taught a moral lesson in order to bring about the economic revolution which alone would permanently end destitution. The essential point was that the attitudes and values of the people had to be changed and this could only be accomplished by a stringent system of relief which would produce moral benefit rather than social harm. The careers of both men in India had brought into even sharper focus for them the gulf between civilised and uncivilised races. Indians, Irish and Highlanders were all inferior but could be raised to acceptable Anglo-Saxon standards by appropriate forms of education and social improvement. As the Central Board evolved different policies between 1847 and 1850 both Trevelyan and McNeill, and also Sir Edward Pine Coffin, were to exert a major influence on the strategy of relief. By using the Board as a front they were able to implement their grand plan for moral revolution without directly incurring the public opprobrium and criticism which it eventually provoked in many quarters.

The first relief organisation to make an impact on the distressed districts was the Free Church of Scotland. Eventually the Church's Destitution Committee raised more than £15,000 throughout Scotland and its schooner, *Breadalbane*, built to carry ministers around the Hebrides, was used to ship provisions into the region. The Free Church's Destitution Committee, though it lasted as an independent operation for only a few months from November 1846 to February 1847, attracted much widespread and deserved praise. It was the only agency active in the field at the most critical time; through its superb intelligence network of local congregations and ministers it was able to direct aid to the areas where destitution was most pressing and its activities were entirely free of any sectarian bias. Grateful thanks for help received came from such Catholic areas as Arisaig and Moidart. The Church also concentrated its relief measures on the cottars, the most vulnerable group by far and through its parish communities was able to organise *ad hoc* relief committees to dispense aid. It also had the advantage of having Charles Baird and Allan Fullarton of Glasgow, who had been prominent in the relief committees of 1836–7, as key members of its organising committee. Not the least of the Free Church's contribution was its highly imaginative plan to transport over 3,000 able-bodied men from the Highlands for work on the railway construction gangs of the Lowlands in 1846–7.

When the Central Board assumed overall control in February 1847, the responsibility for different regions of the Highlands was delegated to the Glasgow and Edinburgh Committees, or 'Sections' as they were now known. Each had considerable independence from the parent body. The Edinburgh Section eventually assumed responsibility for Skye, Wester Ross, the northern Isles and the eastern Highlands; the Glasgow Section was entrusted with Argyll, western Inverness, the Outer Hebrides and the Inner Hebrides, apart from Skye. The Central Board itself had 117 members, including the Moderators of the Church of Scotland, the Free Church and the Relief Church, the Provosts of all the major Scottish towns, several landowners, Bishop Murdoch of the Roman Catholic Church, and the Principals of Edinburgh and Glasgow Universities as 'extraordinary members'. The most significant characteristic of this group, however, was the presence of two government law officers, the Lord Advocate and the Solicitor General. The 'ordinary' members of each Section consisted mainly of the business and professional classes of Glasgow and Edinburgh and the occupations of twenty-seven of the forty-three Edinburgh members can be identified. Thirteen were lawyers or advocates, and there were five ministers, three merchants, three landowners, two doctors and an accountant. Of the thirty-five members of the Glasgow Section whose occupations can be traced, seventeen were merchants, eight were ministers and there were six landowners, two 'manufacturers', one professor and one accountant. These bodies were therefore dominated by the urban upper middle classes and their policies would be shaped by their principles and values.

The most important and influential figures, however, were the two organising secretaries. Charles Baird held the position in the Glasgow Section and William Skene in the Edinburgh Section. As noted earlier, Baird had played a key role in the relief operations of 1836–7 and had also published with Allan Fullarton a pamphlet in 1838 entitled *Remarks on the Evils at Present Affecting the Highlands and Islands of Scotland*, in which the authors acknowledged the Highlander's many virtues, his valour, his religious loyalties and his kindness to kinfolk and the poor. But they also stressed that the people of the western Highlands were feckless, guilty of overbreeding to an alarming extent, were too fond of 'ardent spirits' and were notoriously indolent. Like McNeill and Trevelyan, they saw the Highland population as 'uncivilised' and lacking the proper values which could only be instilled by education and closer communication with the world to the south and east. The Highland work cycle, which involved considerable effort in the spring, summer and autumn but less activity in the winter, was an inevitable result of the nature of subsistence agriculture, the pastoral economy, and the climatic patterns of the north west. But it was deeply offensive to these observers since it jarred with their own profound belief in the moral and material value of regular and disciplined toil. More than any other single factor the middle-class Victorian commitment to the work ethic played a central part in influencing the shaping of relief policies in the Highlands during the famine.

William Forbes Skene (1809–92), the powerful Secretary of the Edinburgh Section, was a member of the family of the Skenes of Rubislaw, lairds in Aberdeenshire. He had strong Highland connections and interests and was actually born in Knoydart, the property of MacDonnel of Glengarry, and lived for a time in the household of the Rev. MacKintosh MacKay, minister of Laggan in Inverness-shire. His interests in the Highlands were further stirred by his association with Sir Walter Scott. Indeed, it was on Scott's personal recommendation that he was able to obtain lodging with the Rev. MacKay. He trained as a lawyer, achieving the rank of Writer to the Signet in 1832, and became clerk of the bills in the bill chamber at the Court of Session, a position which he occupied until 1865.

From his earliest manhood, Skene developed a consuming interest in Highland society and quickly became a recognised expert on Celtic culture, publishing successively *The Highlanders in Scotland* (1837), an introduction to the Dean of Lismore's *Collection of Gaelic Poetry* (1862) and finally his three-volume *magnum opus*, *Celtic Scotland: a History of Ancient Alba* (1876–80).

He was eventually appointed Historiographer Royal for Scotland in 1881.

But Skene's regard for the traditional culture of the Highlands in the past did not dilute his moral disapproval of the habits and customs of the Highlanders of the nineteenth century. His attitude encapsulated the dualism which enabled some of the Scottish middle classes to sentimentalise the world of the 'old' Highlands and, at the same time, vigorously and stridently condemn the way of life of the contemporary inhabitants of the region. From 1847 to 1850 he was also in constant communication with Sir Charles Trevelyan, and from their letters it is clear that they both agreed about the 'inadequacy' of the Highlanders and the need thoroughly to reform their way of life and habits of work. This stereotyping of the population of the distressed districts as both morally and racially inferior was the essential precondition for the enactment of a series of extraordinary schemes of 'improvement' during the famine on a scale which would scarcely have been contemplated for the population of any other region of mainland Britain. To a significant extent, by the spring of 1847, the management of the relief funds had fallen under the control of the officers of the Central Board and a small group of government officials who shared similar views and were determined to use the opportunity of the great subsistence crisis to carry out a social revolution in northern Scotland.

In early 1847, however, all this lay in the future. The distribution of meal was managed initially under the Sections' Local Committees who were appointed from each district or parish from lists of names supplied by local clergymen. The aim was to do enough to prevent starvation, and so allowances were limited to 1½ lb of meal per adult male per day and ¾ lb per female, while children under twelve received ½ lb each. According to the rules of distribution, gratuitous relief was to be avoided and work extracted in return for meal and so all over the western Highlands and islands in the spring and summer of 1847, gangs of men, women and children could be seen labouring at 'public' works such as the repairing and building of walls and the construction of roads and quays. Independent contemporary observers acknowledged that in this period the Central Board's meal supplies saved many in the most distressed areas from malnutrition and even worse, and in spring 1847, the Glasgow Section alone dispatched 7,047 bolls of wheatmeal, 5,695 bolls of oatmeal, 1,980 bolls of peasemeal and 690 bolls of Indian corn. The Central Board also continued to implement the Free Church's policy of assisting the movement of able-bodied men and women to the labour market of the Lowlands.

When judged by the simple and vital criterion of how far it had saved life, the relief programme in the first half of 1847 had been remarkably successful. Mortality which had started to climb from the latter months of 1846, was quickly stabilised and reports of disease became fewer. But this achievement did not satisfy all contemporary opinion and, in particular, some sections of the press, several of the relief officers and their committees or government officials, who had been monitoring the actual implementation of the Central Board's policies at the local level with increasing concern. By the early summer of 1847 the critics were proclaiming that the Highlanders were being encouraged to depend upon 'pauperising' assistance rather than their own efforts. The 'labour test' was everywhere being disregarded, stories were recounted in the press of lavish distribution of meal, often to people who had no need of assistance, and 'evidence' was produced purporting to demonstrate that many were returning from work in the south to take advantage of the liberal provision of food in the north. It was also alleged, with much more foundation, that the works established as part of the 'labour test' were useless, added little of value to the local economy and were carried out in a slipshod manner. The *Final Report* of Sir Edward Pine Coffin, while praising the relief initiative, further added to the developing controversy by arguing that the people were actually better fed than in normal times during the spring and summer of 1847, traditionally the 'hungry' period of the year, and appeared to be much healthier as a result!

All these accusations caused much alarm among members of the Central Board. As early as June 1847, the Edinburgh Section recruited a half-pay Royal Naval officer, Captain Robert Eliot, to inspect the Local Committees and 'purify' them, and his report provided further evidence of broken regulations, liberal provision of relief and maladministration. Three further factors ensured that there would inevitably be radical changes in the relief system in 1848 and thereafter. First, it soon became obvious that the potato failure was likely to persist and destitution would have to be relieved for at least one further year. The opportunity had to be taken now to ensure a radical change in the way of life of the inhabitants of the Highlands so that they would be able to support themselves in the future. Second, adverse publicity provoked a vitriolic campaign in the pages of *The Scotsman* and in pamphlet literature against the 'lazy' Highlander who was taking advantage of the charity and benevolence of the 'industrious' Lowlander. Those who countered with evidence of the hard labour which went into eking out a living in the harsh climate and barren lands of the north went unheeded. *The Scotsman* condemned the 'rash enthusiasm about "the Highlanders"' which had promoted such indulgent philanthropy in the first place. The Central Board should now either use its remaining funds to help the inmates of the hospitals of the Scottish cities or in the next season of relief be as 'sparing and rigid to the utmost limits that common humanity will permit'.[11]

Even more remarkable were the views propounded by one John Bruce in *Letters on the Present Condition of the Highlands and Islands of Scotland* which were serialised in the newspapers and eventually published as a pamphlet. Bruce toured some of the distressed areas in early 1847, and this personal contact lent a spurious credibility to his opinions. One of the key assumptions throughout his lengthy diatribe was the familiar taunt of the racial inferiority of the Highlander: 'In the inns of the Highlands, the Saxon language – the language of civilisation – is keeping its own with the Celtic and the latter is happily doomed to be supplanted by the former'. It was now 'a fact that morally and intellectually the Highlanders are an inferior race to the Lowland Saxon' and their habits had to be changed by southern example, as the 'industrious' Lowlanders were supporting the 'idle and lazy' Highlanders through the agency of the Central Board. These views were not characteristic of all Lowland opinion, and journals such as the *North British Daily Mail*, the *Inverness Advertiser* and pamphleteers like Thomas Mulock and Donald Ross argued just as vehemently that the Highlands required even more liberal aid and support. However, by the autumn of 1847 the critics had the advantage of having the ear of some key officers in the Central Board itself.

Thirdly, and most decisively of all, government officials began to play a more direct role in influencing the strategy of relief. In early 1848, James Loch, the Duke of Sutherland's principal factor, described the close relationship which by that time had grown up between the government and the Edinburgh Section. He referred to it as the organisation which 'communicates with Sir John McNeill and the Government'.[12] From the start of its operations, the Central Board had worked closely with them and McNeill had several meetings with members of the Glasgow Section in the spring of 1847. He encouraged them to form a paid inspectorate to supervise relief, to publicise their proceedings in order to gain the confidence of their subscribers and to ensure that the labour test was implemented with full rigour. When the Glasgow officials voiced their concern that work schemes might benefit Highland proprietors he reassured them that in the circumstances this was inevitable and the only alternative to the moral disease of gratuitous relief. In addition, both McNeill and Sir Edward Pine Coffin were present at a private meeting of members of the Central Board with Charles Baird, William Skene and Captain Eliot when the key principles in the new system of relief for 1848 were decided. Indeed, it is plain that its main elements came not from the members of the Board but partly from a *Memorandum* written by Coffin himself in August 1847 and also subsequent correspondence from Trevelyan to William Skene, the Secretary of the Edinburgh Section. It was the two government officials who produced the detailed blueprint which was to direct the entire course of relief operations from early 1848 until they ceased in 1850.

The central component of this system was the idea of the 'destitution test' by which a pound of meal was given in exchange for a whole day's work. The theory was that only those truly in a condition of severe destitution would accept relief on these stringent terms. The meagre allowance provided but a bare subsistence and only those with no food resources of their own or who did not have the possibility of obtaining gainful employment would endure such a harsh regime for so little in order to avoid starvation. In one sense, it represented the ethic of the new English Poor Law carried to an extreme and imposed on the Highlands. In 1834, the revision of the English Poor Law organised relief under stricter conditions, whereby outdoor relief was to be abolished and all recipients were to be made to enter the workhouse. Conditions in the workhouse were made 'less eligible', i.e. more miserable, than the condition of the lowest-paid worker outside, and a rigorous workhouse test was applied to all applicants for relief in order to deter all but the really 'deserving'. The only differences between the 'workhouse test' and the 'destitution test' were that the latter was applied to outdoor relief and the pittance of one pound of meal per day was even less than the allowances dispensed under the New Poor Law.

But the idea did not come directly from the English experience alone. The allocation of one pound of meal a day was first used in Ireland in 1846 and 1847 and it was Sir Charles Trevelyan himself who pressed its advantages on the Central Board: 'In Ireland we found by the result of our experience which comprehended the feeding of upwards of three millions of persons for several months, that one pound of good meal properly cooked was amply sufficient for the support of an able-bodied person'. He also insisted that only by this bare subsistence could 'pauperism' be avoided: '. . . the pound of meal and the task of at least eight hours hard work is the best regime for this moral disease'.[13] Trevelyan also urged upon Skene the vital need for a paid inspectorate which would not favour the people or sympathise with them and could be relied upon to implement the test with full vigour. The idea of co-operation between the Central Board and local proprietors was also suggested. Out of this came the 'co-operative system' by which the Board and individual landlords shared the burden of relief but the work carried out was devoted to estate improvement and the development of roads. But Trevelyan, and to a lesser extent Coffin and McNeill, were not only the main sources of inspiration of the new system of relief. All new initiatives were also sent to London for personal approval by Trevelyan before they were implemented, and he also found time despite his many other responsibilities to write to the subordinate officials of the Board encouraging them in the resolute execution of the destitution test which he passionately believed was the only effective defence against supposed social and moral disintegration in the western Highlands. But government influence was not only confined to his enthusiastic supervision of the Board's efforts. The posts of paid inspectors required under the new system were filled by Royal Navy officers on half pay, who had had experience of government service during the relief operations in Ireland or who were previously employed by the Board of Supervision of the Scottish Poor Law. Thomas Mulock described them scathingly as 'heroes of the quarter deck, accustomed to rule by means of a boatswain's whistle, to effect at land what they had never tried at sea viz. to exact the *maximum* work for the *minimum* of food'.[14] All the officers were selected on the recommendations of McNeill and Trevelyan.

It is difficult to avoid the conclusion that the Central Board and, in particular, the Edinburgh Section had been virtually transformed by early 1848 into a quasi-government agency. Its principal policies were inspired by government officials who maintained a close supervision of the Board's activities, its relief inspectors were on leave of absence from government employment and the Board had become an organisation for the 'improvement' of the Highlands along the ideological lines defined by Trevelyan, McNeill and Coffin, in close cooperation with Skene, Baird and others. But the costs of the programme now to be executed were not borne by the state or by the ratepayers of the region but by those both at home and abroad who had contributed to the great Relief Fund of 1846 and 1847. It was an extraordinary outcome. But the influence of the government officials remained covert and little explicit reference to their role was made in the published reports and correspondence of the Central Board. Indeed, Skene's original correspondence with Trevelyan, held in the Scottish Record Office, is prefaced with the instruction in Skene's hand: 'Pray do not let these find their way into print'.

V

Relief was suspended in September 1847 in anticipation of the coming grain and potato harvests, as the intention was that even if a programme of relief was found to be necessary it would not commence again until the spring of 1848 as the people could be expected to survive on their own resources until then. But the continued failure of the potatoes and the fact that the southern labour market became depressed from the latter months of 1847 meant that the Central Board was forced to start the provision of relief again from January 1848. When it did so, however, the nature of the system had altered radically from that of 1847.

The Local Committees, long discredited for their lack of rigour, were replaced by 'a paid agency', an elaborate bureaucracy consisting, in the case of the Edinburgh Section, of an Inspector-General, one resident inspector in Skye and another in Wester Ross, and, below these, relief officers and work overseers. The Board acknowledged that this management structure was expensive but that it was necessary in order to secure the efficient application of the destitution test, the central element in the new system. Only staff unconnected with the relief districts were selected for this duty; officers with local contacts might be too sympathetic. The resident inspector in Skye was one Captain E. J. Fishbourne, a man who was enthusiastically committed to the moral value of the destitution test with an almost religious zeal and who justified it in terms of approved Christian doctrine. Trevelyan corresponded with him regularly in 1848, giving him all support and encouragement in his important task, and both were fond of quoting Biblical texts at one another. Trevelyan's favourites were, 'In the sweat of thy face shalt thou eat Bread' and 'If any provide not for his own, and especially for those of his own house, he hath denied the Faith *and is worse than an Infidel*' (underlined in original). Fishbourne replied with a quotation from St Paul: 'If any would not work, neither should he eat'.[15]

The allowance of one pound of meal per adult male was parsimonious even by the standards of other schemes established in Scotland to relieve distress. Relief works for destitute handloom weavers in Glasgow in 1819 paid 7s 6d per week for married men with three dependants, and in Paisley in 1841–2, men with similar responsibilities received 7s, single males 4s, and unmarried women 1s 9d. But the meagre pittance, reckoned by Trevelyan as only enough to sustain life, was not the only unusual aspect of the system imposed on the inhabitants of the western Highlands and islands after 1848. The aim was more to change the values and assumed moral weaknesses of the people than support them through a major subsistence crisis and relief officers were instructed to become 'the hardest taskmasters of and worst paymasters in the district'.[16] They had to select groups who were to be permitted to obtain relief through the destitution test with great care. The able-bodied were not 'primary objects' of relief if they were in a position to obtain employment, and this instruction explains why young single men and women and, eventually, married men with three or less children, were struck off the relief lists from early summer. It was assumed that the labour market in the south was by then sufficiently active to allow them to obtain work there. Again, the criterion of destitution was clearly spelt out: 'Parties who possess means of their own, or who have not consumed the produce of their ground or stock, or whose property is sufficient to enable them to render their credit available are not destitute until their means are exhausted'.[17] Those who were eligible for relief, if fit for outdoor work should be employed in the construction of roads, piers, fishing, enclosure of townships or improvement of land. The unfit worked at spinning, knitting and making fishing nets.

Children under twelve years of age would only receive meal if they attended school regularly because the Board viewed education as an important agency for curing the barbarous and lazy habits of the Highlanders. Special attention was devoted to the 'aged and infirm poor' who had been assisted by the Local Committees in 1847 but who ought to have depended on the official Poor Law. They were to be driven back on to the parish by an especially severe regime. Their allowances of meal were fixed in April 1848 'at the lowest possible scale' in Wester Ross of one half pound of meal per person per day, 'cautioning them that even this aid was irregular, and could only be continued for a short time, and as an interim measure'. Meal allowances for both the able-bodied and the infirm were issued once a fortnight in order to inculcate habits of prudence by teaching the poor to spread their means over an extended period rather than depend upon being fed on a daily basis. Labour books were kept by the overseers in which the hours of work of each recipient were recorded, the fortnight's allowance for each family was calculated and a ticket was then issued to the labourer which he presented to the local meal dealer for his supply. The work books were kept with great care and the correspondence of the Resident Inspectors shows plainly that the destitution test was resolutely put into effect by relief officers who saw it as their sacred duty to teach the people of their districts a moral lesson which they would never forget. The full enforcement of the test from early 1848 provoked anger and hostility in the distressed areas and widespread criticism from sections of the press, and Skene himself observed that opposition 'was almost universal'. The system which was imposed upon the people of the Highlands did not reflect any Lowland or middle-class consensus about the roots of the social problems of the north west or the steps that should be taken to remove them. The policy adopted from 1848 was agreed only by a small group and implemented with the tacit approval of members of the Central Board. The most scathing critic was Thomas Mulock, the editor of the *Inverness Advertiser*, who recognised Trevelyan's role in the whole affair: 'Sir Charles was invited to try his hand in starving the poor Highlanders according to the most approved doctrines of political economy . . . the Highlanders upon grounds of Catholic affinity, were to be starved after the Irish fashion'. Mulock poured scorn on 'the enlightened doctrines of the Economists' which were now used to justify inflicting further misery on a people already ravaged by famine.[18]

The response of the Highland population itself was inevitably hostile. The execution of the policies of the Central Board ensured that two utterly different value systems came into direct and open conflict. The inhabitants of the western Highlands practised subsistence husbandry and their patterns of work were determined by season and climate, the limitations of the land they cultivated and the seas which they fished. They laboured to gain a sufficiency of food, fuel and clothing and for their very basic needs, not to maximise income, and such scanty evidence as survives suggests that in years of scarcity they felt they had a right to be relieved by their landlords in return for rental payment in 'good' years. It was a kind of 'moral economy' totally at variance with the ideology of relief officers of the Central Board. Landlord assistance had been the pattern in earlier crises and was also common in the first year of the potato famine, but support from proprietors was not purely charitable. It was cheaper for a landowner, particularly a non-resident one, to give generously in an emergency rather than find his estate permanently rated for poor relief. By the 1840s, some communities apparently felt that the provision of assistance amounted not only to a moral but almost to a legal obligation. In Lewis, for instance, it was noted that the people were generally under an impression that the proprietor was bound in law to support them. When relief supplies were sent to the region in 1846, the distressed population also felt they had a justifiable right to 'the Committee meal' and to 'the public bounty' which had been collected for their benefit. 'The people had been led to imagine that it was an act of oppression, emanating from the proprietors, to require work as a condition of relief, and that the contributors to the fund never contemplated that work should be exacted'.[19] This attitude was anathema to the key members of the Central Board and their staff and provided unambiguous proof of the corrupt state of the people whom it was now their responsibility to lead to moral enlightenment.

The destitution test brought into even sharper focus the conflict between the expectations of the inhabitants of this peasant society and the ethos of zealots steeped in the orthodoxies of classical political economy. Skene recorded that 'A storm of local vituperation burst upon us for not giving enough'.[20] Local Free Church ministers, who had been in the vanguard of the relief effort in 1846, protested vigorously and Skene noted that the strength of the opposition was even affecting members of the Board itself. At the end of February he confided in Trevelyan that the principle of a bare subsistence for a full amount of labour was seriously threatened and that this would be disastrous because it was the core of the entire system. He sought Trevelyan's *public* support (which he declined to give) but found comfort in the determination of the Resident Inspectors who, despite hostility, were still carrying out their duties responsibly. To him the basic problem was that the critics did not comprehend what the Board was trying to achieve: the 'stringent nature of the test may appear harsh and unfeeling . . . yet we are consulting the best interests of the people in enforcing it and they will in time find their permanent advantage in what we are now doing'.[21]

Not surprisingly the weakened population of the distressed areas did not see it in these terms, and one critic called the test 'systematised starvation'.[22] There was considerable and vocal hostility in Skye and Wester Ross where meetings were held to petition for an increase in allowances and in Kilmuir and Snizort in Skye there was collective opposition to accepting relief under the terms of the test. In Kilmuir, only ten men out of a population of 1,740 were employed at road works in April 1848. The immediate result of the policy was a sharp decline in the numbers on the relief lists, a development which the Board's Resident Inspectors took as certain proof of the efficiency of the system. In Wester Ross, 67 per cent of the population received relief at the peak period in 1847; in 1848, the proportion on relief at the same time slumped to 18 per cent. In Skye, the comparable figures were 56 per cent of the population in 1847 and 22 per cent in 1848. Captain Rose reported from Wester Ross that the test had provoked 'so strong a feeling of opposition' that it was widely refused and this, he reported with satisfaction, was 'a very wholesome symptom'.[23] It was suggested that very few young able-bodied men and women would accept relief under the test and, in consequence, there had been a vast increase in the temporary migration of this group to the Lowlands, despite the contraction of opportunities for employment in the south as a result of the depression of 1848. During that year, at least, in the districts supervised by the Edinburgh Section, most of those relieved under the test were older men and women, the semi-infirm and children. Despite this, one-fifth of the population of Wester Ross and a quarter of the inhabitants of Skye were still forced to accept the destitution test at some point in 1848. It was striking confirmation of the fact that only the allowance dispensed by the Section's officials in return for eight hours of closely supervised physical effort stood between many and potential starvation.

The sufferings of the people of Strathaird in Skye were typical of the plight of the poorer communities. Many were sometimes unable to come to work because of poor nourishment and, in these cases, their allowances were always withheld while they were absent. Their 'payment' of one pound of meal per day compared with 'the ordinary allowance in Scotland for a working man' of 17 lb of meal or bread weekly together with milk and fish. At first the test works were situated four miles away from their homes, but later on they had to travel a distance of ten miles which meant rising normally at 4 a.m. The roads they were required to build, in the view of one observer, did not lead to any place of importance, and a pier which they were constructing and which might have been of some practical benefit was suddenly abandoned and eventually entirely destroyed by winter storms. The heads of families by the end of 1848 were close to despair, but the recurrent failure of the potatoes and the depressed condition of the market for temporary labour in the Lowlands in 1848 ensured that many more of the population of the western Highlands had to submit to the hated destitution test if they were to survive in 1849 and until the operations of the Central Board came to an end in 1850.

NOTES

1 *Extracts from Letters to the Rev. Dr. McLeod regarding the Famine and Destitution in the Highlands of Scotland*, Glasgow, 1847, p. 71.
2 T. Mulock, *The Western Highlands and Islands of Scotland Socially Considered*, Edinburgh, 1850, p. 160.
3 Sir Charles Trevelyan, *The Irish Crisis*, London, 1880, p. 85.
4 H. R. Trevor-Roper, 'The invention of tradition – the Highland tradition of Scotland' in E. Hobsbawm and T. Ranger, eds, *The Invention of Tradition*, Cambridge, 1983, p. 25.
5 W. J. Stewart, *Lectures on the Mountains*, London, 1860, p. 5.
6 *Reports of the General Assembly of the Free Church of Scotland regarding Highland Destitution*, Edinburgh, 1847, Second Statement of Free Church.
7 British Parliamentary Papers, LIII, 1847, *Relief Correspondence*, C. Trevelyan to Mr Horne, 20 September 1846. The phrase is italicised in the source.
8 *Ibid.*, Trevelyan to Coffin, 28 December 1846.
9 *Ibid.*, 17 February 1847.
10 Scottish Record Office, HD6/2, Treasury Correspondence, Trevelyan to Baird, 19 March 1847.
11 *The Scotsman*, 1 September 1847.
12 National Library of Scotland, Sutherland Estate Papers, Dep. 313/1176, J. Loch to Duke of Sutherland, 21 January 1848.
13 Scottish Record Office, HD7/46, Skene to Trevelyan, 2 March 1848.
14 Mulock, *Western Highlands and Islands*, p. 81.
15 Scottish Record Office, HD7/46, Trevelyan to Capt. Fishbourne, 24 January 1848.
16 T. M. Devine, *The Great Highland Famine*, Edinburgh, 1988, p. 133.
17 *Ibid.*, p. 133.
18 Mulock, *Western Highlands and Islands*, pp. 81–2.
19 Devine, *Highland Famine*, p. 136.
20 Scottish Record Office, HD7/47, Skene to Trevelyan, 21 February 1848.
21 *Ibid.*
22 Mulock, *Western Highlands and Islands*, p. 81.
23 Devine, *Highland Famine*, p. 137.

FURTHER READING

T. M. Devine, *The Great Highland Famine*, Edinburgh, 1988.
T. M. Devine, 'The landed class and the great Highland famine' in L. Leneman, ed., *Perspectives in Scottish Social History*, Aberdeen, 1988.
M. Gray, 'The Highland potato famine of the 1840s', *Economic History Review*, 2nd ser., VII, 1955.
J. Hunter, *The Making of the Crofting Community*, Edinburgh, 1976 , ch. 4.
C. Ó Gráda, *The Great Irish Famine*, London, 1989 (for comparative purposes).

12

A CENTURY OF EMIGRATION

Emigration has been a central feature of Highland history over the last three centuries and, for much of that period, the scale of outward movement was significantly greater than that from other areas of Scotland. Its origins were rooted in the dramatic and controversial changes in the region. Clearances, commercialisation, demographic pressures, famine, economic collapse and landlordism all had an impact on the emigration process though there is much debate among scholars about the precise and relative significance of these various influences. Even contemporaries were divided. In the nineteenth century some saw extensive emigration as a necessary cure for the evil of 'over-population', whereas others regarded such an analysis as wholly mistaken and based on a refusal to accept that the region's problems derived from economic difficulties rather than demographic forces. This chapter considers these and other issues.

I

Highlanders had left the Highlands for Europe, England and Ireland for centuries long before the 1700s. But specifically transatlantic emigration, involving large group numbers, dates from the eighteenth century and as early as the 1730s and 1740s outward movement from Argyll and other areas established Highland communities in North Carolina, Georgia and New York. However, the Seven Years War (1756–63) seems to have been something of a watershed. Although precise figures are difficult to obtain, current estimates, based on customs records, the contemporary press and government enquiry, clearly demonstrate a quite dramatic increase in emigration in the years between 1763 and the outbreak of the American War of Independence in 1775. I. C. C. Graham, who conducted a careful survey of the existing evidence, reckoned that 9,500

Highlanders left for North America between 1768 and 1775. Even this total, however, is almost certainly an underestimate because Graham did not take into account the significant number of emigrants of Highland origin who left from Lowland ports. In addition, customs administration in the north was weak and patchy and an unknown number of emigrants must have escaped the surveillance of local officials.

Even given these qualifications, however, the figure is still striking. The 9,500 Highlanders represented over 60 per cent of the estimated total Scottish exodus at this time of about 16,000, although the Highland region contained less than 40 per cent of the Scottish population. Not only was Highland emigration increasing, it was clearly doing so at a much faster pace than that of the rest of Scotland. Indeed, Bernard Bailyn's extensive analysis of *British* emigrants to North America in 1773–6 reveals that more left from the Highlands than from any other British region with the exception of the London area. An astonishing 18 per cent of all British emigrants in these years came from the Highlands and islands of Scotland, one of the most sparsely populated areas of the United Kingdom.

The great exodus of people then all but ceased during the American War. Reliable information on what happened thereafter is even more incomplete and ambiguous than before 1775, but estate papers and contemporary comment indicate that when emigration resumed it did so at a much slower pace and on a reduced scale. Even the serious subsistence crisis of 1782–3 did not produce a significant renewal of emigration and when outward movement became more substantial from c.1785 it still occurred at irregular intervals with great variation between localities. After the outbreak of war with France in 1793 emigration slowed to a trickle until the Peace of Amiens in 1801, but between 1801 and 1803 the scale of the exodus was again reminiscent of the high levels of emigration which occurred before the American War. Figures were quoted of a possible 20,000 Highlanders preparing to leave for the New World and careful enumerations by estate factors and local parish ministers suggested an actual emigration of between 3,000 and 4,000 departures from the Hebrides alone at this time. The magnitude of the planned emigration shook both Highland landowners and the government. The former were concerned about the loss of a labour force at a time of high profits for such labour-intensive activities as kelp and fishing, and the latter was equally sensitive to the haemorrhage of a population which had demonstrated its martial qualities in the imperial armies during both the American and Napoleonic Wars. The immediate consequence of their dual anxieties was the passing of the Passenger Vessels Act in 1803. Its purpose was overtly humanitarian but in reality was designed to increase the costs of the transatlantic voyage and so reduce the incentives to emigrate. The number of emigrants did fall drastically again after 1804 but this probably was as much to with the resumption of hostilities as well as the impact of the new legislation. Nevertheless, despite the Act, individual parties of Highlanders continued to leave their native land up to the wars in 1815, and the following table summarises the rough emigration estimates for the period 1700 to 1815.

Highland emigration, 1700–1815

Period	Estimated number of Highland emigrants to North America
1700–60	Below 3,000
1760–75	*c.* 10,000
1775–1801	2–3,000
1801–3	*c.* 5,000
1803–15	*c.* 3,000

War was a decisive influence on the cyclical pattern of emigration. The departures before 1775 were curtailed by the American War and those of the early 1790s were once again slowed down by the outbreak of conflict with revolutionary France. The chronology of Highland emigration before 1815 suggests that the internal forces making for outward movement were temporarily offset by the effects of hostilities. A clear illustration of this came in 1801 when a brief period of peace almost immediately precipitated a resurgence in high levels of emigration. War limited Highland emigration in several ways. Hostilities raised costs and interrupted sea transport, and by cutting the link with emigrant communities overseas for some years it inevitably delayed the renewal of vital connections. One reason why emigration declined in the 1780s was that the American War severed traditional ties with North Carolina and New York and it took time to establish or renew equally close relationships with the 'new' post-war migrant areas of Upper Canada, Prince Edward Island and Nova Scotia. In addition, the Highlands made a huge contribution to the British army and navy in both the great wars of the later eighteenth century and military service both at home and overseas can be seen as an alternative to emigration. The profits and prestige to be derived from raising family regiments from among the people of their estates encouraged some landlords to postpone the execution of the radical economic strategies which were promoting emigration. In three different properties in mainland Inverness-shire there was a temporary pause in eviction and dispossession in the 1790s as landowners in the district attempted to recruit the tenantry to their personal regiments.

The main outlines of the sequence of emigration from the Highlands in this period are not in dispute. But the reasons why so many people from this particular region of Scotland should seek to emigrate in such large numbers are far from clear. Certainly a new context for mass emigration from northern Scotland had emerged by the second half of the eighteenth century and the foundations of Highland communities in North Carolina, Georgia and New York from the 1730s created the basis for 'chain migration'. The commercial relationship between Scotland and North America was also revolutionised by the remarkable success of Glasgow in the tobacco trade from the 1730s. The American trades helped to provide the transport infrastructure for large-scale emigration from Scotland as most Highland communities were within relatively easy travelling distance of the Clyde ports and vessels were also often chartered from there by organised emigration parties. It was, for instance, the growing trade in Canadian timber to Scotland in the early nineteenth century which partially helped to offset the impact of the Passenger Vessels Act of 1803 on emigration. The British timber market's demand for Canadian lumber radically increased as a result of wartime needs. The timber trade required large vessels but these had low freights on the outward journey and the emigrant traffic to Upper Canada and the maritime provinces was therefore an effective means of utilising surplus capacity and cutting freight costs.

Highland society at all social levels had also become less insular by the later eighteenth century. Reference has already been made to the military service of Highlanders in the Seven Years War, the American Wars and the French Revolutionary War and recruitment on this scale must have accustomed Highland society to greater mobility. This was even more likely when government paid off officers and men in colonial land; these military settlements then provided a point of attraction to kinsfolk at home. A key element in this Highland emigration was the leadership given to many emigrant parties by gentlemen, or lesser gentry who had either obtained land in, or had become familiar with, the transatlantic colonies as a result of their service within the officer class of the British army.

All these influences facilitated mass emigration, but they could not in themselves cause it to happen. In the age before the steamship, transatlantic emigration was tantamount to virtually permanent exile. In addition, most of North America was still a wilderness: an alien land peopled by wild savages, still regarded by Europeans as hostile territory. Few embarked willingly on the long transatlantic voyage. In the search for causation, contemporary commentators and later scholars have addressed both the impact of conditions in the Highlands and the opportunities emerging in North America. Some argue that the increasing volume of emigration reflected the pressure of rising population which led, in turn, to an outflow of 'surplus' peasants and their families. This is a hypothesis which at first glance has much to commend it. Numbers did increase substantially in northern Scotland in the later eighteenth century, the Highland economy was indeed poor and underdeveloped and, in the long run, when the emigration of the Highland people is examined down to the middle decades of the eighteenth century, the Malthusian explanation does have real force. Population loss was inevitable because the regional economy proved utterly incapable over time of generating the necessary level of employment. However, the picture between 1760 and 1815 is considerably more complex and it is by no means certain that the demographic explanation is entirely satisfactory for that earlier period.

There are several problems. First, though numbers were increasing, economic activity was also expanding. There were indeed years of crisis, such as 1772–3, 1782–3, 1801–2, brought about by harvest failure and they did trigger emigration. In addition, the vast majority of the population continued to eke out an existence at, or only marginally above, subsistence level. Nevertheless, in these decades, there was also an increase in employment opportunities, especially in the western Highlands and islands from which most emigrants came, in kelp manufacture, fishing, illicit whisky-making, the seasonal migrant economy in the Lowlands and, above all, military service. Landlord correspondence in these years often reveals a fear of actual labour shortage on some estates, a concern which explains why most lairds were resolutely opposed to emigration from their properties.

Second, detailed investigation of the emigration process does not provide confirmation of the Malthusian hypothesis as this was no flight of the very poor or of the most vulnerable in Highland society. For a start, without some assistance sea migration would have been out of the reach of the impoverished. One historian reckons that '. . . even for indigent emigrants travelling to a wilderness totally supported by charity £10 was a minimum cost per adult . . .'.[1] With the majority of the landlord class firmly opposed in this period, the only evidence of substantial 'assisted' emigration was that which took place from South Uist. This was enthusiastically supported by the catholic church in Scotland because it feared protestant proselytism in this period, and partially explains why the roman catholic islands and the enclaves of the western mainland tended to generate more emigrants than many other areas.

The alternative for the poor and distressed was to obtain passage as indentured servants by which their travel costs were paid in advance in return for a period of bonded service in the colonies, but a remarkably small proportion of all Highland emigrants at this time seem to have travelled in this fashion. Only 150 of the nearly 3,000 Scots emigrants documented in the customs return for 1774–5 were indentured and most of these were Lowlanders. The vast majority of those who left the Highlands for North America in the period did so by using their own resources and belonged overwhelmingly to the tenant group, the middle rank in Highland society, those with some surplus above subsistence, with sufficient stock of cattle, sheep, goats and household goods which, when sold, could raise money for passage and resettlement for themselves and their kinsfolk. Examinations of passenger lists have shown that the movement was led by married tenant farmers of mature years, with their wives, children, other relatives, servants and subtenants. The emigration parties were well organised, usually had close links with established emigrant communities across the Atlantic, carried with them substantial sums of money and consisted of large numbers of related families from specific estates, communities or districts of the Highlands. This was not an exodus born of the stress of hunger and destitution. Rather it was a movement which involved a degree of calculation and a careful weighing of prospects on the part of social groups who were able to exert some choice and could exploit favourable circumstances. One reason for the surge in emigration in 1802–3 was that cattle prices peaked in these years, thus yielding good returns in the sale of stock to help defray the costs of transport and resettlement. At the same time, on some estates, tenants employed the threat of emigration as a means of thwarting or delaying landlord plans for the . reorganisation of their holdings. All this hardly suggests a people driven by the inexorable pressure of demographic forces from their native land.

J. M. Bumsted contends on the contrary that 'the Highlander chose to come to America of his own free will and usually to improve his situation rather than escape grinding depression. This emigration was one of rising expecta-tions'.[2] The explanation recognises the lure of cheap land and freedom from 'feudal' oppression that was clearly significant in promoting emigration. Infor-mation received by letter from earlier emigrants, the work of emigrant agents and reports from returning soldiers had created a powerful image of the New World as a land of opportunity. Bumsted's thesis is also consistent with our knowledge of the social composition of the emigrant parties. They were, as already seen, drawn predominantly from the 'middling' element in the society which apparently had the possibility of some freedom of choice. He also bases his argument on the assumption that there were no fundamental coercive or push forces which could reasonably account for emigration on this scale and suggests that the clearance of peasant communities in order to establish large sheep farms, a pivotal factor in post-1815 emigration, was not significant in the earlier period, especially in the western Highlands and islands from where most emigration occurred. This was then a so-called 'People's Clearance' rather than one directly inspired by landlord action.

Bumsted is correct to an extent in his dismissal of sheep clearances as a causal factor. They were limited before 1815 in most of the Outer and Inner Hebrides where the landed class was creating a labour-intensive economic structure based on kelp, fishing and military employment. But, even in this earlier period, the impact of commercial pastoralism on emigration should not be underestimated. Close direct links can be identified between sheep clearances and emigration in mainland Argyll, several parishes in mainland western Inverness, some parts of Sutherland and at least one estate in Skye. Moreover, it is clear that the relentless movement of the sheep frontier was spreading deep alarm and anxiety throughout the western Highlands and preparation for emigration was often a prudent precaution to avoid the expected future catastrophe of complete dispossession. Fear of clearance in the future may have been as potent a factor as actual eviction in promoting emigration.

The Bumsted thesis also does not fully take into account the extraordinary scale and intensity of the broader social and economic changes which were sweeping across the Highland region. Powerful forces of coercion were at work, quite apart from the familiar expansion of sheep-ranching. Long before the ill-fated '45 rebellion, commercialisation of the society was well under way, and the cattle trade, rent-commutation, landlord 'improving' strategies, seasonal migration and exploitation of slate and timber resources were all symptoms of this process. Only from the later 1760s, however, did the real magnitude of the changes become apparent because only then did southern markets for Highland produce start to expand on a revolutionary scale. In the next few years many landowners systematically subordinated their estates to the pursuit of profit. The methods varied from area to area but the general strategy was to extract more income from the land and to transform the traditional social structure in ways consistent with this new priority. Thus, as seen in chapter 3, the joint tenancy settlements or *bailtean* on many Hebridean estates were broken up and replaced by single croft holdings. This may not seem as dramatic a step as the imposition of sheep clearances, but it nevertheless represented a radical attack on the delicate social hierarchy of the old order as it involved both dispossession and social levelling. Often the allocation of the new crofts was designed to compel the people to depend more on the highly laborious manufacture of kelp to pay rental. The croft system posed a mortal threat to the middle tenantry whose larger holdings were likely to be divided to support the augmented labour force demanded for kelping and commercial fishing. Equally threatened were the tacksmen, or gentry of the clans, whose military role was now redundant and whose position of economic middlemen had no relevance in the new economic order, and this class contributed significantly to the leadership of many emigrant parties. Commercialisation also meant sharp increases in rental which produced acute pressures in such years of distress as 1772–3 when cattle prices were depressed but tenants needed to import more Lowland grain at higher prices. Rent inflation was characteristic of all of rural Scotland in these decades, but it almost certainly caused more stress among the population of the western Highlands because of the relative poverty and hostile climate of that region. There is also a good deal of evidence that rentals were often pushed up to much higher levels than increases in cattle prices justified.

Against this background of tumultuous and massive social change, the Highland emigrations of the period 1760 to 1815 cannot therefore be seen as 'voluntary'. The impact of large-scale sheep-farming had a significantly greater influence on the exodus, especially in certain districts, than some writers have claimed. Even more fundamentally, however, these waves of emigration, consisting mainly of small tenants with some means, were a reaction to the radical changes in land settlement, rentals and tenure which were destroying the old way of life. Dispossession, insecurities and commercial pressures were all intensifying as the new market economy was established. Protest was pointless, would inevitably have invited judicial and landlord retribution, and emigration was a much more rational choice for those who could afford it. Indeed the eighteenth century emigrations are a testimony to the organising capacities and enterprising qualities of the Gael. Highland peasant society often attracted bitter condemnation from Lowland 'improvers' for its supposed indolence, social inertia and conservatism, but the history of transatlantic emigration before 1815 is in conflict with this view. The organisation of large groups of emigrants and their successful transportation to the New World demonstrates initiative and skill of a high order. It was an exercise in self-help made possible by the communal and kin networks within the *bailtean* and parishes and the lines of connection which were rapidly established between particular districts in the western Highlands and areas of emigrant settlement in Canada. It was also achieved in the face of implacable landlord opposition, and there was an obvious irony here. Landlord pursuit of profit and the ensuing commercialisation of estates were the main reasons for the development of mass emigration in the first place.

II

After the end of the Napoleonic Wars the economic and demographic pressures on the population perceptibly increased. Down to the 1830s population in the crofting region continued to rise while sources of employment and income either stagnated or collapsed entirely, and the inevitable response to the crisis was a further acceleration in the expansion of sheep-farming which to many seemed the only hope of economic salvation for the future. Estates where pastoral husbandry had made only a limited impact started to turn more and more arable land over to sheep grazings and many parts of the Hebrides which had been relatively immune before 1815 were now subjected to clearance and dispossession. Large-scale removals became common in Harris, North Uist, Mull, parts of Lewis, South Uist and Skye throughout these decades. At the same time, the crofting population was confronted with falling prices and difficult markets for black cattle, their primary resource, while available land for grazing and wintering was reduced remorselessly by the advance of the big sheep farms.

While the pressures making for mass emigration continued to mount, a new ideological and political climate emerged in these decades which began to favour large-scale expatriation as a solution to the social crisis in the Highlands. The opinions against emigration which had formed the conventional wisdom of the eighteenth century did not change quickly or easily, but gradually by the 1830s, and to a significant degree inspired by the very serious subsistence crisis in the middle of that decade, a new consensus began to emerge. It came to be regarded as axiomatic that the Highlands were 'overpopulated' and that only through extensive migration could the problems of the area be alleviated. In 1841 a Select Committee of the House of Commons solemnly concluded that there was a population surplus in the crofting parishes of 45,000 to 60,000 people. Several years before, in 1827, the restrictions imposed by the Passengers Vessels Act of 1803 had been removed and this was striking confirmation of the transformation in political attitudes to Highland emigration. But the most significant change recurred in the hearts and minds of Highland proprietors. A large population had been vital to the labour-intensive crofting economy of the later eighteenth century with its complex mix of kelping, cattle-rearing and fishing activities. Commercial pastoralism, however, was land and capital intensive and required few workers, and so the people in areas where sheep-farming was triumphant were now deemed to be 'redundant' and their arable land coveted by the flockmasters for wintering ground.

It was not surprising therefore that some landowners became interested in 'assisted emigration' through which they could remove their impoverished tenants across the Atlantic by funding the transport and cancelling rent arrears. In 1826 McLean of Coll successfully shipped around 300 people from the island of Rhum to Canada and in an even more ambitious project Lord MacDonald assisted the emigration of about 1,300 people from his North Uist estate. For the most part the state was unwilling to play any major role in this process, despite the numerous petitions which were despatched to Whitehall by impecunious Highland lairds seeking government support, but in the later 1830s it did become more active. Partly due to the severity of the famine in 1836–7 and the pressing demand for labour in the Antipodean colonies, a scheme of assisted emigration from the western Highlands to Australia was established. Colonial land revenues were used to help cover emigration costs and from 1837 around 4,000 Highlanders were assisted in the long voyage to New South Wales.

Given the enormous stresses to which the Highlands were exposed in the post-war years and the new support of both elites and government for emigration, it is not surprising that the exodus of the people continued. Population which had been growing at an annual rate of 1.46 per annum in the crofting regions between 1811 and 1820, fell back to 0.51 from 1821 to 1830 and to −0.03 between 1831 and 1840. It is also the case that in the early 1840s, when Scottish emigration as a whole can be analysed for a brief period, an estimated two-fifths of all *Scottish* emigrants came from the western Highlands. The outward flow of people, therefore, was maintained. But perhaps the most remarkable aspect of the period from the end of the Napoleonic Wars to the 1840s is that many more did not go. There were profound local and regional differences in the incidence of emigration and some crofting parishes had experienced such significant levels of out-migration that they had already reached their maximum population levels by 1841. Of these sixty parishes, however, 63 per cent were on the western mainland and only 37 per cent in the islands. There were parishes and districts with very strong emigrant traditions alongside others with little or none.

There also seems to have been a change from the pre-1815 period in the nature of emigration. Although there is some evidence of a continuation of the large group forms of movement, most Highland emigrants in the 1820s and 1830s probably travelled in family units or small parties of around a dozen to two dozen people. Marianne McLean's work on western Inverness shows that only one major group emigrated from there to Glengarry in Ontario after 1815 and this was as a result of a government-sponsored experiment at the end of the war. More typical were those who emigrated singly or in small groups and had existing family ties in the emigrant settlements in Canada.

There was no simple relationship, therefore, between economic crisis, demographic pressure and levels of emigration. The basic problem was that sea migration involved considerable costs both of travel and resettlement. Government assisted only sporadically and very modestly, and a few landowners offered subsidised passages but they were still in a small minority. The transfer of Highland estates to new owners of immense wealth, a process charted in chapter 5, was under way but many hereditary lairds were virtually insolvent and incapable of supporting a major programme of assisted emigration. That ambitious initiative would, however, take place during the famine years. Doubtless help was available for those who had kin and friendship links with those who had gone to Canada in earlier years, but remittances from across the Atlantic could only support a fraction of those who might wish to go. For the most part, therefore, the people were thrown back on their own resources and these were being squeezed by poor cattle prices and the pressure on the land from sheep-farming and, in some townships, chronic subdivision of holdings added to the strains. The economic and social crisis, therefore, may well have increased the desire to seek a new life across the Atlantic. But by pushing more and more people towards the margins of subsistence, economic collapse also ensured that emigration was really not a serious option for the majority because they simply could not afford it, and the bulk of Highland emigrants of this period, like those before, possessed some modest means. The strong were able to leave, whereas the poor had no choice but to stay. But many among them did not even wish such a choice and still clung fiercely to the old way of life despite its increasing burdens and insecurities. The minister of one parish in Skye noted with exasperation that the people 'felt a blind and therefore a very powerful attach-ment to the rocks and glens amid which they were brought up – an almost invincible aversion to abandon them'.[3] Even grinding poverty did not easily or quickly dissolve these powerful social attitudes and only during harvest crises, such as 1816 and 1837/8, did the demand for emigration assistance pervade all social classes. But it was not answered to any significant extent until after the potatoes failed in 1846.

III

The emigrations of the period of the potato famine after 1846 were unprecedented in their scale and extent. Between 1846 and 1857 at least 16,533 people were assisted to emigrate to Canada and Australia and this figure does not include an unknown further number who were supported by the Colonial Land and Emigration Commission. Many more paid their own way or were helped by relatives in the colonies, but this group has left hardly any trace in the historical record and it is only, therefore, when the population figures for the western Highlands are considered that the full impact of the famine emigrations becomes apparent. The greatest loss was centred on Skye, Mull, Tiree, the Outer Hebrides and the mainland parishes of the Inner Sound (between Skye and the mainland). In these areas there was an enormous haemorrhage with some parishes losing between a third to a half of their population. This period was also a social watershed in Highland emigration as for the first time the poorest made up the bulk of the emigrant parties and many of those who were assisted by landlords were in a very destitute condition.

However, the failure of the potatoes did not lead to a mass exodus in the short term. In the first years of blight, in 1846 and 1847, emigration though increasing did not reach high levels and in fact during this period many proprietors seem to have been intent on controlling the crisis through providing relief to their small tenants in the way they had done in previous years of difficulty. At the same time the external relief effort, managed by the Central Board for Highland Destitution, helped to stabilise the situation and prevented mass starvation. However, the pressures making for increasing migration soon began to build up as the potato crop did not recover and blight continued to have an effect to a greater or lesser extent for several further years. In addition, the biological disaster was soon followed by economic collapse. Between 1848 and 1852 prices slumped for black cattle, commercial fishing was in difficulty and the industrial recession of the later 1840s reduced opportunities for Highland temporary migrants in the Lowland economy. The net effect of the intensity and long duration of the crisis was to weaken the grip of the people on the land. In many parishes there developed a desperate urge to flee the stricken region, even on the part of the cottars and poorer crofters who were traditionally the most reluctant to contemplate emigration.

The famine also willed the means to find a major programme of expatriation of the destitute, and to a significant extent this came from schemes of assisted emigration financed by Highland landowners. As chapter 5 demonstrated, there had been by now a transformation in the Hebridean landed class as insolvent estates had been acquired by a new breed, many of whom had made fortunes in commerce, finance and the professions. Unlike the old hereditary class they had the means to support and implement assisted emigration of the poor on a huge scale, and it is significant that about 94 per cent of those known to have received landlord assistance in these years were funded by the two ducal families of Argyll and Sutherland and by 'new' proprietors who had purchased their estates shortly before the famine. They included Sir James Matheson, wealthy East India merchant and owner of Lewis and John Gordon of Cluny, the richest commoner in Scotland and proprietor of South Uist and Barra.

Increasingly, the incentives to promote assisted emigration became stronger. The policy of relief provision was short-lived and from 1849 the strategy switched to one designed to export the poor and the destitute as the fear was that the entire burden of maintaining the stricken population would fall on the proprietors. Partly this was because the main organisation for famine relief, the Central Board, intimated its intention to terminate its activities in 1850, but it was also due to the rumours, widely circulating in the region, that the government was contemplating the introduction of 'an able-bodied Poor Law' as the best means of averting the persistent threat of starvation in the Highlands. This would give the destitute, who formed the majority on most Highland properties, the legal right to claim relief, and it would also establish the principle of compulsory rating and so threaten many proprietors with financial ruin. The mere suggestion of such legislation was enough to send tremors of alarm through the ranks of the landed classes. Some suspected that Sir John McNeill, chairman of the Board of Supervision of the Scottish Poor Law, who was conducting an enquiry into Highland destitution in 1851, was likely to report in favour of such a measure but, in the event, however, he advised a programme of assisted emigration as the solution to the problems of the region. Yet before government came to a decision on his report, several landlords had concluded that they were likely to be left with the final responsibility for maintaining the poor on their properties, whether through direct famine relief or through the indirect cost of contributing to a massive extension of the Poor Law. Their eagerness to support emigration derived ultimately from the fact that the costs of assisted passages were in the long run much lower than either of these alternatives.

There was also an obvious economic attraction in thinning the population. During the later 1840s the fall in cattle prices led to an increase in arrears among the small tenants who were also selling stock to buy meal, but in the same period sheep prices were buoyant and there was a sustained recovery from the more difficult market conditions of the 1820s and 1830s. Sheep-farming attracted not only because it yielded higher rentals than traditional cattle-rearing, but also because returns from a few flockmasters were also more secure and more easily collected than from most impoverished crofters. The expansion of sheep-ranching, clearance of small tenants and cottars and assisted emigration schemes all became integrated into coherent programmes of action on several Hebridean estates in this period.

The landlord role was often crucial in translating the social crisis into high levels of emigration and also in fashioning the composition and structure of the emigrant parties and this was not only because proprietors covered transport costs. They also often had a key influence in directly stimulating movement. There can be little doubt that crop failure and economic stress made more of the poor look to emigration, but in some districts even an ephemeral and slight improvement in conditions could quickly change enthusiasm for emigration assistance to an attitude of determined resistance. At the same time, there was considerable variation between estates in social attitudes to emigration, even in the very depths of the famine. In Knoydart, Lewis and North Uist, for example, the people remained at best reluctant and at worst stubbornly opposed to leaving.

Increasingly, therefore, compulsion became a core element in landlord policy and the most popular strategy was the serving of summonses of removal and presenting the bleak choice of dispossession alone *or* loss of land and emigration assistance. After 1848 the volume of summonses of removal granted to landlords in west Highland sheriff courts dramatically increased. One hundred and eighty-seven writs of removal were issued to the Matheson estate in Lewis alone between 1846 and 1848 and in the following three years this multiplied sixfold to 1,180. Yet it is important to note that clearance, or the threat of it, was only one of several weapons employed with great vigour to induce movement. These included the threat of confiscation of cattle stocks for those in rent arrears, prohibition of the right to cut peat supplies during the summer months for winter use and refusal to grant famine relief to those in distress. These techniques were applied with clinical care, and only the most destitute were normally offered support. As the Duke of Argyll noted in May 1851: 'I wish to send out those whom we would be obliged to feed if they stayed at home; to get rid of that class is *the object* (underlined in letter).[4] On his Tiree estate great discrimination was employed in order to remove 'all the poorest and those most likely to be a burden on the property '.[5] Much of the strategy was designed to rid estates of that 'redundant' population which now languished in destitution as a result of the decline in kelp manufacture and this explains why on arrival in Canada many were compared to the Irish because of their ragged appearance. A detailed study of estate policy on the island of Lewis reveals that the administration tried to clear crofting townships in the west which had relied on kelp production while, at the same time, maintaining and consolidating fishing communities on the east coast which had a better record of regular rent payment. Such selective use of emigration assistance ultimately depended on the application of threats, pressure and coercion and it was a policy which must have spread alarm and anxiety throughout the crofting region, even on estates where 'compulsory emigration' was not practised. The overall effect must have been to increase the fear of eviction and hence the attractions of leaving the Highlands forever.

It was probably this background which helps to explain the popularity of emigration to Australia in the 1850s organised by the Highland and Islands Emigration Society. The Society brought together funds from three sources – landlords, the Colonial Land and Emigration Commission and the famine relief committees, and from the landowner's point of view it offered exceedingly attractive terms. Because finance was now available from both government and philanthropic agencies, the contribution of the proprietors was cut dramatically and even landowners of modest means were able to participate as they could secure the passage of an adult to Australia for £1. They could also borrow from the state to assist emigration under the terms of the Emigration Advances Act of 1851. The leading figure in the Society was Sir Charles Trevelyan who had had a major influence on government relief policy during the potato famine in his position as Secretary to the Treasury. He reckoned that the organisation should seek to remove the 'surplus population' of 30,000 to 40,000 people to Australia and that this would be the 'final settlement' of the Highland problem.[6]

This was never achieved. In the first year of operation, 2,605 persons were despatched to Australia and by the time the Society wound up its affairs about 5,000 had emigrated under its auspices. But these numbers do not convey the full importance of its activities. Unlike earlier government-assisted schemes, the Society concentrated its efforts in subsidising the emigration of the very poorest class, precisely those whom landowners wished to remove. A significant number, for instance, were from semi-landless cottar families and many of those assisted were so destitute that they had to be issued with clothing before departure. In addition, the Society drew many of its emigrants from districts, such as Skye, where landlord-assisted schemes did not exist to any great extent. Its activities, therefore, significantly added to the flight of the Highland poor which played such a fundamental part of the emigration history of these decades.

NOTES

1 J. M. Bumsted, *The People's Clearance*, Edinburgh, 1982, p. 12.
2 *Ibid.*, p. 63.
3 *New Statistical Account*, Edinburgh, 1845, XIV, p. 349.
4 Inveraray Castle, Argyll Estate Papers, Bundle 1558, Duke of Argyll to ?, 5 May 1851.
5 *Ibid.*, Bundle 1805, John Campbell to Duke of Argyll, 17 May 1851.
6 Scottish Record Office, HD4/2, Trevelyan to Thomas Murdoch, 31 March 1852.

FURTHER READING

M. I. Adam's articles on eighteenth century Highland emigration in *Scottish Historical Review*, XIV, 1919; XVII, 1920.
B. Bailyn, *Voyagers to the West*, London, 1986.
J. M. Bumsted, *The People's Clearance*, Edinburgh, 1982.
T. M. Devine, *The Great Highland Famine*, Edinburgh, 1988, chs 8–11.
T. M. Devine, ed., *Scottish Emigration and Scottish Society*, Edinburgh, 1992.
M. W. Flinn, 'Malthus, emigration and potatoes in the Scottish north-west 1770–1870' in L. M. Cullen and T. C. Smout, eds, *Comparative Aspects of Scottish and Irish Economic and Social History, 1600–1900*, Edinburgh, 1977.
M. Gray, *Scots on the Move: Scots Migrants 1750–1914*, Dundee, 1990.
I. Levitt and C. Smout, *The State of the Scottish Working Class in 1843*, Edinburgh, 1979.
D. S. Macmillan, *Scotland and Australia, 1788–1850*, Oxford, 1967.
E. Richards, *A History of the Highland Clearances*, London, 1982 and 1985, 2 vols.

13

AFTER THE FAMINE

I

Between 1846 and the early 1850s the Highlands escaped a calamity on the Irish scale but at the expense of a huge increase in emigration and a profound weakening of the crofting economy. Contemporary observers in the 1850s were of the unanimous view that there had been a progressive deterioration in the condition of the people since the potatoes first failed in 1846. The shortage of potatoes in the first year of the blight forced the widespread slaughter of pigs and throughout the famine cattle were sold off to buy meal. In Creich, in Mull, half of the small tenants had sold most of their stock by 1851 and in Skeabost in Skye, thirty of the fifty-eight crofters paying 50s annual rent had no stock left while it was reported from Hangarry in North Uist and Uig in Lewis that stock had fallen by more than one half since 1846. Many of the small tenantry in Barra had been entirely stripped of their cattle, and of 230 rent-paying crofters in 1851 on the island, eighty had no stock left of any kind. Only 16 per cent of families had more than one cow, 56 per cent had no horses and 54 per cent no sheep. In parts of Wester Ross and the Outer Hebrides fishing boats had even been sold off.

All this represented either the substantial erosion or the entire destruction in the basic assets of the small tenant class, and the decline in stock numbers is especially significant. Traditionally, many were prepared to try to sell clothing rather than market an additional cow in times of difficulty and partly for this reason assisted emigrants to Canada were notoriously poorly clad on arrival. The Highland and Island Emigration Society also had often to issue clothing to those it supported. The crofters recognised that the selling of stock was a last and desperate resort, because to do so was to destroy their only capital resource and force their families into chronic and permanent destitution. What made their situation even more parlous was that the Highland cow tended to calve only once in every two years, and even this cycle was not always certain because of the poor feeding which cattle had received in some districts during the famine years. Market reports persistently described the under-nourished state of many Highland beasts when presented for sale at the Falkirk trysts and other fairs.

However, two major pressures often made the erosion of cattle stocks inevitable. First, there was the irresistible necessity to sell in order to buy meal, and this practice was widely reported in 1846 and the early months of 1847. There is also evidence that in 1848 and 1849, when the market for temporary migrants was depressed, small tenants were also compelled to sell cattle in many Highland districts. The meal trade had increased very significantly during the famine: 34,850 bolls of oatmeal were imported into Tobermory in Mull alone between 1846 and 1850, with annual imports rising from 6,184 bolls in 1846 to 8,459 in 1849. This was in addition to the provisions made available through the government stores in 1846–7. Much of this grain was paid for by earnings from work carried out under the Drainage Act and, even more significantly, from temporary migration and fishing, but it is highly likely that a proportion was purchased from funds from cattle sales which, given the depressed condition of the market until 1852, had to increase in volume to yield the same return obtained in the period before 1846. Secondly, landlord tolerance of rent arrears came to an end on some estates in 1848–9 and, in most of the remainder, after 1850. A reduction in arrears could only be achieved quickly by confiscation of some or all of the cattle stocks of the small tenantry.

But it would be wrong to conclude that the famine reduced all the crofting population to penury and ruin, as the evidence indicates a more complex picture. The cottars and those small tenants paying rental of £5 per annum or less suffered most and to some extent, indeed, the distinction between the two groups was an artificial one. Small tenants were often reduced to cottar status by eviction, confiscation of cattle stocks and the selling of their few belongings to buy meal. The kinship links between many cottars and small tenants ensured that both groups endured the same burden of destitution through the sharing of scanty food supplies. But the cottar class was undoubtedly squeezed more than any other. Many lost their potato ground as tenants expanded their grain acreage and they probably did not possess much in the way of savings or of the cattle and sheep stocks which gave the crofters some degree of resilience. More stringent controls over subdivision also threatened their position and even very existence on certain properties.

Yet many inhabitants in the western Highlands were more fortunate than the cottars or the poorest of the small tenants and the data assembled by Sir John McNeill in the course of his enquiry in 1851 reveal some quite fascinating patterns. The progressive decline in the numbers of cattle in individual holdings was widely noted, as was the selling of stock to buy meal. However, only exceptionally, in areas such as Barra, parts of Skye and some other localities, had cattle stocks entirely disappeared from a significant number of holdings. More typically, there was a reduction, but not a complete elimination, of the 'normal' number of beasts per holding. Again, there was considerable variation between districts, with the most serious depletions in stock confined to the Outer Hebrides (except Lewis, outside the parish of Uig and the Carloway district of Lochs), Skye, Mull and Coll. By and large, the numbers of cattle were not significantly below the traditional level in Wester Ross and the western parishes of Inverness-shire. These data may support Sir Edward Pine Coffin's conclusion that effective relief had come early enough in 1847 to ensure that most families did not have to sell all their cattle to survive, but it could also be, of course, that many beasts were in a half-starved condition and so were virtually unsaleable when market demand was poor.

In addition, McNeill found that the majority of communities which depended on white fishing and, to a lesser extent, those which relied on herring, had not been as adversely affected by the crisis as others. This is consistent with the evidence that rent payments from fishing townships were more regular and reliable during the famine and that several landlords endeavoured to preserve these communities while at the same time removing others by clearance and assisted emigration. It is equally clear that the middling crofters – those renting holdings at £5 to £20 per annum – were also partly protected from the worst effects of the great subsistence crisis. McNeill's evidence strongly suggests that the majority of this class managed to retain most of their stock and that they were only rarely threatened with insolvency.

Plainly, this might simply reflect the fact that they possessed more savings than their neighbours, but there were other reasons for their good fortune. Their larger holdings allowed them to diversify cropping more easily after the failure of the potatoes and it was mainly, though not exclusively, from the medium-sized crofts that the reports came of increasing grain cultivation and the sowing of turnips and cabbages after 1847. These holdings also gained considerably from the extension to cultivated acreage which resulted from the works carried out under the auspices of the Drainage Act. Again, their income did not depend solely on cattle sales as most small tenants had a few sheep on their crofts although, on the whole, these were probably used to provide wool for clothing for the family. Only the bigger men, however, sold sheep regularly in the market in significant numbers. The average price for sheep sold at market in 1851 varied between 7s and 9s depending on age, sex and breed, compared with over £2 per beast for marketable black cattle and even in the depressed demand conditions for cattle of the 1840s it still required the sale of six to eight sheep to equal the return from one cow. Because of this, only tenants with a fairly large

Grinding corn in Skye

sheep stock could take full advantage of the increase in wool and mutton prices which occurred during the famine years and the middling crofters in the western Highlands were often in this fortunate position. In Snizort (Skye) a tenant with an £8 holding had an average of eight sheep; in Sorne (Mull), a small tenant paying rental of £9 10s per annum had twenty sheep; in the township of Bernisdale (Skye) there were 105 cows and followers but 150 sheep in 1851. The view that the crofting class as a whole lost out as sheep prices rose and pastoral farms expanded must be qualified in the case of those who possessed bigger holdings than the majority of their fellows.

It could not be too much therefore to conclude that the famine, in the short term at least, may well have increased economic and social differentiation within the crofting community. Few crofters or cottars could remain entirely insulated from the crisis, but some survived better than others. The condition of the poorest deteriorated dramatically, and for a time in 1846 and 1847, and perhaps also in the early 1850s, they were directly exposed to the dangers of starvation and the threat of disease. On the other hand, the position of the less deprived middle ranks of the small tenantry and several of the fishing communities was consolidated both by their resilience during the crisis and by the landlord attempt to get rid of more marginal elements on their estates and then firmly control subdivision of holdings.

Indeed in an economic sense many west Highland and Hebridean estates probably emerged from the famine in a leaner and fitter economic condition than they had been before 1846. Since the end of the Napoleonic Wars the great problem for the landlord class had been the lingering presence of a population which had been rendered both destitute and 'redundant' by the terrible consequences of the economic recession of the 1820s and 1830s. This was a constant drain on resources and a menace to estate solvency because it often had to be fed out of landlord funds during the subsistence crises which occurred at regular intervals throughout these two decades. Chapter 12 showed, however, that though they often lived in grinding poverty, the small tenants and cottars only emigrated with great reluctance, and while the exodus of people did gather pace after the Napoleonic Wars, the movement was not yet on a sufficient scale to markedly reduce levels of destitution in all areas. This was especially so because commercial sheep-farming continued to absorb the sparse arable resources of the peasantry while controls on subdivision of holdings were either weak or non-existent in several districts. In a sense, then, the famine in some areas brutally solved the social problem which had long confronted west Highland landowners. It massively accelerated emigration, not because proprietors cleared their estates, though eviction gave considerable impetus to the movement in some areas, but because the sheer length and intensity of the crisis, for a time at least, weakened the grip of the people on the land. The fears of a potential catastrophe also allowed some proprietors to behave in ways which showed little concern for the social and human costs of their actions, but they were tolerated for a time because the alternatives to such harsh corrective action seemed likely to have even more appalling consequences. This was indeed the application of drastic surgery to the chronic problems of the western highlands.

The landed classes exploited their opportunity with great skill and assisted emigration, in particular, was carried out in a meticulous and selective fashion. There seems to have been a preference in favour of retaining communities which derived most of their income and employment from the sea rather than the land. Crofting townships which had grown up to service the labour needs of the kelp manufacture were especially vulnerable to clearance and consolidation. The result must have been something akin to 'the survival of the fittest', the phrase used by the Duke of Argyll himself when describing the social revolution which he put into effect on the island of Tiree, as whenever possible the very poorest were shaken out of the tenant structure and the more reliable rent payers were retained. Between 1849 and 1854 a series of rigorous surveys was conducted on a number of west highland estates which were designed to separate the weak from the strong in the tenant hierarchy.

Sometimes fundamental changes occurred, such as on the island of Tiree, where the very poor were 'emigrated' and a new structure of bigger crofts and consolidated holdings built up. But such a dramatic transformation was unusual. The more typical pattern appears to have been a major displacement of the cottar class, a marginal reduction in the number of small tenancies, a net increase in the size of the larger pastoral farms and much more effective control of subdivision. On the MacDonald estates in Skye, the number of small tenancies only fell by six 6 per cent between 1846 and 1858, though this apparent continuity probably conceals a considerable turnover in tenant families within the overall structure. In the two western parishes of Sutherland which were most affected by the famine, small tenancies fell by 11 per cent and 31 per cent between 1846 and 1855. Some of this, though, must have been due to redistribution of tenancies within the estate as, by the early 1880s, the *total* number and size of crofts in Sutherland as a whole had hardly changed since 1846. On the Riddell estate in Ardnamurchan, where small tenants paid 54 per cent of the rental in 1851, '. . . the tendency . . . has been to reduce the number of small holdings, several farms of that class are now under sheep'.[1] There was a similar pattern in Barra and South Uist where, in the later 1840s, '. . . there had been many changes from crofts to grazings of late'.[2] Again in Strathaird in Skye, emigration and clearance led to the removal of eight crofting townships and the conversion of their lands to sheep runs.

Sheep-farming was being extended generally throughout the region, but only on a major scale in parts of the Outer Hebrides because in most other areas of the Highlands it was already dominant before 1846. The clearances and emigrations of the famine speeded up the invasion of these last bastions of the crofting population by the Cheviot and the Blackface. By the 1860s the sheep frontier had reached its limit and began to recede from that point in the latter part of the same decade as profits stagnated and deer forests held out even more opportunity for commercial gain. In the meantime, however, the extension of sheep pastures left more proprietors poised to exploit the steep increase in the price of mutton and wool which had started in the later 1840s but advanced even more in the following decade. During the famine years the average annual price of Cheviot sheep varied from 16s to 22s. By the mid-1860s, however, the average had climbed to 26s and 27s.

The experience of the famine also made proprietors more resolved to control subdivision. On many estates cottars were eradicated and formed a considerable proportion of the assisted emigration parties of the 1840s and 1850s. The fall in the number of cottars during the famine gave some owners both the incentive and opportunity to ensure that the problem associated with such a large depressed underclass would not emerge again on the same scale and certainly it is known that successful action to control subdivision was already taking place on some properties, especially along the western mainland, *before* the famine. This probably helps to explain why several parishes in that region had already reached their peak populations by the census of 1841. Again, there are indications that in most areas of the Outer Hebrides *after* the famine, regulations against subdivision were not always implemented as effectively as elsewhere. Nevertheless, for the remainder of the crofting region, there is abundant literary evidence that opposition to subdivision was not only more widespread after the 1850s but that the mechanism for regulating subletting had become more efficient. The result was that by the 1880s, along the west coast north of Ardnamurchan, in Mull and in other islands of the Inner Hebrides, though not in Skye or in the Long Island, the cottar class was disappearing rapidly or had vanished entirely from the social structure. The fear of the burdens they might inflict on the poor rates, the memory of the famine, and the assumption that the proliferation of poor cottar families had been a principal and powerful cause of grievous destitution combined to harden opposition to them. These influences ensured that subtenancy was often crushed whatever the human costs and it was yet another sign of the radical change in landlord policy which had taken place since the early nineteenth century. The boom in labour-intensive activities encouraged fragmentation of holdings to c.1820; their collapse or stagnation thereafter ensured a trend back towards consolidation which grew stronger during and after the great subsistence crisis.

By the later 1850s mass eviction had virtually come to an end, but prohibition of subdivision proceeded in a less dramatic but equally effective fashion. In theoretical terms, the control of subletting implied that no additional or separate households could be created within a single tenancy and only one member of a tenant or cottar family was permitted to set up home after marriage on the holding. Even that could only be done by sharing the father's house until he died. In practice, however, controls were even more stringent than this and were often designed to reduce rather than simply regulate the numbers of households. As one observer put it, 'landlords . . . *weed out* families by twos or threes . . . an absolute veto was placed upon marriage . . . when a young man is guilty of that he may look for a summons of removal'.[3]

These were not the exaggerated claims of an over-enthusiastic pamphleteer. Duncan Darroch, proprietor of the Torridon estate in Wester Ross, admitted to the government's Napier Commission in the early 1880s that the regulations which prevailed on his property meant that when the young emigrated the elderly generally went on the poor roll; as they died the cottages were taken down. In Arisaig it was alleged that any member of a family who reached the age of twenty-one had to seek accommodation elsewhere unless allowed to remain with the written sanction of the proprietor. There had in the past been a good deal of subdivision of crofts on some parts of the Lochaber estate of Cameron of Lochiel but by the later 1840s, however, these practices were outlawed:

> The present proprietor is enlarging rather than subdividing, and his regulations against the increase of population are of the most stringent and Malthusian character. Two families are strictly prohibited from living upon one croft. If one of a family marries, he must leave the croft; and a case has even been brought under my notice, in which the only son of a widow, who is in joint possession of a croft with his mother, has been told that if he marries he will be compelled to leave the estate. Severe penalties are also threatened against the keeping of lodgers. The unlucky crofter who takes a friend under his roof, without first obtaining the consent of Lochiel, must pay for the first offence a fine of £1; and, for the second, shall be removed from the estate.[4]

There is ample evidence in the Lochiel papers in Achnacarry Castle that summonses of removal were issued to any crofters who infringed these regulations.

In Ardnamurchan and Mull, landlords not only restricted subletting but also pulled down cottages on the death of the occupants in order to cause 'a thinning of numbers'. On the Duke of Argyll's estate in Mull the regulations against subdivision were also rigorously enforced, and by the 1830s the older tradition of subletting to kinfolk had disappeared. Instead, the children of tenants had no alternative but to migrate: at Glensheil, regulations against subletting were regarded as the main reason for the reduction in marriages and attempts to limit subdivision on the MacDonald estates in Skye had begun before the famine but were only partially effective. From the 1850s, however, it became the rule that subdivision of lands by crofters was not acceptable. Eldest sons were informed that they alone had the right to succeed to the croft held by their father and it therefore was in their interest to prevent the holding from being divided among other members of the family.

The results of these policies can be seen in the changing balance between rent-paying tenants and cottars which had taken place by the early 1880s. The Napier Commission in the 1880s selected a number of localities for special study as representative of the crofting region as a whole, and these included the parishes of Farr in Sutherland, Uig in Lewis, the districts of Duirnish and Waternish in Skye and the islands of South Uist and Benbecula, where in all 3,226 families lived in the early 1880s. Of these only 21 per cent were classed as 'landless' cottars and squatters whereas in the 1840s, by contrast, subtenants of various types formed as much as one half and more of the total population of Skye and parts of the Long Island. The Napier Commission figure, indeed, is biased towards districts which still contained unusually large numbers of cottars by the 1880s. Of the six districts from which their calculations derived, three (Uig, South Uist and Benbecula) were located in the Outer Hebrides where controls over subdivision were more lax than elsewhere and the 'average' depletion of the cottar class elsewhere in the western Highlands must therefore have been much greater than these figures suggest. Not least, then, of the long-term effects of the famine was a sizeable reduction in the relative size of the most impoverished classes in the Highlands. This had significant implications not simply for the overall material standards of the society but for an understanding of the forces which compelled heavy rates of migration from it. Where controls on subletting were lax, such as in Lewis and South Uist, the rate of permanent migration was relatively slow. Elsewhere, the virtual prohibition of subdivision meant that most of the new generation had to leave the land.

II

It was in early 1856, after a full decade of misery, that the first optimistic reports of recovery began to appear about Highland conditions in the Scottish press. In that year the *Inverness Advertiser* described how more people were at work in the south and east and, more significantly, that the potato crop was more productive. But the potato never again recovered the dominance in the Highland diet which it had attained in the decades before 1846 and there is abundant literary evidence by the 1870s of altered dietary habits in the region. Consumption of imported meal increased markedly and so significant was this that it became common practice to feed the indigenous grain crop and part of the potato crop to the cattle to sustain them during the winter months while reserving imported meal for human consumption. There was an equally important expansion in the purchase of tea, sugar, jam and tobacco. Until the 1850s these articles were rare and expensive luxuries, but by the 1880s tea drinking had become universal in the crofting districts and a familiar part of the way of life.

These alterations in diet were the most obvious manifestations of more fundamental changes in the nature of crofting society in the aftermath of the famine. To some extent, the declining significance of the potato may have reflected the relaxation of population pressure in some districts as emigration persisted and the ranks of the cottar class were thinned in most localities outside the Long Island. But the new dietary patterns were also to be found in the Outer Hebrides where the old problems of population congestion and land hunger remained, and the more varied diet, in fact, was simply one part of a wider and deeper social transition which affected *all* areas. In the 1870s and 1880s the majority of the population of the western Highlands became less dependent on the land for survival and even more reliant on the two sources of income and employment, fishing and temporary migration, which had proved most resilient during the famine itself. They entered more fully into the cash economy, selling their labour for cash wages and buying more of the necessities of life with their earnings rather than producing these themselves.

Manufactured clothes and shoes, 'shop produce' as they were known in the region, steadily replaced the home-made varieties in the two generations after the famine. A new mechanism of credit facilitated these developments. Shopkeepers, merchants and fish curers supplied credit on which meal and clothes were bought until seasonal earnings from fishing and temporary migration became available. The running accounts were then partly paid off on the basis of these returns but more often than not the debts persisted from year to year. In Lewis, for instance, the fishing crews purchased on credit in the curers' shops the meal, clothing and other necessities required for their families. Settlement took place at the end of the season; fishermen were credited with the price of fish delivered by them to the curers and were debited with the price of their purchases.

The entire structure depended ultimately on five factors: the recovery of the prices gained for Highland black cattle; a steep fall in world grain prices in the 1870s and 1880s; a continued expansion in steam navigation in the western

Highlands; the growth of the indigenous fishing industry; and a further increase in the scale of temporary migration and casual employment. These particular influences need also to be viewed against the longer perspective of the decisive change in the economic circumstances of the west Highland population which took place from the later 1850s and continued into the 1860s and 1870s. The period from the end of the Napoleonic Wars to the potato famine had been one of contracting income and falling employment opportunities. The three decades after the crisis saw a significant recovery in both earnings and jobs which was not wholly offset by either rising costs or new demographic pressures. Even given the important qualifications which will be entered below when living standards are considered, there had been a relative improvement in circumstances.

Price trends, between the 1850s and 1870s, were to the advantage of the people in the crofting region and this was a dramatic reversal of the pattern before 1846. Cattle prices continued the recovery which had begun in 1852 and, crofters' stirks in Lewis selling at 30s to £2 in 1854 fetched £4 to £5 in 1883. Those small tenants who possessed sheep stocks gained from the upward swing in prices which lasted until the late 1860s, and the fact that they were much better fed on grain and potatoes during the winter months added to the marketability of cattle. The principal aim was now one of maximising the potential of stock not simply in the traditional manner to pay rent but as a source of the funds employed to purchase meal and other commodities.

A further expansion in sea transport facilitated both cattle and sheep exports and grain imports. In the early 1850s a single small steamer plied the route between the Clyde and Portree once a fortnight, whereas three decades later two larger vessels sailed to Skye and Lewis every week and a further three visited Barra and North and South Uist. These developments in communications were both cause and effect of the changing way of life in the region and the basis of the close involvement of the people in the money economy. Above all, they allowed the population of more areas to take full advantage of the sustained fall in world grain prices which took place after the opening up of the interior areas of North America by railroad and the new steamship connections established with purchasing countries in Europe. In the early 1840s meal imported from the Clyde sold at an average of £2 2s per boll in the Outer Hebrides; by the 1880s, average prices were close to 16s per boll. It was the enormous decline in costs which encouraged the practice of feeding cattle on grain produced at home and allowed earnings from cattle sales and other activities to be devoted to the purchase of cheap meal from outside.

Pivotal to the whole system of increased trade, credit and money transactions was a vast expansion in seasonal employment opportunities, and the

Late nineteenth-century croft house in Skye

A life of hard toil

S.S. Dunara Castle at Loch Maddy, North Uist

West Bay, Portree, Skye

indigenous white and herring fisheries of the Outer Hebrides achieved a new level of activity and prosperity. Fishing stations were set up at Castlebay, Lochboisdale and Lochmaddy and the number of fish curers increased from seven in 1853 to fifty in 1880. In the early 1850s about 300 small boats were active; three decades later around 600. The organisation and capitalisation of the industry were dominated by men from the east coast but the Hebrideans gained from the new opportunities for seasonal employment, and the developing steamer services and the injection of capital from the east had given the winter white fishery in particular a fresh and vigorous stimulus. Casual jobs as stalkers and ghillies were also available on the sporting estates and in the labour squads needed to build the infrastructure of roads and lodges required by the booming recreation economy. There were seasonal opportunities, too, in sheep smearing which involved working a mixture of butter, tar and grease into the fleece to afford protection against vermin:

> Since one man could only smear about twenty sheep a day and since a quarter of a million were annually smeared in Inverness-shire alone, labour was obviously much in demand . . . During the 1860s and 1870s the wages paid for casual labour of this type rose steadily and more or less doubled between 1850 and 1880.[5]

Taking home peats in South Uist

Finally, the expansion in temporary migration which had begun during the famine was sustained after it. Virtually all sectors, agricultural work in the Lowlands, domestic service in the cities, the merchant marine, and general labouring (such as in the gasworks of the larger towns), produced more opportunities for Highland temporary migrants than before. Because of this, as shown in chapter 10, 'seasonal' migration more often became 'temporary' movement with absences extending not simply for a few weeks or months but for the greater part of a year or even longer. The seasonality of different work peaks made it possible to dovetail different tasks outside the Highlands and at the same time alternate labour in the crofting region with work opportunities elsewhere. The classical example of the latter cycle was the interrelationship between the winter white fishery in the Minch, the spring herring fishery in the same waters and the east coast herring fishery during the summer months. This last was the most dynamic sector and the source of a great stream of income which percolated the entire Inner and Outer Hebrides in the 1860s and 1870s. From 1835 to 1854 the annual average cure in Aberdeenshire and Banffshire increased moderately from 428,343 to 495,879 barrels. In the 1860s and 1870s, however, the industry boom really took off and the average cure rose from 602,375 barrels between 1865 and 1874 to 902,665 in the period 1875 to 1884. An increased field of employment opened up for the population of the western Highlands and islands and it was estimated that 30,000 men and women came in a great annual migration to the fishing ports up and down the east coast from the Gaelic-speaking areas of the far west. From Lewis alone 5,000 were involved, or about one in five of the island's population and other parts of the Hebrides with only limited connections with the east coast before the 1850s now also produced many migrants. About 500 came from Harris and it was reckoned that most of the young men of Barra also served on the east coast boats.

None the less the extent of material amelioration should be kept in perspective and the majority of the inhabitants of the region continued to endure an existence of poverty and insecurity after 1860. Despite relative improvement, life was still precarious and could easily degenerate into destitution again if any of the fragile supports of the population temporarily crumbled. Between 1856 and 1890 there was a series of bad seasons which recalled some of the worst years of the potato blight, and conditions in 1864 were briefly reminiscent of the tragic days of the 1840s. On the Duke of Argyll's estate in Mull in that year there was a rapid increase in arrears among the small tenants and cottars and food, seed and labour had to be provided for the people who had suffered great hardship since 1862. Four years later distress was again experienced by the population of an island which had sustained a decline in the number of its inhabitants from 10,054 to 7,240 between 1841 and 1861 and in the Bunessan area, 'many of the poor are actually starving'.[6] Once again meal was made available and public works started. It was successive bad seasons in 1881–2, affecting the whole of the western Highlands, which not only produced much social suffering but also provided the initial economic impetus for the great crofters revolt of that decade. Over 24,000 people received relief in these years. Conditions deteriorated once more in 1888 when in the Outer Hebrides 'actual starvation' was predicted, and the inhabitants once more were supported by charitable organisations from the Lowland cities. The chamberlain of the Lewis estate himself estimated that there had been at least nine seasons between 1853 and 1883 when the proprietor had had to advance varying amounts of seed and meal to distressed crofters.

At best, then, 'recovery' was modest, insecure and interrupted by years of considerable difficulty. Typhus remained common in some localities because of hard living conditions and poor sanitation, and cattle continued to share living accommodation with human beings. Domestic squalor persisted and continued to disconcert observers from outside the Highlands. Mass clearances were a thing of the past but insecurity of tenure remained a fact of life: 'Others, not a few, continue quietly evicting by legal process and clearing by so-called voluntary emigration. The lawyer's pen supersedes the soldier's steel'.[7] At the same time the movement of the young to the New World and the Lowland cities continued unabated. Above all the social calamities of previous decades had not been forgotten, and a bitter folk memory of dispossession lingered on and fuelled the simmering discontent which erupted in the 1880s.

NOTES

1 D. Clerk, 'On the agriculture of the county of Argyll'. *Transactions of the Highland and Agricultural Society*, 4th ser., 10, 1878.
2 British Parliamentary Papers, XXVI, 1851, *Report to the Board of Supervision by Sir John McNeill on the Western Highlands and Islands, Appendix A*, pp. 114–15.
3 Rev. Eric J. Findlater, *Highland Clearances: the Real Cause of Highland Famines*, Edinburgh, 1855, p. 9.
4 R. Somers, *Letters from the Highlands: of the Famine of 1847*, London, 1848, pp. 124–5.
5 J. Hunter, *The Making of the Crofting Community*, Edinburgh, 1976, p. 109.
6 Inveraray Castle, Argyll Estate Papers, Bundle 1764, 25 February 1868.
7 British Parliamentary Papers, XXXII–XXXVI, 1884, *Report of the Commissioners of Inquiry into the Condition of the Crofters and Cottars in the Highlands and Islands of Scotland*, p. 195.

FURTHER READING

A. Collier, *The Crofting Problem*, Cambridge, 1953.

T. M. Devine, *The Great Highland Famine*, Edinburgh, 1988.

M. W. Flinn, ed., *Scottish Population History*, Cambridge, 1977.

J. Hunter, 'Sheep and deer: Highland sheep farming 1850–1900', *Northern Scotland*, 1, 1973.

J. Hunter, *The Making of the Crofting Community*, Edinburgh, 1976.

W. Orr, *Deer Forests, Landlords and Crofters*, Edinburgh, 1982.

E. Richards, *A History of the Highland Clearances*, London, 1982.

14

PATTERNS OF POPULAR RESISTANCE AND THE CROFTERS' WAR, 1790–1886

I

To many contemporary observers and some later historians one of the most perplexing and puzzling questions of the Highland clearances was the failure of the people to show more active resistance to landlord policies. The economic transformation had caused social havoc, enormous displacement of populations and the destruction of an ancient way of life, yet, the people had apparently remained quiet and accepted their fate. It became common to contrast the violent truculence of the Irish and their bitter struggle against an alien landlord class with the passive stoicism of the Scottish Gaels. In a famous and often-quoted comment, Hugh Miller, a strong sympathiser with the plight of the crofters, remarked with great frustration in 1846:

> They [the Irish] are buying guns and will be bye-and-bye shooting magistrates and clergymen by the score; and Parliament will in consequence do a great deal for them. But the poor Highlanders will shoot no-one . . . and so they will be left to perish unregarded in their hovels.[1]

During the famine years of the 1840s the organisers of charitable relief for the Highlands used these stereotypes, and stressed that the Gaels were much more deserving of philanthropic assistance than the lawless Irish. At other times it was asserted that the peaceful nature of the Highland people had intrinsic economic benefits for potential investors in the region and one expert took the view that the real rent of a great Highland estate in 1830 was worth at least 20 per cent more than its nominal level because it had '. . . no *Tythes*, poor *rates* or *Incendaries* to contend with'.[2]

This emerging stereotype of the docile Highlander was a direct conse-quence of the history of Gaeldom. The Jacobite defeat at Culloden and the process of state-enforced pacification thereafter was seen to have effectively tamed a martial people. Their warrior traditions had been crushed or redirected towards the service of the crown in the colonial wars and the systematic betrayal of clan values by the chiefs, together with the sheer scale and speed of economic transformation, had produced cultural disorientation throughout Gaeldom. The people were stunned as their world fell apart rapidly and lacked either the spirit or the confidence to resist, and evangelical protestantism then completed the process of transforming a warrior society into a timid and God-fearing community.

So compelling and apparently convincing were these images that it is only in recent years that some scholars have started to question them, both in terms of the actual historical experience of the Highlands and its relationship with the wider comparative study of peasant rebellions. Already, however, it is clear that the traditional interpretation is at best an oversimplification and at worst a considerable distortion of the reality. For example, comparing the Highland case with events in Ireland is not particularly fruitful. Hardly any peasant society in western Europe experienced the levels of intense and recurrent violence which characterised certain parts of Ireland before the Great Famine and virtually any country would have seemed relatively 'peaceful' by comparison. The chronic instability of Ireland was due to very special factors such as Irish colonial status, the existence of an alien landed class, and the unusually severe demographic and economic stresses which intensified in many areas of the country in the early nineteenth century.

Eric Richards has shown that Highland resistance was indeed muted in comparison with Ireland but much greater than previous observers imagined. Indeed, many episodes of clearance are known to historians precisely because the opposition of the people attracted considerable press attention which then resulted in the compilation of a documentary record of events which could be examined by posterity. In all, between 1780 and 1855, there were around fifty known occasions when the forces of law and order were challenged. Sometimes resistance took place on a considerable scale, as in 1792 in Easter Ross when the population of several districts rose and tried to drive the sheep which posed such a threat to the old way of life out of the area. More often, however, it was highly localised, sporadic and unco-ordinated, a spontaneous and desperate response to the threat of eviction and, while estate factors, police and sheriff officers might be assaulted, protest usually crumbled when the army intervened. Only sticks and stones were used as weapons, and in most cases women, and men dressed as women, played an important part in such acts of defiance.

These disturbances have placed a question against the received notion of the 'docile' Highlander. However, the significance of these episodes needs to be kept in perspective as the overwhelming majority of clearances still took place

The crofting agitation of the 1880s

with little fuss and no physical response from the people. The Richards data also show that much of the disorder was concentrated on the great Sutherland estate and adjacent areas in the decade or so after the end of the Napoleonic Wars and then there was a major gap of more than twenty years, until the famine period, in which little physical resistance has been documented. In addition, while some disturbances may have slowed down or delayed clearance, in virtually all cases, before the 1850s, dispossession was eventually successfully enforced. Increasingly some episodes, especially those at Sollas in North Uist and Suishnish and Boreraig in Skye during the potato famine, drew attention to the crofters' plight

Steamer with the Sheriff, Procurator-Fiscal and Chief Constable

and elicited growing sympathy outside the Highlands. But the acts of resistance did not significantly impede or slow down the process of clearance itself.

This is hardly surprising. One of the weaknesses in the case of some of those who have looked at this problem is the expectation and assumption that there *ought* to have been more mass resistance to clearance. But various studies of peasant rebellions in South America, Asia and eastern Europe have all shown that small farmers are very slow to protest and when they do it is notoriously difficult for them to engage in sustained and effective conflict, either with landlords or the state. Where acts of defiance become generalised and are successfully maintained over time, as in the case of nineteenth century Ireland, there are usually exceptional circumstances which do not normally apply to most peasant communities. The sociologist Eric R. Wolf has characterised the general pattern in this way:

> Peasants cannot rebel successfully in a situation of complete impotence; the powerless are easy victims. Therefore only a peasantry in possession of some tactical control over its own resources can provide a secure basis for on-going political leverage . . . the poor peasant or the landless labourer who depends on a landlord for the larger part of his livelihood, or the totality of it, has no tactical power: he is completely within the power domain of his employer, without sufficient resources of his own to serve him as resources in the power struggle. Poor peasants, and landless labourers, therefore, are unlikely to pursue the course of rebellion, unless they are able to rely on some external power to challenge the power which constrains them.[3]

In the Wolf thesis the powerless are unlikely to rebel and if they dare to do so, failure is almost inevitable. The Highland people were mainly devoid of power during the clearances. They did not own the land and only had access to it through short-term leases at the landlords' will, and cottars and squatters, who were in the majority on some Hebridean estates, had no rights of tenure at all. The power of the authorities was overwhelming and the landowners had full legal control over their properties. The army was engaged on ten occasions to uphold the law against anti-clearance rioters, although they were never actively involved in hostilities, and on the appearance of troops from Inverness, Aberdeen, Fort William or Glasgow, resistance tended to disintegrate rapidly.

Again, after 1815 the crofting population had little economic bargaining power against the proprietors as the labour-intensive activities which had given them a degree of leverage during the Napoleonic Wars collapsed or stagnated. In addition, as shown in chapter 8, their language and culture had long been under sustained attack. Gaelic was synonymous with backwardness in the eyes of the outside world, and some argued that these aggressive attitudes of cultural

Marines land at Uig in Skye, 1884

contempt had devastating effects on the morale of the Gaels. In the 1880s, John Murdoch, the energetic and influential champion of crofters' rights, argued that:

> The language and lore of the Highlands being treated with despite has tended to crush their self-respect, and repress that self-reliance without which no people can advance. When a man was convinced that his language was a barbarism, his lore as filthy rags, and that the only good thing about him – his land – was, because of his general worthlessness to go to a man of another race and another tongue, what remained that he should fight for?[4]

Marines on the march in Skye

The intrinsic weakness of the people's position was compounded by the lack of external support. At the time of the Sutherland clearances, southern newspapers, such as the *Military Register* and the *Star*, publicised and bitterly criticised the evictions, and similarly in the 1840s, the Free Church journal, *The Witness*, and the radical *North British Daily Mail*, were hostile towards landlordism. In the following decade there was also evidence of growing sympathy for the crofters and one writer in the relatively conservative *Inverness Advertiser* asserted as early as 1850 that 'No human being should have a right to evict nor to be tempted with such power. Even good men cannot be safely trusted with it'.[5] But despite this growing concern, there was still little effective political and intellectual challenge to the economic principles behind the removals. The dominant belief was that they were a necessary evil in order to allow the economy to develop and demographic crisis to be alleviated. Only in the second half of the nineteenth century, and particularly from the 1870s could the Highland people count on vigorous support from external political forces and by then mass clearance had come to an end.

In earlier decades the Gaels were thrown back on their own resources and these were not enough for sustained and widespread protest. The history of the Highlands was a powerful handicap in this respect. Long after chiefs had become commercial landlords, the people seem to have clung to the concept of *duthchas*, the principles which obliged clan elites to provide land and protection

Disturbances in Lewis

for their followers, and they experienced acute difficulty in adjusting to the realities of the new landownership. Even during the Crofters' War of the 1880s, the Napier Commission observed that after almost a century of eviction and dispossession there was still, '. . .on the side of the poor much reverence for the owner of the soil'.[6] Unlike Irish Gaels, confronting an alien landed class, Highland Gaels could not easily break with traditional loyalties. There was a continuing belief in the notion that if the landlord only knew of the circumstances of the people he would provide justice. Gaelic poetry of the nineteenth century demonstrates a tendency to blame factors, tenants, tacksmen, sheepfarmers and even sheep but rarely individual landowners. When the landed class was criticised it was usually in anonymous terms; even Mary MacPherson, whose vigorous poetry emerged from the land agitation of the 1880s, did not attack the hereditary landed families of her native island of Skye.

The Highlanders were therefore weakened in economic, legal, political and cultural terms. Peasant rebellion on anything like the Irish scale would have been impossible and even if attempted would have resulted in speedy retribution. But this is not to say that the population had been broken by the social havoc of the clearances or that they were so enfeebled as to be incapable of resistance. It was overt, collective and organised physical protest which was problematic and other forms of opposition were both more widespread and less risky. The advance northwards of the big sheep farms was marked by growing

Disturbances in Lewis

popular hostility. This was shown not in the form of collective resistance, which the authorities could easily crush, but by sheep stealing and occasional mutilation. The Rev. Norman MacLeod stated in evidence to a Select Committee of the House of Commons in 1841:

> The flocks of large sheepfarmers are annually thinned by those who feel the pinching of famine; and to such an extent is this system carried on that it has led to the proposal of establishing a rural police throughout the island.[7]

On the MacLeod estate on Skye, for example, in the later 1830s, inflammatory proclamations were posted on the church doors and numerous sheep mutilated and killed, and from other parts of the country around the same time came reports of petty violence and a simmering hatred for the sheep-farmers. The absence of dramatic public agitation does not in itself mean that the people were either submissive or resigned to their fate.

Indeed, arguably the most remarkable demonstration of a collective response to the new order, was through mass emigration rather than physical resistance. Migration both to the Lowlands and across the seas was a safety valve which dissipated some of the social tension building up in the Highlands, in the southern cities and the transatlantic emigration communities. By the last quarter of the nineteenth century, however, second generation Highlanders in urban Scotland were among the most enthusiastic supporters of the crofters agitation of the 1880s, and even more significant were the emigrations of the period c. 1760 to 1815 to North America. As shown in chapter 12 they were neither automatic responses to demographic forces nor the desperate exodus of a cowed and despairing people. Rather these emigrations were a collective rejection of the new economic structures developing in the Highlands. The emigration parties were well organised and successfully transported several thousand Highlanders to the New World against the open opposition of both landowners and the state in that period and as one of the earliest examples of large-scale group emigration from western Europe to North America, it hardly seems the response of a docile and helpless population. As one scholar has remarked: 'The evidence of surviving emigrant letters is striking – for the writers refer repeatedly not only to their new-found ease, but to their exultation in colonial freedom and to their contempt for the landlord class back in the Highlands'.[8]

For those who remained, of course, the outlook was grim as eviction intensified after 1815 and the crofting economy degenerated into acute crisis in the 1820s and 1830s. Most of the west Highland population in these decades did not possess either the modest means or the limited freedom of action of the middle tenantry who made up the emigrant parties of the later eighteenth century. Increasingly they looked towards evangelical religion for consolation, support and for a greater sense of emotional security. However, it might be too simple to see the revivalism in Gaeldom of these years as the means by which potential protest was channelled away from political action into religious hysteria as it is unlikely, for reasons already advanced, that effective resistance would have occurred anyway. Again, in some ways, evangelicalism produced yet another arena of conflict between proprietors and people. This was the case in the patronage disputes which became more frequent in this period as congregations opposed the induction of unpopular ministers who might not show the evangelical commitments of the majority of the people. In a sense the great Disruption of 1843, which split the Church of Scotland and drove the majority of the population of the Hebrides (outside the catholic enclaves) into the Free Church, can be partly seen as a climax to these earlier struggles because it too was in large part about the landowner's rights of patronage. The Disruption was the result of a belief in a particular kind of Christian commitment. It was neither a class struggle nor an overt expression of anti-landlordism, but the sheer scale of the exodus of the people from the established Church was deeply significant since it came about in the teeth of the opposition of established authority in the Highlands. It was later said of the Free Church, '*Thainig an Edglais a mach*' ('the Church came out'), as if no one was left behind after 1843. This act of collective independence was followed by some landowners refusing to make sites available for church building and many of the new congregations were forced to worship in the open air. The hostility of the proprietors provoked the establishment in 1847 of a full-scale enquiry into the matter by a Select Committee of the House of Commons, and 1843 therefore showed that the people could be defiant and demonstrate considerable powers of courage and organisation. The ravages of economic devastation and large-scale clearance had not entirely demoralised them.

II

Yet, to suggest any direct link between the success of the Disruption years and the crofting agitation almost half a century later is hardly convincing as if anything, indeed, the possibilities of revolt diminished in the 1850s. This was the decade of most widespread evictions when, amid continuing famine, the removals reached unparalleled levels. Even when the scale of eviction died down, chronic anxiety and fear of dispossession remained endemic and, on many estates, the factor came to resemble an absolute monarch or petty tyrant who ruled the people with an iron hand. John Murdoch found the crofters on the Gordon estate of South Uist in the 1870s in such 'a state of slavish fear' that, although they had many grievances, they dared not complain to the factor, Ranald MacDonald, for fear he might drive them from their estate lands. In South Harris, Murdoch also noted how the crofters were 'paralysed by terror'. It was at a land reform meeting at Dunvegan in Skye that the speaker, Donald MaCaskill, openly admitted: 'I am ashamed to confess it now that I trembled more before the factor than I did before the Lord of Lords'.[9]

In the light of these statements it is all the more remarkable that a full-blooded land agitation did finally emerge in the Highlands in the 1880s. It is true that in some ways the early incidents of that decade were partly reminiscent of the sporadic acts of defiance which had occurred over the previous half century and the events in Skye in 1882, which the press soon dubbed 'the Battle of the Braes', and eventually became the catalyst for a much wider crofters' campaign, had several familiar features. The protest began in the townships of Gedintailor, Balmeanach and Peinchorran, which constitute the district known as Braes or the Braes on Lord MacDonald's estate on the east coast of Skye some eight miles south of the island's capital of Portree. The crofters petitioned their landlord to have traditional grazing rights on Ben Lee returned to them. The factor rejected this request but the crofters replied by stating they would no longer pay rent to Lord MacDonald until their rights were restored. The landlord then attempted to serve summonses of removal on a number of tenants on the grounds that they were in rent arrears. On 7 April 1882, however, the sheriff officer serving the summonses was accosted by a crowd of around 500 people, the notices were taken from him and burned. Ten days later, the law returned in force, strongly supported by no less than fifty Glasgow policemen. They managed to arrest those who had assaulted the sheriff officer but not before about a dozen constables received injuries at the hands of a large crowd of men and women throwing stones and wielding large sticks. The Battle of the Braes was followed by similar forms of action at Glendale in Skye at the end of 1882.

These disturbances had several features which recalled the ineffectual protests against clearance in the decades before the 1860s including the use of rudimentary weapons; the central role of women; the deforcement of the officers of the law; the intervention of the police and the localised nature of resistance. However, the Battle of the Braes has come to be regarded as an historic event because it also signalled a decisive change of direction from past episodes of protest. For one thing, the people took the initiative to try to regain grazing rights which they had lost seventeen years before. This protest was proactive rather than reactive. For another, the rent strike, which had been employed with deadly effect on numerous Irish estates in earlier years, was a tactic which was extremely difficult for proprietors to combat without contemplating mass eviction, and policy which was becoming politically unacceptable by the 1880s.

The Battle of the Braes and other disturbances suggested that landlordism was now encountering a different type of opposition, but it was still small in scale, confined to only a few estates in Skye and at this stage the authorities were dealing with a minor land dispute. This soon changed. Previous episodes of resistance had petered out in failure and imprisonment for the participants, but the Braes skirmish was the prelude to more widespread acts of subordination sustained on many Highland estates for several years which involved the consolidation of rent strikes, occupation of sheep farms, the destruction of farm fences, deforcement of sheriff officers and mutilation and killing of stock. *The Scotsman* reported in some alarm in October, 1884 that:

> men are taking what does not belong to them, are setting all law at defiance, and are instituting a terrorism which the poor people are unable to resist . . . Rents are unpaid, not because the tenants cannot pay them, but because in some cases they will not, and in some cases they dare not.

It asserted that if the law was not enforced quickly: 'the condition of the islands will soon be as bad as that of Ireland three years ago'.[10]

The Scotsman was likely to exaggerate since the paper was a close ally of the landlord interest. There was little 'Irish'-style agrarian terrorism in the Highlands at this time and most disturbances were confined to particular districts. The western mainland was peaceful for the most part and even in the Hebrides, where there was most overt discontent, illegal activity was mainly concentrated in Skye and, to a lesser extent, Lewis. Direct action did occur in South Uist, Tiree and Harris but tended to be much more intermittent than elsewhere. In part the notion that the entire region was aflame and lawlessness everywhere rampant was the result of the extraordinary success of the publicity given the disturbances by the Scottish and English press. The incidents in Skye were deemed so serious that the government sent an expeditionary force to the island, the first since the time of the last Jacobite rebellion in the eighteenth century, and this produced an almost hysterical reaction from certain sections of the press. A violent armed confrontation between troops and people was eagerly anticipated, the *North British Daily Mail* carrying such sensational headlines as, 'Threatened General Rising of Crofters' and 'Dunvegan Men on the March to Uig'. The sixteen newspaper correspondents who were sent from the south and two artists from the *Graphic* and the *Illustrated London News* were disappointed, however, when expected violent conflict did not take place. Marine detachments did stay on in Skye until 1885 and on their departure from Uig in June of that year they received a friendly farewell message from the local people. The troops stationed at Staffin seem to have developed a particularly close association with the local inhabitants and according to one observer they had shown a considerable interest in the women of the district: 'They gave more of their time to the god of love than to the god of war'.[11]

In fact, the distinguishing feature of the events of the 1880s, or the 'Crofters' War' as they have come to be described, was not so much the spread of violence, intimidation and lawlessness throughout the Highlands as the fusion of an effective political campaign for crofters' rights with a high profile series of acts of resistance, of which the refusal to pay rents and the 'raiding' of old lands were the most significant. By the early 1880s a crofting lobby had already grown up in the southern cities consisting of land-reformers, Gaelic revivalists, second and third generation Highland immigrants and radical liberals. From these groups and existing committees there was formed the Highland Land Law Reform Association (HLLRA) with a strategy loosely based on that of the Irish Land League. It sought fair rents, security of tenure, compensation for improvements and, significantly, redistribution of land. This was a decisive development because not only did the HLLRA link the crofters' cause with external political interests it also, through its proliferating branches and district committees, helped to end the localism which had impeded collective action in the past.

The most remarkable example of this came with the appointment of a Royal Commission into the condition of the crofters and cottars in the Highlands and islands under the chairmanship of Lord Napier and Ettrick. The Government had responded to the perceived scale of civil disobedience and growing public sympathy for the Highlanders, so that the Commission took evidence throughout the region from the spring to the winter of 1883 and its Report was finally published in 1884. When it appeared it was much criticised, not surprisingly by landlords, because it recommended controls on their powers of ownership, but also by the majority of the people because its proposals fell far short of their aspirations. The proposals ignored the problem of the cottars and were confined to those who possessed holdings of more than £6 and less than £30 per annum. Nevertheless, the Napier Commission's Report was also a symbolic victory for the crofting agitation as, for the first time, a public body had admitted the validity of the land rights of the people, even though these were not recognised in law. The Royal Commission also proposed that the state should provide a degree of protection for their interests. The Report was reluctant to offer perpetual security of tenure but advocated that government should instead assist crofters to purchase their holdings. It was a radical change from the kind of assumptions which had governed external intervention in the Highlands during the famine years of the 1840s and 1850s.

The subsequent legislation, enshrined in the Crofters Holdings (Scotland) Act differed in some key respects from the Commission's recommendations, but it too represented a decisive break with the past and began a new era in landlord–crofter relations in the Highlands. Security of tenure for crofters was guaranteed as long as rent was paid and fair rents would be fixed by a land court; compensation for improvements was allowed to a crofter who gave up his croft or was removed from it; crofts could not be sold but might be bequeathed to a relative and, with certain restrictions, the compulsory enlargement of holdings could be considered by the land court.

As will be shown in the next chapter, this legislation did not immediately find favour with the land reformers, especially since it gave only very minor concessions to crofters' demands for more land. But its historic significance should not be underestimated. The Crofters' Act made clearances in the old style impossible, breached the sacred rights of private property, controlled landlord–crofter relations through a government body and afforded the crofting population secure possession of their holdings. The balance of power between landlords and small tenants had been irrevocably altered by 1886, but in fact was already becoming apparent earlier. In December 1884, Cameron of Lochiel noted that the current of political and public opinion was flowing fast against the landed interest and the following month about fifty Highland proprietors and their representatives met at Inverness to discuss the crofting agitation and agreed to provide crofters with leases, consider revision of rents and guarantee compensation for improvements. It was a remarkable and tardy attempt at developing a more benevolent form of landlordism induced by the weakening position of the elites. The proposals were rejected as a sure sign that the landowners were finally on the run. As the *Oban Times* gleefully declared, 'the Highland lairds are on their knees'.[12] Final victory seemed only a matter of time.

III

In historical perspective the events of the 1880s are quite remarkable. The crofters had not secured the return of lands from which they had been removed during the clearances, that would have amounted to expropriation of property and remained politically unthinkable. Yet by imposing legislation which made the tenancy of a croft heritable, the state had in effect deprived the landlord of most of his former rights of ownership. No other class or group in late nineteenth century mainland Britain were given such protection as were the crofters in this way. How and why they managed to achieve such privileges is the question which will be discussed in the final section of this chapter.

The agitation in Skye was triggered in part by economic crisis. The winter of 1882–3 was reckoned to have been one of the worst since the disasters of the 1840s. The potato crop was partially destroyed and earnings of migrant labourers from the east coast fisheries, a key source of income in Skye and the

Long Island, had fallen dramatically. Problems became more acute after a great storm in October 1882 which damaged or destroyed many boats (one estimate suggested over 1,200), nets and fishing gear. The resulting economic stresses may help to explain why no rent campaigns became so popular within the crofting community. Even when there was some recovery from the difficulties of 1882–3, cattle prices collapsed throughout most of the remainder of the decade and by the late 1880s stirks which might have fetched £7 or £8 in 1883 were worth less than £2. The period was also one of difficulty in sheep-farming as the British market for wool and mutton was swamped by imports from the Antipodes. The big flockmasters suffered most with many surrendering their leases and there was wholesale conversion of sheep farms to deer forests. But small tenant income was also affected as, by this time, it was also usual for crofters to keep a few sheep.

It is very possible these continuing economic difficulties in the western Highlands fuelled social tensions. But there had been bad times before and little unrest. The people had accepted suffering as God's judgement or as part of the natural law, not as a consequence of the injustice of man, but the difference in the 1880s may have been partly because the generation of that decade had become accustomed to the better times of the 1860s and 1870s and could have experienced frustrated expectations as living standards collapsed. But the movement of the 1880s was not one of the hungry and distressed. If it had been it would probably not have endured for long. Economic factors do not really explain how a few minor land disputes became the catalyst for a widespread land agitation which eventually resulted in a political and social revolution in the Highland counties.

One factor was a changing attitude among the people. Some scholars have noted that they had more iron in their souls by the 1880s. Certainly the Gaelic poetry of the land war period, as analysed by Sorley McLean, transmits a more powerful mood of confidence and optimism, and even before the Battle of the Braes, there was evidence on some Highland estates of a new level of tenant truculence. By 1880, for example, on the Sutherland estate, the agents were apparently willing to allow rent arrears and breach of regulations, rather than provoke the people into acts of defiance. It is also interesting to note that virtually all the famous incidents of the Crofters' War were the results of the initiative of the local population rather than responses to landlord action as had been the pattern in the past.

This new-found confidence may reflect the growth of a new generation in the western Highlands. All commentators stressed that it was young adult men and women who formed the backbone of protest. They had been brought up in the more secure and prosperous times of the 1860s and 1870s and had not known at first hand the anguish of the famine decades which had demoralised many of their parents and grandparents. The press often drew attention to the fact that many of the older people in the crofting townships were sometimes timorous and meek while the young were bold and defiant. A decisive factor prompting them to action was the example of the Irish. Rural agitation in Ireland had led in 1881 to a famous victory when Gladstone's government passed the Irish Land Act. This granted to tenants the rights known as the '3 F's' , fair rents fixed by a land court, fixed tenure as long as the rent was paid and free sale of the tenant's interest in the farm which allowed for compensation for improvements. The Irish victory had obvious implications for Highland crofters. In part information on the Irish agitation was conveyed through the regional Highland press, especially in the columns of the *Highlander*, edited by John Murdoch who had lived in Ireland. Indeed, it was suggested by some that he devoted most of the last few issues of his journal more to Irish than Highland matters. Even more important, however, was the personal connection between Skye and Ireland. From about 1875, many Skye men became labourers in Campbeltown and Carradale fishing boats for the summer season in Irish waters and there can be little doubt that these annual sojourns gave them experience of such Irish tactics as rent strikes. Indeed, the Irish connection goes a long way to explaining why in its early years, the agitation concentrated mainly on Skye. In a remarkable letter to Lord MacDonald's Edinburgh agent, his factor in Skye noted:

> Shortly before the term of Martinmas a body of young men, the sons of tenants, most of whom had been fishing at Kinsale in Ireland and had imbibed Irish notions, came to my office and presented a petition which they had almost the whole tenants to sign, to the effect that they demanded Ben Lee in addition to their present holdings without paying any additional rent.[13]

But despite the new boldness of the men of Skye the dispute would probably not have lasted for long if it had not been for significant changes in external attitudes to the land issue. As late as the 1850s protests against clearances had been effectively crushed, the law enforced and the rights of landed property upheld, but such brutal assertions of proprietorial privilege were politically unacceptable thirty years later. At first the due process of law in Skye was followed against deforcement and land raiding and both the police and the military were employed, but the government recognised that it could not contemplate the full use of force because public and political opinion would not permit it. The only alternative, therefore, was to eventually concede some of the crofters' demands in order to restore law and order.

The climate of opinion was already changing in the 1870s. In 1879 the estate of Leckmelm on Lochbroom was purchased by A. C. Pirie, an Aberdeen paper manufacturer. He tried to organise 'improvements' on his property which resulted in some evictions, but the removals produced a huge outcry in the Highlands and resounding condemnation from all sections of the national press, with the predictable exception of *The Scotsman*. Four years later J. B. Balfour referred to 'a considerable body of vague and floating sentiment in favour of ameliorating the crofters' condition' which had influenced several members of the Liberal Party.[14] These feelings were apparent at the very highest levels of government. They were shared by the Prime Minister, William Ewart Gladstone, himself and the Home Secretary in 1882, Sir William Harcourt. Harcourt had a key role to play in the unfolding of events in the Hebrides as he had spent many years on yachting holidays there and had developed a sympathy for the condition of the people of the area, and his actions showed this. In November 1882 he refused permission for a military expedition to be sent to Skye and in the same month suggested to Gladstone that a Royal Commission be established instead. Significantly he observed that among 'decent people' there was now a view that the crofters had real grievances, and in the age of an extending franchise such opinions could not easily be ignored.

These latent sympathies for the crofters were exploited to the full by pro-crofter propagandists and one of the most effective was Alexander McKenzie, editor of the *Celtic Magazine*. McKenzie had been using this publication to draw attention to the social problems of the western Highlands since 1877. In 1883, however, he published his bestseller, *A History of the Highland Clearances*, which conveyed in emotive prose the harrowing details of some of the most notorious mass removals. It was not a work of historical detachment but a compendium of landlord misdeeds. Works like McKenzie's portrayed Highland proprietors as heartless tyrants who had ruthlessly betrayed their responsibilities and their people.

The contemporary press played an even more central role in publicising the crofters' cause and influencing public opinion further in their favour. This was a publicity machine which even the wealthiest landowner could never hope to equal. As one reporter who covered the events of the 1880s noted later: 'Printed paper in the shape of newspapers proved the most deadly tool against the Highland landowners'.[15] The fact that coverage was so extensive, not only on the part of the Scottish papers but also the English press, reflected the deep interest which existed throughout the country in the Highland problem and this was facilitated by the revolution of communications in the Western Isles. By the 1880s a network of steamer connections had spread throughout the Inner and Outer Hebrides. In addition, the telegraph now allowed eyewitness reports of disturbances to be published soon after they took place, and this made the Crofters' War one of the first popular agitations in Britain in which the media of the day played a significant part not only by reporting but also by actually influencing developments.

External political and cultural forces were also important. Crofter political awareness was raised by the methods and campaigns of Charles Stewart Parnell's Irish Nationalist Party and the Irish Land League. Though the disturbances in the north were not as some suggested a 'fenian conspiracy' there can be little doubt about the general Irish impact, especially through the writings and speeches of the charismatic John Murdoch, editor of *The Highlander*, who had been politically active in Ireland for several years and was acquainted with some of the leading personalities of the Irish agitation. There was also powerful support from the Highland societies which were now active in the Lowland towns. Until the 1870s they had been almost exclusively devoted to conviviality and cultural pursuits, but by the end of that decade, however, the Federation of Celtic Societies was being criticised in some quarters as being too political. Activists, such as the eloquent and energetic Professor John Stuart Blackie of the University of Edinburgh, projected a potent message of literary romanticism and political radicalism. The regional Highland press was increasingly sympathetic, notably the *Oban Times* from 1882 when Duncan Cameron became editor, and provided a faithful record of speeches, meetings of the HLLRA at local level which lent both cohesion and momentum to the agitation. Land reformers in mainland Britain and Ireland took up the crofters' cause and it received particularly important support from some reformist sections of the Liberal Party in Scotland. Second generation Highlanders in the southern cities were also deeply influential in certain areas.

This motley alliance became in time an effective crofter's lobby. The people of the disturbed districts did help themselves, but they gained a great deal from the unparalleled levels of external support which provided experienced leadership, political muscle and organising expertise. The most remarkable demonstration of this contribution came in the months after the setting up of the Napier Commission. Government may have seen this as a way of defusing tension and deflecting opposition, but instead it became a catalyst for further agitation and the creation of a more effective organisation especially when it became apparent that the witnesses to the Royal Commission would be guaranteed immunity from intimidation. This was a crucial development since bitter memories of the reign of terror of the clearance period endured among the older men whose evidence of past events was vital to the crofters' case. Until the Napier Commission sat for the first time in May 1883 at the Braes in Skye, every effort was made to prepare evidence. Alexander McKenzie and John Murdoch toured the region and provided advice, and at the end of 1883 the HLLRA of London published three pamphlets in Gaelic and English addressed to the crofting community, highlighting past wrongs and encouraging agitation in favour of security of tenure, fair rents and reallocation of land as well as other aims. They were urged to form district branches and use peaceful and constitutional methods in pursuit of their demands. When branches were established the rules were drawn up by central headquarters in London.

But the crofters' movement did not simply become the creature of external sympathisers in these years although they did do much to raise expectations. One of the most significant events in the organisational process was the decision taken by west coast fishermen at a mass meeting in Fraserburgh in August 1883 of men engaged in the herring fishery to form land reform associations on their return home. Furthermore, subversive and illegal activity on some estates persisted despite the official opposition of the HLLRA. The successes achieved represented a joint victory for the crofters and their new allies who were able effectively to exploit the new and more sympathetic climate of opinion which had emerged in the last quarter of the nineteenth century. It was this which gave the power that previous generations had lacked.

NOTES

1 Quoted in J. Hunter, *The Making of the Crofting Community*, Edinburgh, 1976, p. 89.
2 Quoted in E. Richards, *A History of the Highland Clearances*, Edinburgh, 1985, vol. 2, p. 295.
3 E. R. Wolf, 'On peasant rebellions' in T. Shanin, ed., *Peasants and Peasant Societies*, London, 1971, p. 268.
4 Quoted in C. W. J. Withers, *Gaelic Scotland*, London, 1988, p. 333.
5 *Inverness Advertiser*, 20 November 1850.
6 Quoted in Hunter, *Crofting Community*, p. 91.
7 British Parliamentary Papers, VI, 1841, *Select Committee on Emigration (Scotland)*, p. 80.
8 Richards, *Highland Clearances*, 2, p. 287.
9 Quoted in I. M. M. Macphail, *The Crofters' War*, Stornoway, 1989, p. 1.
10 *The Scotsman*, 15 and 18 October 1884.
11 Quoted in Macphail, *Crofters' War*, p. 120.
12 *Oban Times*, 24 January 1885.
13 Quoted in Macphail, *Crofters' War*, p. 38.
14 Quoted in Hunter, *Crofting Community*, p. 143.
15 Quoted in Macphail, Crofters' War, p. 11.

FURTHER READING

T. M. Devine, 'Unrest and stability in rural Scotland and Ireland, 1760–1840' in R. Mitchison and P. Roebuck, eds., *Economy and Society in Ireland and Scotland*, Edinburgh, 1988.
J. P. D. Dunbabin, *Rural Discontent in Nineteenth Century Britain*, London, 1974.
F. Grigor, *Mightier than a Lord*, Stornoway, 1979.
H. J. Hanham, 'The problem of Highland discontent, 1880–1885', *Transactions of the Royal Historical Society*, 19, 1969.
J. Hunter, 'The politics of land reform 1873–1895', *Scottish Historical Review*, 53, 1974.
J. Hunter, *The Making of the Crofting Community*, Edinburgh, 1976.

K. J. Logue, *Popular Disturbances in Scotland*, 1780–1815, Edinburgh, 1977.

I. M. M. Macphail, *The Crofters' War*, Stornoway, 1989.

E. Richards, 'How tame were the Highlanders during the clearances?', *Scottish Studies*, 17, 1973.

E. Richards, *A History of the Highland Clearances*, London, 1982 and 1985, 2 vols.

E. R. Wolf, 'On peasant rebellions' in T. Shanin, ed., *Peasants and Peasant Societies*, London, 1971.

15

THE INTERVENTION OF THE STATE

I

The great drama of the clearances had been played out between the landowners and the people with occasional interventions from external forces of law and order. With the passage of the Crofters' Act in 1886, however, social and economic conditions and relations in the western Highlands and islands could never be the same again. The state had become a major factor in influencing the future development of the region both through statute law, which established in 1886 new controls on the relationship between landlord and tenant, the formation of new agencies such as the Crofters Commission and, from 1897, the Congested Districts Board, and the provision of financial support for distressed areas, emigration and communications development. The problem of civil disorder had originally drawn government into the Highlands, but by the eve of the First World War the original aim of bringing a measure of stability to a troubled area had been replaced by a vague and ill-defined commitment to a policy of economic and social improvement for the inhabitants of the region. The notion of the Highlands as a special case deserving special treatment was already established in the thinking of British policy-makers by 1914.

The legislative foundation of this revolution in the role of government was the Act of 1886. Both its origins and its impact in the short and long term have engendered heated debate among scholars. It would be wrong, for example, to see a causal relationship between the general election of 1885 and the legislation of the following year. The crofters' movement had put up candidates in all the crofting counties and northern burghs in 1885, and five were successfully returned to Parliament. However, these new members had little effective influence on the passage of the bill. Most of the main clauses had been framed the year earlier, the government successfully resisted such pressures as the crofting lobby was able to bring to bear and crofter MPs were too few in number to have any real impact. In essence, they arrived on the political scene too late as the key elements in the legislation had already been agreed by the former Liberal Government which had unexpectedly fallen in the summer of 1885.

The Crofters' Act was the government's main response to the problems in the Highlands in the early 1880s and its structure reflected a complex series of influences. There was a desire to defuse the agitation and restore law and order through concessions to the crofters, but to interfere with the rights of private property could have serious repercussions for the maintenance of social hierarchy elsewhere in Britain. Key ministers responded to this threat by accepting that the Highlanders were a special case, and what gave them this status was not their poverty but their history. Gladstone argued that the people had a historic right to the land which had been expropriated from them by commercial proprietors in the eighteenth and nineteenth centuries. The crofters had suffered a profound injustice which should be redressed by Parliament. In terms of land law the historical basis of this contention was false, but these 'historicist' beliefs were fundamental to the passage of the 1886 legislation. As Gladstone stated in early 1885:

> For it is, after all, this historical fact that constitutes the crofters' title to demand the interference of Parliament. It is not because they are poor, or because there are too many of them, or because they want more land to support their families, but because those whom they represent had rights which they have been surreptitiously deprived to the injury of the community.[1]

He also indicated that legislation would be confined to any parish with a history of common pasturage over the previous century and in this way the crofters were isolated from other social groups suffering material disadvantage. They were, by definition, an exceptional case and legislation for them could proceed without necessarily being regarded as a dangerous and politically unacceptable precedent.

The government was also helped by the position of the landowners and the people in 1884 and 1885. A conference of proprietors took place in Inverness in January 1885 on the initiative of Donald Cameron of Lochiel and, partly because they feared government intervention was likely, they put forward their own voluntary proposals. Where possible, more land was to be offered to crofters; so also were revised rents and compensation for improvements. In addition, the government was encouraged to make loans available to the Highlands for development in the manner proposed by the Napier Commission. These suggestions fell short of the demands of the HLLRA, but there was sufficient convergence to justify the belief of the key ministers, Harcourt, the Home

Secretary, J. B. Balfour, the Lord Advocate, and Gladstone, the Prime Minister, that a compromise bill might have support among both only moderate land-owners and crofters. The demands of the crofters' movement were also relatively limited. The HLLRA did not seek land expropriation but the return of some land, security of tenure, fair rents and compensations for improvements. These, if granted, would all control the freedom of action of proprietors but they did not threaten the institution of landlordism itself.

The fact that the main thrust of policy was to draw the teeth of the agitation without endangering other interests too much can also be seen in the treatment of the Napier Commission's recommendations. Napier did not simply see the Highland problem solely as a law and order issue. He was not interested in short-term expedients which would bring temporary stability, but not lead to long-term economic benefit and so fail to cure the deeper malaise of the region. Lord Napier talked of the need to encourage the people 'to shake off the torpor which besets them and induce in them habits of industry and self respect'.[2] Because economic reformation was essential, the Irish land legislation was not in his view appropriate for the Highlands. He therefore proposed not only limited security of tenure but an ambitious scheme of assisted emigration and opportunities for extension of holding size.

However convincing this was as a programme of improvement, it was anathema to government and this was not simply because of its potential costs. Far from defusing discontent, the Napier proposals might have intensified it. The central principle that large-scale emigration was a solution to the area's problems was in direct conflict with the argument advanced by the crofters' movement that there was no shortage of land, only the existence of artificial legal and political obstacles preventing access to it. Ministers' dismissal of the Napier Commission's suggestions more or less ensured that the Crofters' Act of 1886 would be determined by political factors and by a judgement of what would be acceptable to the people without entirely undermining the rights of private property in land. The legislation was not designed to be a long-term economic panacea but a pragmatic response to particular political difficulties.

The final legislation was modelled on the Irish Land Acts of 1870 and 1881. It granted security of tenure to all crofters (defined as tenants paying rent of less than 30 and holding land on an annual basis in parishes with rights of common grazing), provided they did not sublet and maintained their rental payments. A Crofters' Commission was established to adjudicate on fair rents and arrears. Crofters were entitled to compensation for improvements and to assign their tenancy at death to a lawful heir, and there was provision in the legislation to allow a group of five crofters to apply for extra grazing land. However, this was surrounded by such an array of conditions that it had little impact in practice, but overall the Liberal government judged that all this was enough to take the heat out of the situation and bring stability to the north west.

At first, this expectation was disappointed. The passing of the Crofters' Act produced a good deal of bitterness and disillusion and a subsequent return to violence and confrontation in some parts of the Hebrides. The crofter MPs had opposed the legislation with their allies the Irish nationalists, but to no avail. Their principal bone of contention was the absence of any clause which might allow the restoration of land to the people, and this shortcoming drew angry condemnation from such militant districts as Kilmuir and Glendale in Skye. Even more disappointed were the cottars, the landless or semi-landless people, for whom the 1886 Act had made no provision and this excluded group demonstrated their discontent and frustration through land raids on several estates over the next four decades. Concern about the limitations and weaknesses of the Act became apparent at the HLLRA's annual conference in September 1886 when it reconstituted itself as the Highland Land League and committed its members to 'restore to the Highland people their inherent rights in their native soil'.[3] The scene was set for further confrontation when Gladstone's government fell on the issue of Irish Home Rule and was replaced by a Conservative administration from the autumn of 1886. This government determined on a more resolute policy of coercion in the Highlands and the new Scottish Secretary, Arthur Balfour, saw no need for further concessions to the crofters. The 1886 Act had gone far enough to meet their grievances; continued disorder should therefore be punished and malcontents brought to justice since there was no longer any justification for lawlessness.

The immediate aftermath of the passage of the Crofters' Act therefore saw several episodes of significant unrest in 1886 and 1887 and the return of military and naval forces to the Highlands in support of the civil power. Following a land raid in Tiree, troops intervened to assist the police on the island who were losing control of the situation. Similarly, there was another military expedition to Skye in late 1886 when civil administration on the island was in danger of collapse because of the accumulation of arrears of rates. The following year the military was also used in Lewis and in Assynt in Sutherland after land raids in these areas. The disorder had taken a change of direction and, instead of rent strikes, the emphasis was now on the occupation of land. Increasingly too the cottar class assumed a higher profile in several of the incidents. The courts also took a more stringent attitude to lawlessness and handed down much heavier prison sentences, and there seemed to be a new climate of opinion emerging that the major grievances of the crofters had been answered in the 1886 Act and there was little legitimate reason for further disorder.

Over time the Crofters' Act itself became more acceptable. In January 1887 the Crofters Commission published its first set of judgements on crofting rentals, and the results were a revelation. The *Oban Times*, a few days afterwards, admitted that the 1886 Act had been misjudged and, on the basis of the Commission's decision, was likely to inaugurate a new era for the Highlanders. The Commission examined 1,767 holdings in 1886–7 and recommended an average rent reduction of almost 31 per cent, and in subsequent years, down to 1892–3, the reductions ranged on average from 30 per cent to 21 per cent. Equally significant was the action taken on rent arrears which had risen dramatically as a result of the economic crises of the early 1880s and the series of rent strikes over many estates in the western Highlands and islands. In Wester Ross and Lewis the cancellation of arrears between 1886 and 1895 was 72 per cent, in the Inverness-shire islands it was just over 71 per cent and in Argyll around 63 per cent.

It is also apparent that the Commission was consciously used as an instrument of pacification. Repression was one means employed by government to establish stability, but the other was the Commission's systematic reduction of rentals and cancellation of arrears. It was besieged with requests by landowners to visit their estates as soon as possible because the small tenantry were clearly reluctant to pay their rents until the levels had been subjected to critical examination by the new authority, but the commissioners tended to focus first on such troubled areas as Skye and Tiree because they saw themselves as having an overtly policing role. Not surprisingly, given the scale of rent reduction as a consequence of their adjudications, they quickly gained the respect and trust of the crofting population and the favourable perception of the work of the Commission was in turn a major factor in the acceptance of the legislation of 1886 in the Highlands. The decade of the 1890s has been characterised as one of relative peace in the region after the difficult years of the 1880s, and in part this may have been due to the fact that in the later 1880s the law was being enforced with more rigour. Moreover, stock prices recovered over earlier levels and the cost of imported grain dropped significantly. Economic conditions for crofters in most areas (though not, as will be seen below, for the cottars in the Hebrides) eased somewhat and all this made for greater stability. But the implementation of the policy of 'fair rents' was also influential and there was general satisfaction with the Commission's decisions. After a seven-year period crofters could apply for rent revision, but only a relatively small number did so and only 333 applications were made in 1894–5, the first year for revisions, out of a possible total of several thousands. Significantly too the rent issue began to fade rapidly from the political agenda in the Highlands by the 1890s. Attention became focused on land rather than on rents and on the position of the cottars whose problems had been virtually ignored by the 1886 Act.

Among the crofters, however, the legislation soon came to be regarded as the fundamental basis of life in the western Highlands. Adam Collier described the Act of 1886 as 'the Magna Carta of the Highlands' and a historian writing in the 1970s concluded that even at that time minimal interference with it was likely to cause alarm and concern. It is hardly surprising that the Act quickly became widely popular and attracted intense loyalty, and the Crofters Commission, established by it, ensured the credibility and practical value of the legislation. As one crofting activist put it, there was 'not an institution . . . except perhaps the Sabbath, that the Highland people clung to with more determination'.[4] The Act gave security of tenure and made mass eviction virtually impossible which meant the clearances were now a thing of the past. However, it must be stressed that widespread removals had come to an end by the 1860s, the climate of public opinion was rendering eviction on any significant scale difficult and the contemporary malaise in sheep-farming had itself undermined the economic rationale for population displacement. In a sense, therefore, 1886 gave a legal basis to an historical process which was not only already under-way but practically completed. At the same time, however, the powerful psychological impact of the legislation should not be underestimated on a population which had endured arbitrary land management and a life of profound insecurity and hardship for several generations.

Indeed the Act of 1886 placed the crofter in a unique position, as has been said, 'by conferring on him most of the advantages of ownership – security and power of request – without its drawbacks'.[5] In the two decades after its passage there was substantial material improvement in the crofting counties, and during that period an estimated 40 per cent of crofters in Barra, the Uists, Skye and Harris built new homes. The Crofters Commission in 1912 noted how cottages were replacing 'black houses' in many districts. A Royal Commission of 1895 also took the view that the legislation had given a fresh impetus to crofting society and generated a greater sense of confidence and security. The knowledge that improvements to the holding would not necessarily result in increased rent had produced a new context for development. As the Commission concluded:

> we found that more attention is being paid to cultivation, to rotation of crops, to reclamation of outruns, to fencing and to the formation or repair of township roads; but most conspicuous of all the effects perceptible, is that upon buildings, including both dwelling-houses and steadings. In a considerable number of localities we found new and improved houses and steadings erected by the crofters themselves since the passing of the Act.[6]

But the improvements should not simply or even mainly be regarded as the result of legislation. The last quarter of the nineteenth century was a period of modest amelioration for many groups in addition to the crofters, but the fall in world grain prices was especially significant for the Highland population because there was an increasing tendency to buy in food for human consumption and use crops produced on the croft for animals. On the west coast of Sutherland grain prices fell by about 50 per cent between 1880 and 1914. In addition, money income in many households rose as a result of remittances from migrants.

In the longer term, critics have argued, the 1886 Act became a powerful force for conservatism and condemned crofting society to a future of inertia and stagnation. It froze an existing structure of smallholdings and ensured by its constraints and limitations that any evolution of holding size as circumstances changed was virtually impossible. What compounded the problem was the loyalty the legislation inspired which made any attempt at amendment politically unpopular and unattractive. The Act had provided the Crofters Commission with powers to grant enlargement of crofts, but these were inadequate and resulted in only marginal changes. In addition, there was no provision at all for the creation of entirely new crofts. The assumption behind the Gladstonian policy of 1886 that in some way the government was preserving an ancient way of life threatened in the past and the present by the forces of commercial landlordism was fallacious. The crofting system had itself been created in the later eighteenth century as a response to the economic imperatives of the age of improvement and was not an inheritance of the distant past of clanship. Nor did the benevolent legislation of 1886 provide any long-term remedy for the fundamental economic problems of the region, and for much of the twentieth century depopulation proceeded apace. The assumption behind Lord Napier's proposals was that crofting had lost much of its rationale in the first half of the nineteenth century when several of the by-employments linked to each holding, such as kelp manufacture and distilling, went into decline. As previous chapters have shown, the croft was not designed to produce a full subsistence which could only be secured by combining other activities with the working of the land, and it was this essential problem between population and land resources which the more radical proposals of the Napier Commission attempted to address. Given the political impossibility of wholesale landlord expropriation, Napier concluded there was not enough land available to provide an adequate living for all, and therefore some consolidation and reorganisation was necessary which should be linked to a programme of emigration. This approach was rejected by the Liberal Government which was not in the business of producing economic panaceas. The favoured policy was based on more pragmatic and short-term criteria. The 1886 Act came about for political reasons, was a political response to a problem of public order and it is therefore hardly surprising that its long-term economic consequences have generated considerable controversy. It was not designed to be a blueprint for economic recovery.

II

The Crofters' Act did nothing either to help the problem of the landless cottars. This class was distributed unevenly throughout the Highlands, and clearance and draconian controls over subletting on many estates after the potato famine had resulted in a decline in their numbers along much of the western mainland and some of the Inner Hebrides. But cottar families were still very numerous in parts of Skye, Mull and, even more significantly, in the Outer Hebrides, particularly in Lewis, Harris and the Uists. Popular agitation in the years after the passage of the Crofters' Act began to become more common in these districts and the centre of discontent switched to Lewis from Skye. The political agitation had probably raised expectations among cottars and these were doubtless frustrated by the 1886 legislation which had ignored their interests, but this Act, however, was proof that popular action could bring political rewards. In addition, the cottar economy in the Hebrides was hit by a devastating crisis from 1884. The income of most families depended on the earnings of seasonal workers on the east coast fishery. Herring prices fell between 1884 and 1886 as a result of record catches and higher European import duties, and wages also went into decline and became more insecure as curers moved from fixed-price arrangements with the boats to one where the returns depended on the fluctuating market prices for fish. The average earnings of Hebridean seasonal workers collapsed from £20 to £30 in the early 1880s to a mere £1 or £2 later in that decade.

This was the economic background to a series of land raids by the cottars designed in large part to draw attention to their plight. The most celebrated was the occupation of the Park deer forest in Lewis when several hundred young men raided part of the Matheson estate and slaughtered many deer in the process. This was a well-organised and effectively publicised incident with lurid and exaggerated details of the mass killing of hundreds of deer reported in the press, and once again the government had to draft in the military to restore order, this time in the form of the Royal Scots. The *Oban Times* concluded in December 1887 that the crofters' agitation had come to an end. It was now the turn of the cottars, the class descended from those who had lost their lands during the clearances. For this reason, the agitation concentrated on the recovery of land. It was a movement of the expropriated.

The Park raiders were acquitted on a technicality which probably served to encourage more disturbances and further raids took place at Aignish in Lewis in early 1888, which led to a bloody confrontation with troops, and in Assynt in Sutherland. Throughout the Outer Hebrides more covert cottar protest became endemic, with nocturnal dyke breaking being commonplace and almost impossible to control. In the interim, the government responded to the lawlessness not simply by sending in the army but also by establishing an enquiry into the social and economic conditions of Lewis. The subsequent report demonstrated that the breakdown in law and order was not the work of hot-headed agitators but derived ultimately from the conditions of destitution, poor housing and congestion in which the landless population lived. The scale of the human crisis, reminiscent in some ways of the terrible years of the potato famines of the 1840s, and a desire to restore stability and order prompted government intervention. The problem demanded other responses in addition to those of repression and coercion, and in formulating these the state became involved directly in the Highlands to an unprecedented extent and in the process attempted to evolve a strategy of development for the region to remove once and for all the causes of instability and economic crisis.

There were several elements in the emerging policy. First, a short-term need existed to assist with the immediate problems and a subsidy of £30,000 in relief of rates was made available by the Conservative government in 1888. In subsequent years the Highlands received £48,000 in relief of local taxation under the Local Government (Scotland) Act of 1889 and these monies helped to relieve the acute difficulties of the late 1880s and early 1890s. Second, an ambitious scheme of assisted emigration was planned to reduce congestion in the Hebrides in which one of the authors of the report on Lewis had envisaged the removal of 30,000 families. Lord Lothian, the Secretary for Scotland produced a plan in 1887 by which the British government would provide a loan of £120 for each emigrant family while the Canadian authorities made available 160 acres of free land. In the event only £12,000 were forthcoming from government, the organisation of the venture was less than efficient and the two settlements in Manitoba and the North West Territories met with only limited success. Thirdly, there was a commitment between 1888 and 1892 to develop the infrastructure of the region and promote the fishing industry. This, however, would be done in parallel with planned emigration. By December 1890 the Treasury had agreed to expenditure of nearly £10,000 for harbours, roads, steamboat subsidies and the extension of the telegraphic system.

All this represented a remarkable extension of government activity in the Highlands, but it is too simple to say that recurrent agitation forced the hand of the state. Certainly the problem of law and order was a real one and it was hoped that prosperity would bring eventual stability, but the ruling Conservative administration specifically eschewed the crofters' and cottars' demands for more land and matters relating to land tenure were consciously excluded from all policy initiatives. Indeed, by helping to support fishing it was hoped that land hunger would diminish as non-agricultural employment became more available. The government's emphasis on emigration as central to the strategy was also in direct conflict with the view taken by the crofters' lobby that there was sufficient land if only it were to be redistributed.

State action could in fact be justified because there was a growing view that the Highland problem was a chronic one which could only be alleviated by external intervention. Without this the crofting districts would lurch from crisis to crisis, with recurrent destitution and disorder compelling emergency government action which would itself be a drain on national resources. It was better by far to stabilise the situation and move the region towards a more secure economic system with a linked programme of assisted emigration, fishing expansion and development of the infrastructure. Significantly, as they pointed out in a Memorial to Lord Lothian in 1888, most of the major Highland proprietors favoured such a strategy and their initiative did much to convince the Conservative government of its value. However, despite progress in road and harbour building and in the development of the telegraph system, the policy was not brought to a successful conclusion. Investment was limited and few initiatives were completed, and the government therefore failed to make any significant impact on the long-term social and economic problems of the western Highlands, despite alleviating the crisis of the later 1880s. It was not, however, the last Highland development plan which would founder, as later policy-makers discovered to their cost.

III

Public policy in the western Highlands and the west of Ireland had often run in parallel in the last quarter of the nineteenth century as both areas suffered from chronic problems of economic difficulty which often stimulated phases of popular unrest, and Irish land legislation was also used as the model for changes in Highland land tenure. Irish developments had yet another effect in the 1890s. In 1891 the Conservative government set up the Congested Districts Board in the west of Ireland to promote economic improvement by providing new holdings on land acquired for the purpose, support industry and give instruction in farming. The Board had a major impact and was deemed to have achieved many of its objectives even in the poorest areas.

Such was its success that the government established a Congested Districts Board in 1897 to improve those parts of the Highlands perceived to be suffering from the same problems of over-population as Ireland. Fifty-six parishes in the crofting counties were judged to be 'congested' and the Board's remit extended to all the islands from Barra and Tiree northwards together with most of the maritime districts of the western mainland from Ardnamurchan. Its objectives were to promote agriculture, provide land for settlement among crofters and cottars, extend road communications and develop the fishing industry. Most of these aims had been familiar parts of government policy since the later 1880s, but what was new was the commitment to the redistribution and resettlement of land and the recognition that 'congestion' could not be reduced by encouraging emigration alone. This acceptance of the principle of land settlement was of great political significance. Even if its practical effects were limited before the First World War, it became a basic factor in public policy towards the Highlands thereafter and drew the state much further into the life of the region than could have been imagined during the land wars of the 1880s.

However, the Congested Districts Board had raised expectations among the land-hungry cottars which it could not fulfil, although some aspects of its activities during the fifteen years of the Board's existence were deemed to have been a success. It assisted through providing improved seed and stock, roads, bridges and piers were constructed, and vegetable growing was encouraged throughout the congested districts. But the Board would be judged mainly by its creation of new holdings and policies of land settlement. Between 1897 and 1912 it did successfully establish 640 new holdings and complete enlargements totalling 133,000 acres, but this was very far from the land transformation which the population of the western Highlands had expected and the frustrated expectations were demonstrated in a fresh series of land raids which punctuated the years of the Board's existence. Barra, South Uist and Lewis were all affected and the threat of land occupation was often made in numerous other localities.

The evidence suggests that the cottar population expected the wholesale restoration of the lands they believed their forefathers had lost during the clearances, but this the Board could in no way deliver as it did not possess powers of compulsory purchase and therefore could not take the initiative in the land market but had to wait until a proprietor was willing to sell. It acquired no large estates up to 1904 and after 1906 its activities were considerably restricted because of changes in government policy and it was also hampered by inadequate funding with a budget of £35,000 compared to the Irish Board's final income of £231,000. It was therefore hardly surprising that the impact of the two bodies was very different. The Congested Districts Board in Ireland is credited with transforming the poorer districts of that country, but in the Highlands the effects were much more problematic. The Irish Board had greater powers to cajole and finally compel landlords to sell land than its Scottish counterpart and, in addition, Highland crofters were much less willing to purchase holdings than Irish tenants and this reduced the Scottish Board's potential income. There was a greater desire to obtain tenancies under the protection of the Crofters' Act of 1886 than assume the burdens of ownership which could lead to higher outlay on rates. More generally, the policy of land resettlement was doomed in the western Highlands because of the deep reluctance of the people in most districts to migrate. Some argued that this was because planned resettlement, no matter how potentially beneficial, was still associated with clearance. The deep scars left by the great social trauma of the nineteenth century were still there and would affect the implementation of public policy for some time to come.

The Congested Districts Board was wound up in 1912 and its functions taken over by the Board of Agriculture and its demise brought to an end a period of increasing state involvement. Governments of different political colours had recognised the Highlands as a special case, requiring the development of policies, the creation of agencies and the supply of subsidy not thought appropriate in the rest of the country. A striking example of this was the establishment of the Highlands and Islands Medical Services Board in 1913 by which a grant of £42,000 was made available to allow doctors in the region to charge fixed low fees. This was a recognition of the exceptionally high costs of delivering a medical service in sparsely populated and remote districts and the very poor health record of the western Highlands. On the eve of the First World War the state was assuming responsibilities for the welfare of the Highland population which would have been unthinkable a few decades previously. This was not simply a result of the general increase in social expenditure which occurred in the Edwardian era, it was also because of the peculiar history and circumstances of the Highlands. Ironically this was also one reason why public policy failed to regenerate the economy of the region. Governments could not afford to concentrate exclusively or even mainly on economic rationalisation of land use and so policy had to be based on what was acceptable to the people and also meet to some extent the widespread desire for land. More profit and greater output might have been produced if land had been concentrated in bigger holdings, but such an approach whatever its potential merits was politically and socially impractical. As the Committee on Land Settlement in Scotland stated in 1929, 'their [the crofters] conditions were a reproach to the nation of which they formed a part and the only way to remove that reproach was to give them the only available land'.[7] It was an unambiguous declaration that social priorities were of paramount importance in the approach to the Highland problem.

NOTES

1 Quoted in E. A. Cameron, 'Public policy in the Scottish Highlands: governments, politics and the land issue 1886 to the 1920s', unpublished Ph.D. thesis, University of Glasgow, 1992, p. 19.
2 British Parliamentary Papers, XXXVI, 1884, *Report of the Royal Commission to Inquire into the Condition of the Crofters and Cottars of the Highlands and Islands of Scotland*, pp. 22, 41.
3 Quoted in J. Hunter, 'The politics of Highland land reform, 1813–1895', *Scottish Historical Review*, LIII, 1974, p. 57.
4 Quoted in J. Hunter, *The Making of the Crofting Community*, Edinburgh, 1976, p. 179.
5 A. Collier, *The Crofting Problem*, Cambridge, 1953, p. 98.
6 British Parliamentary Papers, XXXVIII, 1895, *Royal Commission (Highlands and Islands, 1892), Report and Minutes of Evidence*, XII.
7 Quoted in Collier, *Crofting Problem*, p. 104.

FURTHER READING

E. A. Cameron, 'Public policy in the Scottish Highlands: governments, politics and the land issue 1886 to the 1920s', unpublished Ph.D. thesis, University of Glasgow, 1992.
A. Collier, *The Crofting Problem*, Cambridge, 1953.
J. P. Day, *Public Administration in the Highlands and Islands of Scotland*, London, 1918.
C. Dewey, 'Celtic agrarian legislation and the celtic revival: historicist implications of the Scottish and Irish Land Acts, 1870–1886', *Past and Present*, 64, 1974.
J. Hunter, 'The politics of Highland land reform, 1873 to 1895', *Scottish Historical Review*, 53, 1974.
J. Hunter, *The Making of the Crofting Community*, Edinburgh, 1976.
A. I. Macinnes, 'The Crofters Holding Act: a hundred year sentence', *Radical Scotland*, 25, 1987.
W. Orr, *Deer Forests, Landlords and Crofters*, Edinburgh, 1982.

16

DIASPORA: HIGHLAND MIGRANTS
IN THE SCOTTISH CITY

In the winter of 1850 the Scottish press reported in full and harrowing detail the sufferings of a group of crofters and cottars from the island of Barra who had been evicted by their landlord, John Gordon of Cluny, and forced to make their way to the mainland and from there to the southern cities. They were destitute and hungry, subsisting by begging and charity in a society of strangers, and seemed to symbolise the plight of the evicted Highlander and the social catastrophe that had engulfed the crofting region during the clearances. Their experience and that of others faithfully reported in contemporary journals helped to create a stereotype of the dispossessed Highlander, compelled to move to the Lowland towns and cities by eviction and famine and there condemned to a life of poverty and insecurity amid the burgeoning urban slums. In this view, the catholic Irish migrants and the Highlanders formed the depressed underclass of the industrial regions, the pool of casual and general labourers vital to the new manufacturing economy, but who were at best able only to eke out an uncertain living as a result of poor wages and irregular employment. As one observer of the time put it, while some Highlanders of means were able to emigrate, the more deprived were forced to stay in Scotland and '. . . crowd into the towns and add much to the existing mass of pauperism and distress there'.[1]

However, recent and careful research on the social and occupational patterns of Highland migrants in the nineteenth century city has revealed a more intriguing and complicated picture. Not surprisingly Highlanders do feature in the poor law and charity records of the larger towns but they were never a significant group and were always vastly outnumbered by the Irish. Again, Highland involvement in general and casual labouring was not surprising since many migrants came to the Lowlands on a temporary or seasonal basis and sought employment mainly in the unskilled labour market. It does not necessarily follow, however, that those who were more permanently settled in southern towns and cities were similarly confined. Fortunately, through a scrutiny of census, church and other records it is possible to penetrate behind the rhetoric of contemporary comment to a more realistic appreciation of how the Highland migrant fared in the Lowland world in the nineteenth century.

Highland migration to southern towns did not start in the age of transformation. There had always been 'crisis migration' of 'puir Highlanders' when the more precarious harvest failed in the north and, even in less disturbed times, a slow trickle of small farmers, traders and fishermen to the Lowland burghs. In 1717, for example, it was reported that there were considerable numbers of persons 'having the Irish language' residing in the city of Glasgow and the 'town of Grinok',[2] and the Glasgow Highland Society was founded as early as 1727. Nevertheless, it is clear that substantial migration only accelerated in the later eighteenth century as emerging employment opportunities in the growing urban areas combined with agrarian and demographic changes in the Highlands to increase the rate of outward movement considerably. Significantly it was in this period that a series of Gaelic chapels were founded in several towns, including Dundee in 1791 and Perth in 1787. Highlanders comprised an estimated 6 per cent of the population of Greenock in the early eighteenth century but around 30 per cent by the 1790s, and the number of Gaelic-speakers in the town had risen from less than 500 in the middle decades of the century to over 5,000 by its end. It seems to have been a similar story in other major towns close to the Highlands, but there was, nevertheless, one distinctive feature. While migration was accelerating in most areas, it was the urban areas of the western Lowlands which attracted most Highlanders and the Gaelic communities in Glasgow, Greenock and Paisley were much greater than those of the eastern towns. A special investigation into the Highland population in Edinburgh in 1850 suggested a community of 1,200, and the 1,277 Highlanders in Dundee in 1891 made up less than 1 per cent of the city's population. On the other hand, Glasgow, at the census of 1871, had a Highland-born population of over 20,000, showing that the migration trail seems to have led primarily from north to south rather than from west to east.

Not all areas of the Highlands contributed in equal measure to these movements. Indeed, especially in the first half of the nineteenth century, a distinctive migration hinterland is apparent and, overwhelmingly, the majority of migrants came from parishes and districts on the Highlands frontier and only a relatively small fraction, until the later decades of the century, from the more distant areas of the far north and west. Over three-quarters of the Highlanders in Perth in 1851, for example, were natives of Highland Perthshire, and the adjacent parishes of south and east Argyll produced most of Greenock's migrants. The majority of the Highlanders settled in Glasgow in the 1850s also came from the county of Argyll and those southern and eastern Highland parishes on the edge of the Grampians.

This distinctive pattern is significant for two reasons. First, it is a further illustration of the arguments advanced elsewhere in this book, that permanent mobility in many crofting districts was limited by the potato, temporary migration and the prevalence of subletting among kinfolk. Only when this structure was threatened and partially destroyed by the famine of the 1840s did permanent movement from the crofting parishes of the north and far west to the Lowland towns become really significant. By the last quarter of the nineteenth century, for instance, the relative number of migrants to Greenock, Glasgow and Perth had visibly increased from these more remote parts. Second, the source areas of most Highland migrants have implications for the study of their experience in the urban labour markets as the majority were natives of southern Argyllshire, eastern Inverness-shire and Highland Perthshire and these were not areas of acute deprivation or destitution. When the potatoes failed in 1846 these districts experienced hardship but, unlike the less fortunate areas to the north and west, they quickly weathered the storm and soon were able to survive without external support. In some parts, commercial fishing and textile manufacture, especially the making of linen cloth, were well established, and literacy levels were markedly above the Highland average. In 1826 the Church of Scotland estimated that in the Hebrides and other western parts of Inverness about 70 per cent of the population were unable to read but in Argyll and Highland Perthshire the figure fell to about 30 per cent. Village and small town development was widespread throughout the region and the migration rate to the south from these settlements was often considerably higher than from surrounding rural areas. For much of the nineteenth century, therefore, many Highlanders who settled in Lowland cities came from districts with a varied occupational structure and not all had been the victims of clearance and removal. Significantly, for example, studies of the Highland migrant population in Dundee and Perth reveal that precious few new arrivals came as family groups which might have been expected if wholesale dispossession had been a major influence on movement and only a little over 6 per cent of the Highland-born population in late nineteenth century Dundee are recorded in the census enumerations as being within a family group. The vast proportion of the Highlanders who migrated to these two towns were single men and women, almost certainly driven south and east by limited economic opportunity in their rural parishes and the hope of employment and advancement in the cities.

The migration process, where it can be examined from the fragments of evidence available, was often exceedingly complex and the change of location from Highland croft or farm to urban tenement did not necessarily occur in either a single or a direct fashion. For a start, the distinction between 'temporary' and 'permanent' migration was very blurred. Doubtless when urban economies were depressed, there was some 'return migration' to the Highlands and, equally, periods of urban prosperity must have been an incentive for many to move to the towns even if only on a short-term basis. That such mobility was common is shown by the large number of young Highland men who lived as lodgers either in lodging houses or in subletted accommodation in nineteenth century Scottish cities and one senses a transient group who were likely to move many times during their adult lives. The parochial board records of Dundee, investigated by Charles Withers, give a tantalising insight into this migrant world. There is, for instance, the case of the 'Widow MacDonald' who was born in Kenmore parish in Highland Perthshire in 1793 and married in Crieff parish in 1823. Around the same time she moved to Edinburgh, remained there for ten years before migrating to Denny in Stirlingshire for a further period of three to four years, and from there moved to Cardross for eight years before settling in Perth in 1836. Similar life histories suggest a pattern of intricate short-term movement, of 'stage' migration between Highland parish and Lowland city, rather than a single, decisive act of resettlement.

It is possible to reconstruct the occupational profile of Highlanders in Lowland towns from the census records. In Edinburgh, they were employed mainly as domestic servants, shopmen, chairmen, porters, policemen and labourers, and Highlanders in Dundee worked in the linen and jute mills as well as in general labouring. In Glasgow, domestic service was far and away the biggest single outlet for Highland women, while Highland men found employment in the police, construction, metalworking, fishing, machinery and the shipbuilding industries. Overwhelmingly they entered the working-class occupations of the great Scottish cities, though their prominence in them varied between different sectors.

But closer scrutiny of the migrant Highlanders' occupational and status position does not suggest that they represented an underclass eking out an existence in the urban slums on the paltry and insecure earnings from general labouring. In all the major cities, the Highlanders seem to have been significantly better off than the catholic Irish with whom they are often compared. For a start, not all Highlanders were unskilled manual labourers and indeed, in some towns, those with some skills were almost in the majority. Over 43 per cent of the Highland-born population of Dundee in 1891 were classified in the census as skilled, semi-skilled or professional and in Perth at the same date around 60 per cent of Highlanders were listed as either skilled or semi-skilled. Highland men active in the metal, machine and shipbuilding sectors in Glasgow were also mainly skilled and in 1851 about two-thirds of those employed in these industries in the Anderston area of the city were skilled workers: carpenters and joiners, blacksmiths, boilermakers, engineers, and shipwrights.

The Irish penetrated the skilled sector to a greater extent than is often believed but not on the same scale as the Highlanders. Highland-born building workers were largely in the better-paid and more exclusive trades of mason, carpenter and joiner whereas the Irish were more likely to be unskilled labourers. In Greenock, the arduous employment in the sugar factories was dominated by the Irish while the Highlanders were dominant in fishing, joinery and cooperage. The most striking and significant point of contrast between the two groups, however, was that in a limited way the Highland-born were able to penetrate the high status professional and managerial occupations from which the catholic Irish were almost entirely excluded. This in large part reflected the varied social mix of the Highland population. The Irish migrant stream on the other hand was more homogeneous and comprised poor small farmers, weavers and labourers whose catholicism was an additional constraint on upward social mobility in a protestant society. Around 10 per cent and 7 per cent respectively of Perth and Dundee Highlanders at the end of the nineteenth century belonged to the managerial and professional classes, and these were the prime movers in the Highland and Celtic societies which became part of the social life of the town elites in Victorian times. But even the majority of their fellow Highlanders did better than the Irish, and William Sloan's careful analysis of the two groups in mid-nineteenth century Glasgow is very revealing in this respect. Levels of over-crowding were significantly higher among the catholic Irish and they were also more vulnerable to epidemic disease. Both Irish and Highland migrants lived in the worst slum areas of Glasgow, around the Cross, High Street, Gallowgate and Saltmarket, but while the Highland presence was relatively limited, the Irish were concentrated in very large numbers and some streets in the district had become virtual Irish ghettoes. All in all, the evidence seems to suggest that the Highlanders did not live on the margins of society to the same extent as many Irish immigrants. Destitution, ill health, poverty and unemployment were a constant threat in the lives of all the working classes in the nineteenth century city, but there is little reason to believe that Highland migrants were peculiarly vulnerable to them.

However, the material experience of Highlanders in urban Scotland is only one part of the story. Another important question is the extent to which they attempted to perpetuate any sense of communal and ethnic identity in the new context. The Gaels possessed a distinctive language and culture and it is an intriguing problem how far these were maintained or diluted by the urban experience. Traditionally, sociologists and historians have often seen urban life as an alienating process where the anonymity and ·insecurities of the city dissolve old cultures and loyalties and produce a more amorphous way of life. More recently, however, attention has been given to the development of urban 'subcultures'. Some migrants may decide to ignore and eventually reject their ethnic backgrounds, but others find it a vital resource and those from a common culture can combine to face the challenges of urban life. This is rendered easier if those belonging to the subculture share a common language and religion which differentiate them from the majority and, in addition, residential segregation in the city along ethnic lines can work to the same end. 'Chain migration', the process by which highly specific traditions of mobility develop between particular rural districts and certain neighbourhoods in the city, also supports the subculture development.

The model outlined above fits the history of the catholic Irish in urban Scotland very well. A sense of ethnic identity was preserved and strengthened by religion, education, parish social life and the hostility of the host community, and residential patterns in the cities and Irish dominance of specific employments also added to a continuing collective awareness which was maintained into subsequent generations. How far, however, the model can be as readily applied to the Highlanders is much less certain. At first sight, of course, there is evidence of continued ethnicity with the building in several towns of Gaelic chapels, the foundation of Highland Societies and the proliferation of Highland clubs of various sorts. But it is reasonably clear that these organisations mainly attracted middle-class migrants for 'social' reasons and were ignored by many ordinary Highlanders. The Gaelic churches did have a much more popular appeal but they did not perform the same central role played by the catholic chapels as the foci of a distinctive identity for the Irish and only a minority of Highland migrants had any formal connection with the Gaelic churches. In Perth the figure was around 10 to 20 per cent of the Gaelic community in the middle decades of the nineteenth century and most members were relatively affluent. By the 1840s there were four Gaelic churches in Glasgow with accommodation for up to 4,250 people, but only a minority of the city's Highland migrants attended. It has been estimated by Sloan that about a quarter came to church services regularly and many of these went to mainstream English-speaking churches rather than to the Gaelic chapels. Certainly the social mission of the latter should not be underestimated. Gaelic churches organised aid and support for distressed Highlanders and leading ministers, such as the Rev. Norman McLeod, provided valuable assistance and advice to those seeking employment, but they had no commitment to maintaining a separate cultural identity. On the contrary, the city's Gaelic ministers accepted it as inevitable, indeed desirable, that many church-going migrants themselves, and certainly their offspring, would eventually join regular church congregations. Gaelic services were a short-term means to a longer-term end, the successful adaptation of Highland migrants to urban life, and English speech was essential for that.

Other indicators confirm that the urban Highland community had a much weaker collective identity than the migrant Irish. Gaelic speech was common among first generation migrants, though given the prevalence of anglicising cultural forces in the southern Highlands, many were bilingual. By the second generation, however, the linguistic tradition was weakening and in 1891 only 17 per cent of children of Gaelic-speaking parents in Greenock spoke the language. Significantly, in the cases where a Highland parent was married to a Lowlander, the figure fell to less than 7 per cent. Language was shed rapidly but so also was social solidarity. In the Irish catholic community, inter-faith marriages became less frequent over time as the Church established an effective structure of parishes and social networks to influence the young, whereas intermarriage between Highland migrants and others, even in the first generation, was much more common. In the 1850s well over half of the heads of household from the Highlands living in the centre of Glasgow had married a partner born outside the Highland counties. The scale of intermarriage was even greater in Dundee and Perth, perhaps because of the smaller size of the Highland community, with the great majority of single male and female migrants eventually obtaining a non-Highland partner.

The Highlanders also differed from the catholic Irish in their residential patterns. In certain streets and districts of some western Lowland towns there were heavy concentrations of Irish. The best-known area was the thoroughfares running off Glasgow Cross and especially in the tenements of the back lands in High Street, Trongate, Saltmarket and Gallowgate. But on a lesser scale, there were localities such as this elsewhere in Glasgow, like the Bridgegate, and also in parts of Paisley and Greenock, and here the inhabitants, whether or not they were active churchgoers, identified with the culture and symbolism of catholicism in a way which marked them out from the neighbouring protestant Irish and Scots. Such residential concentration did not exist to any great extent among Highlanders. In Glasgow they sometimes clustered in a few localities like the George Street area of the city and some tenements were also dominated by Highlanders. However, there was little evidence of Highland ghettoes and residential patterns primarily seemed to reflect such factors as proximity to work and income levels rather than ethnic background.

Clear differences therefore emerge when the two migrant groups are considered in detail. The catholic Irish seem to have successfully preserved a subculture in the Scottish cities, much of it derived from a sense of shared religion and awareness of the overt hostility shown them by many in the host society. Their religion had a powerful social function and the catholic parish provided a cultural identity for a despised immigrant group, reinforcing feelings of self-worth and supplying one means of adapting to an alien and often unfriendly environment. The Highland migrant experience was markedly different. Some sense of ethnic identity was preserved through the formation of Gaelic churches and Highland societies, but these attracted only a minority of migrants and the clubs and societies in particular were normally the preserve of the better-off rather than of the ordinary Highlanders. Over time too a sense of ethnicity was diluted by the erosion of Gaelic speech, intermarriage and by the scattered distribution of Highlanders within the urban areas. It is plain that no coherent subculture was perpetuated and Highland migrants were relatively quickly assimilated into urban society.

In part these different patterns reflected the source areas of most Highland migrants to urban Scotland. The southern and eastern rim adjacent to the Lowlands was the region subjected earliest to modernising forces in the economy and anglicising influences in education and culture, and migrants from these districts were already experiencing a change in culture and values before they left. Significantly, for instance, the level of bilingualism seems to have been high among them. In addition, there were profound differences in class, occupation, status and background among the Highland population and these divisions must have weakened any sense of common ethnic identity. Upper-class Highlanders may have supported the Celtic societies but they did not regard themselves socially as Gaels. Their class ties were with the urban professional and business elites, not with the mass of ordinary migrants of more humble background. The Irish also had their social disparities but they were much more homogeneous and hence more easily united around religious faith and ethnicity.

In addition, Highlanders as a group did not attract the powerful hostility encountered by the Irish and so had much less incentive to establish a collective cultural defence against social prejudice. Highland migration was never as significant in numerical terms as the Irish movement and contemporary observers regarded the increasing waves of Irish immigrants as an alarming threat to jobs, health, civilisation and the protestant religion itself. But the Highlanders were more easily absorbed. Many came from a less deprived economic background than the catholic Irish and there were also far fewer of them. At the census of 1851 there were 16,534 Highland-born in Glasgow but over 60,000 Irish, and Highland migration seems to have peaked relatively early. For instance, the Highland-born population in Greenock reached a peak in 1801 but declined thereafter. In the 1790s, 30 per cent of the town's population were from the Highlands, but by 1891, the proportion had fallen to 6 per cent. Highlanders, therefore, never really posed a threat: they were not a numerically vast alien intrusion. They were Scots, protestants for the most part and came from a regional society being sentimentalised by Lowland writers and artists throughout the nineteenth century as the authentic heartland of Scottish nationhood. At most they attracted humour and derision for their 'teuchter' accents and strange ways, but rarely provoked overt antagonism.

NOTES

1 Rev. T. McLauchlan, 'The influence of emigration on the social conditions of the Highlands', *Transactions of National Association for Social Science*, 1864, p. 606.
2 Quoted in C. W. J. Withers, *Highland Communities in Dundee and Perth 1787–1891*, Dundee, 1986, p. 11.

FURTHER READING

T. M. Devine, 'Highland migration to lowland Scotland, 1760–1800', *Scottish Historical Review*, LXII, 1983.

M. W. Flinn, ed., *Scottish Population History*, Cambridge, 1977, part 6.

R. D. Lobban, 'The migration of Highlanders into Lowland Scotland, 1750–1890', unpublished Ph.D. thesis, University of Edinburgh, 1969.

R. D. Lobban, 'Highland migration to Lowland Scotland', *Scottish International*, 1971.

W. Sloan, 'Religious affiliation and the immigrant experience: Catholic Irish and Protestant Highlanders in Glasgow, 1830–1850' in T. M. Devine, ed., *Irish Immigrants and Scottish Society in the Nineteenth and Twentieth Centuries*, Edinburgh, 1991.

C. W. J. Withers, 'Highland clubs and Gaelic chapels: Glasgow's Gaelic community in the eighteenth century', *Scottish Geographical Magazine*, 100, 1984.

C. W. J. Withers, *Highland Communities in Dundee and Perth*, 1787–1891, Dundee, 1986.

INDEX

Kathy
01466
740229